Mark David Sheftall is Assistant Professor in the Department of History at Auburn University, Alabama, United States. He specialises in the history of Britain and the Dominions, especially their military and cultural history.

ALTERED MEMORIES OF THE GREAT WAR

Divergent Narratives of Britain, Australia, New Zealand and Canada

MARK DAVID SHEFTALL

I.B. TAURIS

LONDON · NEW YORK

Published in 2009 by I.B.Tauris & Co Ltd
6 Salem Road, London W2 4BU
175 Fifth Avenue, New York NY 10010
www.ibtauris.com

Distributed in the United States and Canada exclusively by Palgrave Macmillan
175 Fifth Avenue, New York NY 10010

ISBN: 978 1 84511 883 9

A full CIP record for this book is available from the British Library
A full CIP record is available from the Library of Congress

Library of Congress Catalog Card Number: available

Printed and bound in India by Thomson Press India Ltd
From camera-ready copy edited and supplied by the author

Contents

Acknowledgements

This book is based primarily on my doctoral thesis completed at Duke University, so I would first like to thank my major Ph. D. advisors, Professors Tami Davis Biddle and Alex Roland for their guidance and inspiration. I also benefited from the invaluable support and advice of the other members of my dissertation committee: Susan Thorne, John Thompson and Malachi Hacohen. Their patience, constructive criticism and confidence in my project were indispensable at every step on the road to its completion. I would also like to express my appreciation to the helpful and patient staffs of the various archives, libraries and museums where I conducted research for this work. I am particularly grateful to the archivists and librarians of the National Archives of Canada, the National Library of Canada, the Canadian War Museum, the Australian War Memorial, the Australian Archives, the National Library of Australia, Archives New Zealand, the Alexander Turnbull National Library of New Zealand, the Auckland War Memorial Museum, the Provincial Archives of Newfoundland and Labrador and the Imperial War Museum.

Finally, I would like to thank all of my friends and colleagues not already named for being there to commiserate, celebrate and provide more help of every kind than can possibly be repaid. Above all I want to dedicate this book, with much love, to my mom and dad, who I hope understand that I literally could not have done any of this without them.

Introduction

In 1928, Siegfried Sassoon, a popular and critically acclaimed novelist and poet who had served as a junior officer in the British Army on the Western Front in World War One, penned his reaction to the New Menin Gate, a memorial commemorating 54,000 British soldiers missing and presumed dead from one of the war's most notorious battle zones, the Ypres salient. Sassoon wrote:

Who will remember, passing through this Gate,
The unheroic Dead who fed the guns?
Who shall absolve the foulness of their fate, –
These doomed, conscripted, unvictorious ones?

To the poet, the memorial did not honour the memory of the slain it named, but instead blasphemed their senseless sacrifice. In Sassoon's words:

Here was the world's worst wound. And here with pride
"Their name liveth forever," the Gateway claims.
Was ever an immolation so belied
As these intolerably nameless names?
Well might the Dead who struggled in the slime
Rise and decried this sepulchre of crime. [1]

Two years after the publication of Sassoon's poem, a popular Canadian novelist and First World War veteran named Will Bird returned to France, where construction was underway on a memorial commemorating the 3,000 of his countrymen who fell at Vimy Ridge, one of the Western Front's most celebrated battles. For Bird, the monument testified to the outstanding military achievements of Canada's soldiers in the Great War, and affirmed in stone the searing martial rite of passage that helped transform Canada into a nation. He wrote that, 'Europe, when viewing the finished work, will change her impressions of the Canadians as a people.'[2]

The contrasting reactions of these two literate World War One veterans to the war memorials at Menin Gate and Vimy Ridge represented more than simply the distinct subjective impressions of two individual ex-soldiers from different countries. The strikingly divergent tone, language and imagery with which each author appraised the particular monuments illustrated larger cultural phenomena as well. Essentially, Sassoon's poem and Bird's essay exemplified how the process of representing, interpreting and assimilating the experience of the First World War was unfolding in profoundly different ways within the inter-war culture of Great Britain, and within the cultures of Canada, Australia and other imperial Dominions.

The imperial Dominions referred to in this work are those countries that at the time of the First World War were often described as the Empire's 'White Dominions'. These were defined as the Empire's self-governing former settlement colonies where inhabitants of British heritage enjoyed political dominance, if not demographic majority. This category included Canada, Australia, New Zealand, Newfoundland and South Africa. The focus here is on Canada, Australia, New Zealand and, to a limited extent, Newfoundland. South Africa presents a case too singular and complex to be encompassed within the confines of this work. The value of focusing this study on more than just a single country is this: Most studies of the First World War and its aftermath have been confined within the geographical parameters of the nation-state, despite the global scope of the conflict. By using a comparative approach, it is possible to extend the range of the investigation to include phenomena that exist above and beyond any specifically national context, which is especially appropriate in the case of countries such as Canada, Australia and New Zealand, whose identities were determined to such a large extent by their status as part of a trans-national empire.

The inter-war years in Britain witnessed the increasing prevalence in literature, art, film, media commentary, commemorative texts, historical works, and other cultural products, of depictions and interpretations of the First World War experience that emphasized the disillusioning human, material, social and spiritual cost of the conflict. In Canada, Australia and New Zealand by contrast, the dominant narrative of the war for the duration of the inter-war period focused on what was achieved between 1914 and 1918 by the nation and its soldiers, rather than on what was lost in the process, despite the fact that the human cost of the war for each Dominion was proportionally comparable to or greater than that experienced by Britain. In inter-war Canada, Australia and New Zealand, the themes, language and imagery associated with this narrative were remarkably congruent, except for relatively minor nationally specific nuances and variations here and there. In the Dominions, the narrative of loss and disillusion was successfully marginalized during the inter-war years, while in Britain, it proved a compelling and eventually dominant alternative to interpretations of the war experience that validated and affirmed the sacrifice of those who died in the conflict.

There is currently a significant body of scholarship that documents and debates the *nature* of Britain's Great War narrative. Paul Fussell, in his groundbreaking 1975 work, *The Great War and Modern Memory,* described the narrative of disillusion and discontinuity which he argued became during the inter-war period the predominant mode of representing and interpreting the country's war experience. Fussell in fact presented the Great War as the seminal event leading to the birth of the 'modern' literary and artistic idiom.[3] Subsequent scholars, including, most significantly, John Onions and Samuel Hynes, while not necessarily making such a sweeping cultural claim, essentially validated Fussell's assertion that the narrative of disillusion he described was how Britain 'remembered' the Great War. Indeed, building on this premise, Hynes charts in great detail the evolution of this narrative within Britain's high culture during the war and the inter-war years, conflating, as Fussell did, the narrative's increasing literary and high-artistic presence in this period with the nation's overall 'cultural memory' of the conflict.[4]

By contrast, more recent scholarship focusing on Britain, including that by Jay Winter, Adrian Gregory and Rosa Maria Bracco looks beyond the elite cultural sources mined by their predecessors and finds that the most *common* inter-war representations and interpretations of the conflict strove to incorporate the war experience within a continuum of traditional values and ideals.[5] These contradictory perspectives are reconciled here by showing how the narrative of disillusion, while primarily articulated in inter-war Britain by an elite – but not marginal – cultural vanguard, nevertheless proved over the course of this period an increasingly formidable and subversive challenge to more conventional understandings of the war experience.

While the 1990s witnessed a considerable amount of scholarship devoted to Australia's 'memory' of the Great War, Canada and New Zealand have been studied far less. Without exception, scholars of this topic for Australia, Canada and New Zealand document the inter-war dominance of the proud, validating narrative of the country's war experience described above.[6]

This is the first project to compare the emergence within Britain and the Dominions of the distinctive collective narratives that are associated with each country's experience of the First World War, and to locate such phenomena within the broad context of each nation's culture by focusing primarily on how this process relates to evolving conceptions of collective identity. The questions central to this study are: What factors explain the resonance and appeal of these divergent narratives within the societies where they were most prevalent? Why did Canadians, Australians and New Zealanders typically reject the more bitter representations of the war and its meaning that many men and women in Great Britain found particularly compelling, despite the fact that Britain, Canada, Australia and New Zealand endured equally grim experiences on the First World War battlefield, despite the fact that all four countries experienced major social upheaval as a result of the war, and in spite of how much these countries shared in terms of traditions, heritage and outlook?

Answers to these questions can only be found by exploring how 'new' narratives of the unprecedented experience of the conflict were shaped by 'old,' long-standing conceptions of identity. To a significant extent, whether or not a given narrative proved compelling within a society depended to a great extent on the degree to which it struck familiar and appealing chords in the hearts and minds of those who encountered it. In other words, to understand why in the Dominions disillusion played such a marginal role in the pre-eminent inter-war collective memory of the conflict, we must first and foremost examine how those who took part in the process of interpreting and representing the war – including men and women, elites and non-elites – brought with them pre-existing discourses, and previously constructed identities. In many cases, these discourses and identities were transformed and re-defined by the experience of the war, but they in turn also frequently influenced the meanings that individuals attached to that experience.

At the same time, in order to fully comprehend how different ways of 'remembering' the war became more or less prevalent within the societies in question, it is necessary to investigate the often bitter ideological, sectarian or ethnic contests that took place in each country between various institutions and interest groups with opposing political and social agendas, as they sought to appropriate the meaning of the war in ways that served their claims to authority and legitimacy, while undermining the claims of their rivals. Such a study of war and memory that emphasizes the contextualizing role played by identity and its relationship to political and social forces might take to heart Joan Scott's admonition that 'We cannot simply accept at face value the written records or people's memories… Instead we must read the evidence we accumulate for what it reveals about how people appropriate and use political discourse, how they are shaped by it and in turn redefine its meaning.'[7]

Wars, and particularly wars on the scale of the First World War, are, as Samuel Hynes has said, not only extraordinary military and political events in the history of a society, but also extraordinary imaginative events.[8] Collectivities, like individuals, must rationalize and render coherent experiences that are perceived as abnormal, bewildering, and very often traumatic. Collectivities, like individuals, do this by recollecting, or perhaps more accurately, re-imagining, the experiences as narrative, through a process discussed in greater detail below. This process both shapes and is shaped by identity, which acts simultaneously as a prism and a mirror, refracting and reflecting experience. War, particularly total war, in the stress and destabilization that it typically inflicts on individuals and societies, provides what Margaret Higonnet calls a 'clarifying moment' in which the discursive constructs underpinning the edifice of identity may be illuminated to an extraordinary degree.[9]

This work is guided by a research methodology derived from the postulate that there is such a phenomenon as *collective memory*, and that it is visible within the realm of culture. This idea owes much to the work of Pierre Nora, as well as to more recent scholarship by Peter Novick and Daniel Sherman, among others.[10] Collective memory is, in this case, an expression of collective experience, in that it emerges out of events that are experienced, in one way or another, by practically every cognizant member of a given social group. For collectivities, no less than individuals, memory provides the coherence that underpins a sense of identity. Even though no two individuals remember a shared experience in exactly the same way, the cohesion of the social group is enhanced if most of its members share an understanding of the *meaning* of a particular communal experience. Fundamental to this definition of collective memory is the idea that these understandings can only be shared if they are transmitted, and in order to be transmitted, they must be articulated. Thus, collective memory is necessarily articulated memory. The transmission of memories collectively is facilitated if experience can be articulated as a *narrative* that structures and interprets the event through language and imagery that is comprehensible and meaningful to the entire group. Significantly, it is possible for certain narratives of a given communal experience to coalesce as the *dominant collective memory* of that event. Dominant collective memories are those that achieve centrality within the public realm, and their centrality is discerned by their near-ubiquity in the domain of public culture. The means by which they attain ubiquity often involve the effective suppression or marginalization of competing or contrasting narratives, and the establishment of a connection with widely held notions or ideals within a society.

In Canada, Australia and New Zealand during the inter-war period the dominant collective memory of the national war experience portrayed the conflict as a rite of passage in which the Dominions' costly contribution to Allied victory helped solidify their identity as nations, rather than colonies, loyal to, but not subordinate to, the British Motherland. Furthermore, this narrative celebrated the widely acclaimed battlefield performance of the nation's fighting men, and represented these soldiers as paradigms of a distinct and proud national identity revealed by the war. For the duration of the inter-war period, even in the face of alternative and contradictory interpretations and depictions of the Canadian, Australian or New Zealand war experience, this narrative could be represented in these countries as established truth in, for instance, school textbooks, and also by countless authors, filmmakers, scholars and others, without fear of widespread dispute. At the same time, understandings of the war that called into question various tenets of the dominant narrative were greeted by large cross sections of the Canadian, Australian and New Zealand public with reactions ranging from disinterest to vitriolic hostility. In addition, as the scholar Alistair Thomson demonstrated in a 1994 study based on interviews with Australian veterans of the First World War, this dominant narrative of the war experience could colour the memories of many ex-soldiers to such an extent that individual recollections of their personal wartime experiences which did not conform to the established orthodoxy might be altered or suppressed.[11]

The question then becomes, what was it about this particular narrative that explains why so many men and women in Canada, Australia and New Zealand found it compelling? The facts underlying many of its central assertions allow for, at the very least, far more ambivalent readings of the war's meaning for the Dominions. For instance, despite all of the rhetoric, widely expressed in Canada, Australia and New Zealand during and after the war, that hailed the ascendance of these Dominions to nationhood as a result of their role in the conflict, the formal Constitutional status of Canada, Australia and New Zealand within the Empire changed very little in the wake of the war. It can be argued that even the creation of the Commonwealth by 1931 largely formalized the degree of Dominion autonomy that had been an informal reality even by the outbreak of the First World War. In reality, the most significant changes wrought by the war on the imperial relationship between Britain and the Dominions occurred within the minds of men and women in these countries, and manifested most visibly within the realm of culture. It is easy to survey the years between 1914 and 1939 and find ample proof in the Dominions of the diminishing hold of the British mystique on popular imagination, and of the increasing celebration of distinctly Australian, Canadian and New Zealand identities, accompanied by more and more assertive expressions of national self-esteem.[12]

Along the same lines, the dominant Canadian, Australian and New Zealand narratives of the war reserved pride of place for their nation's soldiers, who simultaneously embodied and were the wellspring of the heightened national consciousness and self-respect arising out of the conflict. [13] The distinguished battlefield record of Canadian, Australian and New Zealand fighting men during the First World War certainly did garner the accolades of friend and foe alike. The Canadian Expeditionary Force (CEF) was one of the most successful fighting units on the Western Front, particularly when it was allowed to exercise a degree of tactical independence from the British. The performance of Canadian units in battles like St. Julien and Vimy Ridge, as well as the unwillingness of senior Canadian officers to allow British commanders to squander Canadian lives, or to break up the CEF and sprinkle its troops throughout the British Army, led to the increasing battlefield autonomy, and eventual full tactical independence, of Canadian fighting units as the war progressed.

Likewise, Australian and New Zealand troops initially earned worldwide acclaim for their extraordinary bravery in battle at Gallipoli in 1915, as members of the Australian and New Zealand Army Corps (ANZAC). By 1917, they were heavily employed on the Western Front, and regarded as one of the theatre's elite forces. By the summer and fall of 1918, Canadian, Australian and New Zealand units, alongside newly arrived troops from the United States, served as the spearhead of the Allies' final victorious offensives, cementing in the process a reputation for courage under fire and tactical innovation. Over the course of the war, Dominion soldiers were celebrated as paragons of a particular kind of masculine martial ideal associated with the 'colonial fringe': What they lacked in spit and polish, or even discipline out-of-the-line, they made up for in raw courage, toughness, resourcefulness and enthusiasm. Moreover, and perhaps most importantly, by the war's end, many Australians, Canadians and New Zealanders, both soldiers and civilians, expressed the belief that their fighting men were in fact superior to the vaunted legions of the British Army.[14]

In an age when widely prevalent ideas of romantic nationalism and Social Darwinism presented the notion that nations could only be forged in the crucible of war, and that the performance of a 'race' in battle best proved their fitness for survival, the conception that they might be superior warriors could make a profound impression on a populace. Furthermore, the martial prowess of Canadian, Australian and New Zealand soldiers, in comparison to the perceived ineptitude of British troops, was proof to many colonials that the greater egalitarianism and rugged 'frontier' lifestyle of their homelands produced a breed of warrior superior to the soldiers drawn from Britain's class-ridden and over-urbanized society. In reality, Australia was one of the most urbanized countries on earth at the time, and the overwhelming majority of recruits to its army came from cities and towns. Similarly, most of the Canadian and New Zealand volunteers recruited during the war came from major cities.[15] Still, even if myth underlay much of the image of Canadian, Australian and New Zealand soldiers that emerged from the war, their idealization struck a resonant chord with many people in the Dominions who were now able to fashion positive and unique identities from long-standing and previously unflattering stereotypes.

However, success on the field of battle came with a terrible cost in human terms for Canada, Australia and New Zealand. The North American Dominion suffered approximately 60,000 war dead between 1914 and 1918. Australia lost around 60,000 personnel as well, and about 16,000 New Zealanders perished. Of course, the more than 700,000 British servicemen who died in the First World War dwarfed these figures. However, Great Britain's wartime population totalled about 40 million, while that of Canada was under eight million, Australia's population by 1914 stood at around four million, and New Zealand's at a mere one million. Consequently, the loss of tens of thousands of their young men was as keenly felt by the Dominions as the numerically greater casualties were in Britain.[16]

In all four nations that are the focus of my study, the years immediately after the end of the Great War witnessed a tremendous flurry of commemorative projects, which is not surprising given the scale of the carnage. Countless memorials to the war dead were erected in cities and towns throughout the British Isles, Canada, Australia and New Zealand. Remembrance holidays were established. In all four countries, with very few exceptions, the language and imagery associated with these commemorative projects, from the design of the memorials to the rituals and speechmaking related to the commemorative ceremonies and holidays, was traditional and conservative. To a great extent, this can be explained by the fact that commemorative projects were primarily designed to achieve two inter-connected aims: To provide consolation to the bereaved, and to legitimate the reasons for which so many had died. In addition, commemorative projects generally reflected the consensus of a given community about how to best to accomplish these aims.

Commemorative projects were just one of many ways that men and women in the aftermath of the Great War struggled to make sense of the immense cataclysm that they had endured, and to render the bewildering and traumatic experience meaningful in some fashion. The narrative that in Canada, Australia and New Zealand dominated each country's inter-war collective memory of the conflict was one form of this process. This narrative provided citizens in the Dominions a way to mitigate their sorrow over the war's human cost with a compensating pride in the achievements of their soldiers and their young, emerging nations. In so doing, the narrative did, in many ways conform to the commemorative ideal.

However, an equally rational response to the war experience might be to derive meanings from the conflict that were not at all consistent with the project of consoling the bereaved and validating the enormous collective sacrifice. In many cases, such interpretations of the war could not be expressed in the language and imagery of the commemorative ideal, but required new and unorthodox modes of representation. It was in Britain, far more than in Canada, Australia or New Zealand, where a narrative completely antithetical to attempts to derive solace or positive inspiration from the war experience would take root and flower within the nation's inter-war culture.

The seeds of this particular understanding were planted primarily in the years shortly after the Armistice, with the publication of a few novels and essays written by individuals seeking to debunk the mythology then being cast in stone on thousands of memorials in Britain and overseas. None of these authors was a war veteran, but most were respected members of the country's cultural elite. They included H. G. Wells, John Maynard Keynes, C. F. G. Masterman, Philip Gibbs, and C. E. Montague.[17] Of these, Gibbs, a war correspondent, and Montague[18], had personal experience of the trenches. Isolated though their voices were in the war's immediate aftermath, they were nevertheless influential in articulating an alternative interpretation of the war. The overarching theme to all of their works was the idea of loss. The physical loss of men and material had its spiritual corollary in the form of lost values, lost order and lost faith in many of the concepts and convictions that were valid before the war. Fuelling this bitter assessment was the sense of disorientation and dislocation that many individuals experienced in the wake of the tumultuous war years, along with the anger, suppressed during the conflict, that they felt over the disparity between the true nature of the war and the fiction that had been fed to the home front by the government and the mainstream press.

Still, whatever authority these disillusioned literati claimed about the war, the fact remained that most of them were civilians. Personal accounts of the war produced by former soldiers could be expected to achieve a level of authenticity, legitimacy and poignancy unattainable by non-combatants, but such works were largely absent from the British cultural scene for most of the 1920s. This drought ended abruptly in the late 1920s and early 1930s. Roughly between 1926 and 1933, the country witnessed a torrent of memoirs and novels penned by ex-soldiers, including Robert Graves, Siegfried Sassoon, Edmund Blunden, and Herbert Read. Wilfred Owen's volume of wartime poems was also published posthumously in these years, and R. C. Sherriff's play, *Journey's End* was performed for the first time.[19] Many of these works were best sellers, and received glowing reviews from literary critics. But more importantly, most war books shared many literary elements as well, including common themes, a common language and a common range of tones (irony being the dominant one), alongside a common interpretation of the war experience and its meaning. These narratives emphasized the physical and spiritual destruction, dislocation and discontinuity wrought by the war, and the language in which they unfolded was utterly devoid of romantic embellishments.

There is compelling evidence that the especially traumatic war experienced by members of Britain's elite lies at the heart of the bitterness and disillusion so palpable in most war writings. Almost without exception, ex-soldier authors hailed from the country's aristocracy or upper-middle class. Consequently, most of them had served during the war as junior officers, the rank befitting their age and status. Most of the war authors were also volunteers, and had spent their tour of duty on the killing fields of the Western Front. As junior officers, these men led troops into combat on the battlefield, which exposed them to disproportionately high levels of danger, and caused them to suffer disproportionately high casualties as a consequence. The attrition that resulted within the junior officer ranks devastated the psyche of at least some of those who comprised it, and by extension, and perhaps on a greater scale, that of the elites on the home front whose sons, husbands, fathers, brothers, friends and lovers were dying in droves overseas.[20] Moreover, many of Britain's junior officers adhered to an ethos of masculine behaviour on the battlefield, one that was consistent with ideals of heroism and masculinity promoted in the public schools that many of them had attended, and with the examples set by the heroes venerated in the popular annals of Empire. This ethos encouraged almost reckless disregard for one's own life in the face of danger. Thus, for many in this cohort, the juxtaposition of this 'romantic' ideal with the speed, lethality and range of modern industrial-age weapons cast their tragic decimation in a particularly ironic light, and contributed to decisively to the remarkable bitterness of their disillusionment.[21]

The narrative of disenchantment represented in the war books and other works by ex-soldiers never achieved the degree of ubiquity within the realm of public culture in inter-war Britain that would allow it to be characterized in these years as the country's dominant collective memory of the First World War. However, it exercised a profound, and perhaps disproportionate, influence on British inter-war culture as a subversive challenge to the most commonly expressed consoling, validating interpretation of the war that had been established by the commemorative project.

The years leading up to the Second World War saw the influence of the narrative of disenchantment grow more conspicuous, not only with the increasing prevalence of its language, imagery and tone within the culture, but also with the infiltration of its tenets into politics and society. One example will have to suffice: In February 1933, when the young students of the Oxford Union debating society approved a resolution stating that they would 'in no circumstances fight for King and Country' (a declaration that would have seemed almost as unthinkable in 1924 as in 1914), their motion served as an explicit rejection of the jingoism, imperialistic sentiment and patriotic high diction excoriated within the narrative of disenchantment as the 'Old Lies' with which the 'Old Men' lured the country's youth to their destruction between 1914 and 1918.

In Canada, Australia and New Zealand during the inter-war period, unlike in Britain, the narrative of the war that mitigated the losses, horror and turmoil of the nations' war experiences by emphasizing the 'positive' outcomes of the war remained largely unruffled on its pre-eminent perch within Dominion culture. This despite the fact that Canada, Australia, and to a much lesser extent, New Zealand, experienced a surge in war books around the same time as Britain. Most of the Dominion authors were veterans of the same experience of industrialized warfare on the Western Front that so disillusioned many of their counterparts in Britain. However, with a few notable exceptions, the sense of loss and spiritual desolation that pervades the works of Graves, Sassoon and other British ex-servicemen is entirely absent from the typical Canadian, Australian or New Zealand war book.[22] On the contrary, while seldom actually glorifying war, Dominion authors generally celebrated the character and achievements of the nation's soldiers with obvious pride. In the words of one Australian author: 'Through all the horror, filth, and suffering there shone something inspiring, stimulating, sacred. This was the heroism, the selflessness of the men who fought for their country, died for their country, taking only what consolation there is in the submerging of self in country.'[23]

Granted, there were often concrete reasons in the Dominions for not contradicting the dominant version of the war. To do so was sometimes to invite the heavy hand of censorship. *All Quiet on the Western Front*, *A Farewell to Arms* and Robert Graves' *Good-bye to All That* were all banned in Australia. The only anti-war novel of the First World War written by a veteran of the Canadian army, Charles Yale Harrison's *Generals Die in Bed,* was banned in Canada. Furthermore, whereas in Britain the disenchanted narrative was cultivated and nurtured by members of a strong cultural vanguard whose ideological agenda compelled them to oppose nationalism that portrayed war and dying for one's country in a sacred light, in Canada, Australia and New Zealand, the prevailing interpretation of the war was disseminated and protected by groups and institutions belonging to or controlled by the powerful loyalist establishment. Especially in Canada and Australia, bitter wartime domestic political battles, particularly over the issue of conscription, had polarized societies to a degree unmatched in Britain. In struggles with their home front enemies during the war, members of each nation's political, social and cultural leadership who were 'loyal to the cause' (these were typically English Canadians in Canada and middle class Protestants of British descent in Australia and New Zealand) had mobilized their considerable political and media resources to paint dissenters as traitors to the Empire, the nation, and particularly, to the heroes in uniform dying overseas. In the post-war period, the loyalist establishment promoted and safeguarded the version of the war experience that validated their support for the country's involvement in the terribly costly conflict.

Uncovering the tangible mechanisms of power employed by various political interests and social and cultural institutions that tried to define collective understandings of the war is crucial to comprehending how particular narratives did or did not achieve prevalence within British and Dominion societies. However, it is important to recognize that the complex process by which the Great War came to be 'remembered' within Britain, Canada, Australia and New Zealand was no more a purely top-down elite project than the war itself had been. This process operated at all levels of society, and a hallmark of the most successful narratives was that they appealed to broad cross-sections of the public.

During the inter-war years, men and women throughout the Empire struggled to come to terms with the Great War's heavy toll. Certainly many of those left behind gazed, like Bird and Sassoon, upon the thousands of names etched in stone on countless memorials to their nation's dead, and asked, 'What does it mean?' In Canada, Australia and New Zealand during these years, the standard response to that question remained fundamentally unchallenged, at least within public culture. In Britain, this was not the case. Understanding why sheds light on the inextricably intertwined, and heretofore largely unexplored, relationship between collective identity and the memory of the Great War.

1

'Heroes of Their Own Epic'

The Last of the Gentlemen's Wars?

Writing thirty-five years after the end of the South African War, Major-General J. F. C. Fuller, the influential military theorist and prophet of modern mechanized warfare, nostalgically recalled the 1899–1902 conflict in which he had served as a subaltern as 'the last of the gentlemen's wars.' His memoir of the experience, published in the lull between 'the first of the cad's wars – the unsportsmanlike war of 1914–1918,' and the even more brutal conflict that loomed on the horizon, vividly depicts some of the more unpleasant aspects of the South African campaign: the unremitting heat and dust, the fever-ridden field camps and hospitals, the constant fear of an unseen, lethal enemy. However, for Fuller, these and other negative features of the war were largely redeemed by the atmosphere of chivalry that prevailed among combatants, and by the 'sporting' way in which hostilities were conducted. Such behaviour characterized Boer and British soldiers alike, but British officers particularly exemplified the ideal, because, as Fuller explained, 'during the long years before the war we had been brought up to believe that war was a sport, and that the height of soldiership was to be a sportsman.'[1]

Fuller's memoir pays tribute to certain martial virtues that he contends made the South African conflict the ultimate exemplar of a romantic and relatively more humane mode of warfare that was dealt a mortal blow by the industrialized carnage of the Great War. Of the underlying ethos that motivated his and his fellow officers' chivalry, Fuller writes:

> It belonged to the days when kings fought kings, and not to a democratic age when demented, newspaper-fed masses of men vilify and tear each other to pieces. It belonged to the days of the sword and the lance and not to those of the magazine rifle and machine-gun.[2]

For Fuller to wax nostalgic about the gallant conduct of belligerents in this particular war might seem more than a little strange. Latter-day historians and commentators looking back across the shattered landscape of two world wars have been more inclined to see in the South African conflict harbingers of the vicious and indiscriminate warfare so prevalent in the twentieth century. The last two years of the contest seem to offer especially chilling portents of the shape of wars to come. Decisively defeated on the battlefield, the Boers after 1900 waged a fierce and tenacious guerrilla campaign against the militarily superior British forces, who responded with sometimes-brutal reprisals against Afrikaner civilians. Thousands of Boer homesteads were burned as part of a British 'scorched earth' policy designed to deprive Afrikaner guerrillas of their primary source of support in the countryside. Of the huge numbers of Boer refugees inevitably created by this tactic, over 100,000 were placed in badly prepared, disease-infested concentration camps, where about 28,000 of them, mostly children, starved to death or died of illness.[3]

Fuller does not deny the sordidness of the British farm-burning policy (though he does downplay its brutality, and he hardly mentions the concentration camps at all), but rather argues that the ugly side of the war in South Africa was largely mitigated by the conspicuous civility displayed by the combatants toward one another. He cites as an example the famous incident at Paardeberg in 1900, when the British commander, Lord Roberts, having surrounded and commenced to bombard the laager of his adversary, the formidable Afrikaner general Pieter Cronjé, offered upon learning of the presence of Boer women and children in the line of fire to allow them to pass through the British lines to safety. That Cronjé turned down this offer was hardly the fault of the chivalrous Roberts, contends Fuller.[4] To further support his argument, the author might have related the anecdote of the dashing and flamboyant French general Georges Henri Anne-Marie Victor de Villebois-Mareuil, shot down in battle while serving as a volunteer commander in the Boer army. The Frenchman's gallant last stand so impressed his British adversaries that he was buried with full military honours by the regiment responsible for his death, and the commander of that unit, Lord Methuen, personally paid for the gravestone, wrote a letter of condolence to Villebois-Mareuil's daughter, and sent an officer to Paris with the dead general's ring.[5]

In light of such ostentatious displays of sportsmanship, it is easy to understand why Fuller lamented that the nature of war had changed irrevocably for the worse in the years since his baptism of fire in South Africa. If the reality of the war he fought on that scorching veldt was nowhere near as humane and sporting as he subsequently portrayed it to be (it was certainly no 'gentleman's war' for South African civilians, Boer and black, caught up in the maelstrom), it is clear from his memoir that his first experience of war as a young subaltern did little or nothing to defy his naive expectations of soldiering, or to shatter the underlying illusions that allowed him to transplant, without irony, the customary attitudes of the playing field to the battlefield.

For Fuller, however, and for a generation of subalterns whose introduction to war occurred in the conflagration of 1914–18, the unprecedented bloodshed and brutality of that conflict irreparably tarnished, if not completely obliterated, the veneer of charm and romance that had often gilded nineteenth-century warfare.[6] The revelation of war's darkest actuality was devastating to many of these men largely because the convictions and delusions that it contradicted were so deeply held. The way Victorian and Edwardian males throughout the British Empire, particularly young men who hailed from the upper and upper-middle-classes, regarded and conceptualized war before 1914 was a crucial component of the ethos that lay at the heart of how they defined themselves within society.

Martial Paragons

Ironically, the development of this ethos, and of the martial components so integral to it, took place during the long century of relative peace that Britain experienced following the end of the Napoleonic Wars – the same century that saw the world's scientists and arms makers invent and manufacture the increasingly deadly and technologically sophisticated military hardware that would, in large part, spell the doom of 'gentlemen's wars.' Over the course of the nineteenth and early twentieth centuries, many members of the British aristocracy and upper-middle-class were indoctrinated with a self-awareness of their status as the country's 'leading class,' and inculcated with certain ideals of masculine behaviour that shaped their understanding of what was expected of them in a martial context. These ideals would help to ensure their disproportionate slaughter when they collided with the industrialized lethality of modern warfare. As we will see in a later chapter, it was largely ex-soldiers hailing from this group whose novels, poems and other works of art compellingly represented the war primarily in terms of disenchantment and loss.

To understand how the collision on the battlefield of class-based illusions with murderous reality contributed to the way the First World War came to be imagined after 1918, it is first necessary to examine the reciprocal relationship between war and the ethos that underpinned the British elites' conception of who they were. This chapter will deal solely with the experience of the British elite, as it seeks to illuminate how pre-war conceptions of identity within the country's pre-eminent class contributed decisively to the increasing prevalence within inter-war Britain of a particular understanding of the war's meaning as a national ordeal. Aspects of pre-war Australian, New Zealand and Canadian identity that would play a crucial role in determining how the memory of the war developed in each country will be explored in the next chapter.

On October 21, 1805, Admiral Horatio Nelson, architect of Britain's greatest naval victories in the war against Napoleon, was mortally wounded while directing his fleet to victory in the battle of Trafalgar. Paralysed and in excruciating pain, his spine shattered by a French sniper's bullet, Nelson was carried below the decks of his flagship, where he lived long enough to know Britain's fleet had prevailed. Having exhorted his men before the battle with the famous rally, 'England expects that every man will do his duty,' witnesses reported that the admiral's last words were, appropriately, 'thank God I have done my duty.'[7]

Already a national hero in Britain at the time of Trafalgar, Nelson's death in the midst of his greatest triumph assured his elevation to the status of a secular saint in the eyes of many of his countrymen. The image of the Great Man struck down at the moment of victory, with its Christ-like connotations of a victorious, transcendent death, proved particularly compelling to a number of the nation's best-known painters and writers, as well as to a host of imitators. The poet Robert Southey, in his immensely popular 1813 biography of Nelson, canonized the admiral with these lines:

> The most triumphant death is that of the martyr; the most awful, that of the martyred patriot; the most splendid, that of the hero in the hour of victory: and if the chariot and the horses of fire had been vouchsafed for Nelson's translation, he could scarcely have departed in a brighter blaze of glory. He has left us, not indeed his mantle of inspiration, but a name and an example, which are at this hour inspiring hundreds of the youths of England: a name which is our pride, and an example which will continue to be our shield and our strength.[8]

Nelson's martyrdom was represented on canvas as well, most famously in Arthur William Devis' 1805 painting, *Death of Nelson*. The artist depicts the wounded admiral lying on his deathbed beneath the decks of his flagship *Victory*, naked except for a white shroud, an expression of serene triumph on his face. Nelson is surrounded by twelve of his loyal officers (an appropriate number, given the Christ-like imagery), as well as by a few suitably grief-stricken members of the lower ranks. His body, illuminated by the ship's lantern, seems aglow with angelic inner light, and the massive wooden beams of the ship's deck arch above the tableau like a crucifix.

In terms of style, tone and subject matter, Devis' painting of Nelson is representative of an artistic genre that achieved widespread popularity with Benjamin West's 1770 composition, *The Death of General Wolfe*, and continued to flourish in one form or another until the end of the Great War. The American-born West's innovation was to render the subjects of this and his subsequent epic narrative paintings as unmistakably contemporary in terms of dress and accoutrement, while posing them in a manner meant to recall the martyrs and heroes depicted in traditional works devoted to Biblical or Classical themes. In so doing, West, and counterparts such as Devis, John Singleton Copley, Johann Zoffany, and David Wilkie, explicitly invited Britons to imagine their martial heroes, and possibly themselves, as figures comparable to the legendary paladins and revered saints of old.[9]

By the early nineteenth century, a warrior of Nelson's stature, particularly if he made the ultimate sacrifice for King and Country, could be elevated by artists, poets and other purveyors of culture to the pinnacle of what was an emerging pantheon of national secular deities. Enshrined in their country's Valhalla, these great military men were the main characters in Britain's heroic myths of the nineteenth century, and they provided role models of patriotic, manly virtue worthy of reverence by the general population, and emulation by the patrician class from which they typically originated.

An embryonic version of this phenomenon was evident in the late eighteenth century, as the art of West and his contemporaries attests, and developed in the context of Britain's expanding power and consequent acquisition of a global empire. However, it was the French Revolutionary and Napoleonic Wars between 1793 and 1815 that proved the decisive catalyst for the consolidation of warrior worship as a force in British culture. In a contest that required an unprecedented mobilization of manpower and resources across British society, as well as compelling sources of patriotic inspiration to rival the enemy's revolutionary ideology (which many Britons unquestionably found appealing), paragons of British superiority such as Admiral Nelson and the Duke of Wellington tapped the deep wells of chauvinistic sentiment essential to sustaining loyalty and maintaining enthusiasm for the struggle.

Moreover, as the historian Linda Colley has convincingly argued, for Britain's traditional aristocratic elite, the promotion of a cult of heroism in which the heroes glorified were almost always genteel members of the military officer class helped to reinforce their continued dominance over society during an era in which their control was threatened by the economic and political turmoil swirling around them. The cult of the martial hero allowed Britain's aristocracy to redefine themselves as a service elite providing the patriotic, heroic and self-sacrificing leadership cohort of the nation's military. Thus the gentry in Britain were able to provide a cultural justification for retaining their elevated status in society at a time when members of the ruling class across the Channel were lucky just to keep their heads.[10]

It is fair to say that the heroes of the wars against France provided the mould for the legion of martial idols that were created in later years. The century between the defeat of Napoleon and the outbreak of the First World War was an era of relative peace for Great Britain, in that the nation managed to avoid any significant conflicts with the other major European powers (with the possible exception of the Crimean War fought against Russia in 1853–56).[11] However for Britain, despite stable, albeit tense, relations between the Great Powers, the years between 1815 and 1914 were characterized by almost constant military strife, if only of a very

limited form. In this period Britain was busy expanding what was already the largest empire in history; not only was the country's military engaged in the conquest
of territory, but in the policing of the territory that it already held. In an empire that
encompassed one-quarter of the world's land surface and population, there was
bound to be unrest, particularly among the millions of foreign peoples subject to
British rule. During the 64-year reign of Queen Victoria there were about 70 'little'
imperial wars and punitive expeditions, in latitudes and climates ranging from the
wilderness of northern Canada, to the deserts of Egypt, to the jungles of Burma.[12]

For Britain, the conquest and consolidation of empire throughout the nineteenth century proved a national endeavour on a par with, if not greater than, the
earlier struggle against France. So, like their forebears, Victorian and Edwardian
Britons were greatly in need of martial paragons, in this case to inspire enthusiasm for the nation's efforts to achieve and maintain dominance over millions of
other human beings. At the same time, there were cultural forces at work in the
nineteenth century that would build upon the heroic warrior archetype that had
been prevalent in the Napoleonic Wars and would help to spawn a clutch of imperial icons commensurate with the expansionist tenor of the times. By the beginning of the Great War, the halls of the national Valhalla would be crowded
indeed, and the cult of the martial hero would be an increasingly pervasive presence within society.

Despite the fact that Victorian-era British society was less militarized than many
other European societies of the day, and its empire was more civilian in nature than
some of its rivals, the nation's most celebrated heroes in this period overwhelmingly tended to be military champions. The French wars had established the ideal
of the martial man of action, a romantic figure whose genius, indomitable will, and
above all, courage and willingness to sacrifice himself for the country, gave him the
capacity to almost single-handedly shape the course of history. Exemplars such as
Nelson and Wellington were seen as having saved the nation from the threat of
foreign tyranny. The paladins of Empire, on the other hand, while conforming to
the aforementioned ideal, would be represented as the standard-bearers of British
civilization and culture, extending Christianity, capitalism and the rule of law into
distant, exotic and benighted realms. Of course, within this paradigm there was
often room for glorifying the explorers, entrepreneurs, colonial administrators and,
in particular, missionaries, who also played a fundamental role in accomplishing
this imperial mission. However, civilian celebrities of Empire, despite some notable
exceptions, seldom really captured the public's imagination as heroes in the same
way that military figures did.

Without a doubt, the watershed event in the development of an archetypal martial hero for the age of Empire was the Indian Rebellion of 1857–58. This brief but
bitter struggle was one of the bloodier episodes of imperial history, and nearly cost
the British control of India. Savagery characterized the conflict on both sides, as

Indian rebels massacred European civilians, including women and children, and vengeful British troops carried out brutal reprisals against captured or defeated rebels and their alleged supporters. In Britain, men and women avidly followed the progress of the conflict in the popular press, and the generals who played conspicuous roles in the nation's eventual triumph were showered with glory and immediately elevated into the country's heroic pantheon. Those most celebrated were, of course, the warriors who had sacrificed their lives in the cause of victory. The ferocious fighting that characterized the Rebellion produced quite a few such individuals, and they are typically represented in Victorian-era biographies or accounts of the Rebellion as part of a long tradition of outstanding British military leaders who died splendidly, and consequently earned a particularly exalted status among the paragons of martial gallantry.[13]

Brigadier General John Nicholson, mortally wounded leading the assault on Delhi, was eulogized by one of his contemporaries as an heir to the tradition of General Wolfe, who fell on the Plains of Abraham in 1759. Nicholson was like Wolfe 'in the number of his years, like him in his noble qualities and aptitude for command, like him in the confidence he inspired in all around him, and like him in the wail of sorrow, which told him his death marred the joy of the nation in the hour of victory.'[14] Another chronicler of the Rebellion expressed similar sentiments:

> It has often been the misfortune of England to have the lustre of her brightest achievement dimmed by the death of the victor: Wolfe fell at Quebec – Abercrombie at Acre – Nelson at Trafalgar – and now, no unworthy comparison, Nicholson at Delhi.[15]

When Sir Henry Havelock, perhaps the most controversial and celebrated British commander in the conflict[16] died of dysentery after helping to relieve besieged Lucknow, *The Times* of London had this to say:

> We must think of him upon his death-bed at the Dil-koosha, when he was about to resign his devout and fearless spirit into his Creator's hands, as we think of Wolfe on the heights of Abraham, of Abercrombie on the Egyptian sands, of Moore on the cliffs of Corunna. Never was there a more glorious death than that of the most gallant soldier, when he sank to his long rest, his duty discharged to the last.[17]

Along the same lines, the standard contemporary account of the death of Sir Henry Lawrence, fatally injured by artillery fire during the siege of Lucknow, is hauntingly reminiscent of Nelson's death as depicted by Devis. In fact the admiral's famous last words were echoed in the epitaph the dying general requested for his own tombstone: 'Here lies Henry Lawrence, who tried to do his duty. May God have mercy on him.'[18]

The gallant self-sacrifice of heroic martyrs like Nicholson, Havelock and Lawrence, as celebrated in the popular press, art and literature, helped standardize the code which defined the appropriate behaviour of the British warrior *in extremis*. As with the troopers of the Light Brigade in the famous 1854 poem by Tennyson, death was often depicted as inherently glorious and noble if it occurred as a result of having courageously performed one's duty, even if the battle in which the soldier fell was a hopeless fiasco. It was certainly no secret to Victorians that the British military was far from immune from the occasional shocking defeat at the hands of some underestimated colonial foe. Disasters like Isandlwana in Zululand (1879) and Majuba Hill in the Transvaal (1881) were scandalous blows to national prestige and incited virulent criticism of the Army in the press. However, the men who met their tragic fates with requisite good form were spared any disparagement, and their courageous ends even acquired a certain poignant grandeur in the public imagination. For instance, Major-General George Colley, who was killed while leading the defence of Majuba Hill, is regarded by some present day historians as being largely responsible for the hopeless position in which he and his men found themselves in that ill-fated battle. Nevertheless, at the time of his death, he was memorialized with the appropriate reverence by his contemporaries, one of whom praised him as a 'Homeric hero.'[19]

Perhaps no incident better illustrates the depth of sentiment that could be aroused by the martyred warrior than the last stand of Gordon at Khartoum in 1885. General Charles Gordon was certainly one of the more unusual figures ever to ascend into Britain's heroic pantheon. An extremely devout Christian, he had made his reputation as a mercenary, first in the service of China's emperor, and later in the employ of the Khedive of Egypt. In 1884 he was sent by the British Government to the Sudan to evacuate Khartoum, which was in danger of being overrun by insurgent Dervishes led by the charismatic Mahdi. Upon arriving in Khartoum, it soon became apparent to Gordon that evacuation would be impossible, so he decided to hunker down for a siege, in the forlorn hope that British leaders would mount a relief expedition to rescue the beleaguered city. After much debate, delay, and prodding by the press (and Queen Victoria) the Government finally dispatched forces to the Sudan, but it was too late. After holding out against all odds for 317 days, Khartoum fell only sixty hours before the relief expedition reached the city. Gordon was dead, killed defending his headquarters at the Governor's palace.[20] Shortly before he died, he had written his sister that, like Henry Lawrence in the Indian Rebellion, he had 'tried to do his duty.'[21]

With his death, Gordon became perhaps the most exalted icon in the cult of the fallen warrior since Admiral Nelson. When news of his sacrifice reached Britain, a day of national mourning was declared, on which memorial services were held at

Westminster Abbey, St. Paul's Cathedral and other churches throughout the country. Among those who paid their respects were the Princess of Wales, the Duke of Cambridge, Commander in Chief of the Army, Lord Granville, Archbishop of Canterbury, the Chancellor of the Exchequer and many peers of the realm and members of Parliament.[22] Like Nelson, Gordon's death scene became the stuff of legend, and was also immortalized on canvas, most famously by G. W. Joy. In this highly romantic (and highly dubious) representation of the event, Gordon stands at the top of the steps to the Governor's palace, resplendent in the uniform of his command, a revolver in one hand, his un-drawn sword dangling from his hip. Below him, several Dervishes climb up the steps toward their quarry. One of the two nearest to him is frozen in awe on his hands and knees, almost in a crouch of supplication, while the other stands poised with a spear to strike the general down. To this man, Gordon directs an impassive gaze, and with his empty hand placed over his heart, indicates where the assassin should make the fatal thrust.

Here then, presented in unambiguous visual terms with Joy's painting, was the ideal of the heroic warrior whose gallant death upheld some of the best traditions of the culture, and whose supreme example could help ensure that those traditions continued to be upheld by future generations. And certainly, the didactic uses of Gordon's martyrdom were not lost on his contemporaries. One biographer, writing a decade after the hero's death, had this to say:

> it is as a perfect model of all that was good, brave and true that Gordon will be enshrined in the memory of the great English nation which he really died for, and whose honour was dearer to him than his life ... the qualities which made Gordon superior ... to all his contemporaries ... are attainable; and the student of his life will find the guiding star he always kept before him was the duty he owed his country.[23]

Indeed, the lessons of Gordon and the heroes who preceded him certainly do not seem to have been lost on Britons in the decades before the Great War. By the turn of the century, there were a number of well-known examples of non-warriors who faced danger and death with the same gallant valour as the famous martial icons. For instance, when the Titanic sank in 1912 (in a civilian maritime disaster at least as preventable as the military fiascos at Majuba Hill and Khartoum), contemporary press accounts of the tragedy emphasized the chivalry and bravery of the upper-class male passengers, many of whom sacrificed their lives so that the ship's women and children might have seats in the few available lifeboats.[24]

Only ten months after the Titanic disaster, Britain was again rocked by tragedy, this time by the news that the polar explorer Robert Falcon Scott, along with the other four members of his party, had died as they attempted to become the first men to reach the South Pole. In death, Scott achieved glory that he never had in life. St. Paul's Cathedral held a memorial service that was attended by the King. One national newspaper devoted an entire edition to the life and career of the lost hero.[25] Perhaps what most captured the imagination of the public was Scott's last message, written on the day he died. That facsimiles of these handwritten lines were reprinted in countless British newspapers and journals, and also hung in classrooms throughout England and the Empire, testifies to their resonance[26]:

> We are weak, writing is difficult, but for my own sake I do not regret this journey which has shewn [*sic*] that Englishmen can endure hardships, help one another, and meet death with as great a fortitude as ever in the past … Had we lived, I should have had a tale to tell of the hardihood, endurance and courage of my companions which would have stirred the heart of every Englishman. These rough notes and our dead bodies must tell the tale, but surely, surely, a great rich country like ours will see to it that those who are dependent on us are properly provided for.[27]

The Flower of England

Neither Scott nor most of the well-heeled men on the Titanic would have been likely to see any overtly martial connotation in their attitudes toward facing death. Rather, they described themselves as dying like 'gentlemen.' For instance, when an injured member of Scott's party walked off alone to certain death in a raging blizzard, so as not to slow the progress of his healthier compatriots, Scott praised his action as that of 'a brave man and an English gentleman.'[28] Similarly, a great many of the upper-class British and American passengers on the doomed luxury liner rationalized their self-sacrifice as the only proper response of a gentleman under such circumstances.[29]

However, whether or not they would have articulated the connection, there was a definite link between the way these self-described gentlemen faced death and the way they imagined a long line of heroic martial antecedents had faced death. In addition to figures from the national pantheon, these antecedents included examples drawn from the myths and legends of antiquity and the age of chivalry, thus establishing continuity between the values of past heroic ages and those of the present. Martial paragons, whether ancient or recent, provided the most obvious models for gentlemen to try and emulate when facing danger or the prospect of death. And certainty about how they would respond under such dire circumstances was an absolutely fundamental component of the larger ethos that underpinned the idea of the gentleman.

For many of the men in Victorian and Edwardian Britain who comprised the elite social cohort vaguely and broadly defined as 'gentlemen,' the idea that they belonged to an inherently heroic class was an essential component of their self-identity. For, while being able to call oneself a gentleman presumed a certain degree of wealth (though not necessarily, by the mid-to-late nineteenth century, an aristocratic lineage), it was equally important to possess certain attributes of character and behaviour that marked the individual as a person of quality. While many of these attributes were superficial traits related to manners and appearance, the most sublime qualities revolved around the moral code that guided the gentleman's conduct under almost every circumstance. The nature and resonance of that moral code was one of the fundamental characteristics that distinguished the ruling class of the nineteenth century from that of the previous centuries.

Before the nineteenth century, the landed gentry's right to rule society rested solely on their ownership of property and titles. However, as the century progressed, Britain's ruling class, which had always been relatively more open to upward mobility than was typically the case elsewhere in Europe, welcomed an increasing number of bourgeois newcomers into its ranks. The fact that this nouveau elite lacked a noble pedigree could be overlooked as long as they embraced the ethos and semi-mythical landed tradition of their genteel brethren, and many of them did so with apparent relish. To a great degree, the permeability of the British upper echelon provided a means by which landed aristocrats could maintain at least a share of power in a rapidly industrializing society in which the burgeoning middle class loomed as a force that could potentially wipe them out altogether. By accepting and co-opting non-noble well-to-do bourgeoisie into their cultural paradigm, the gentry ensured that, even if their bloodlines did not survive, the customs and attitudes of their caste would continue to flourish among the elite strata of society. [30]

However, once lineage was no longer the primary justification for their status, then on what basis could the ruling class claim a mandate to lead the country? By the mid-to-late nineteenth century, particularly for many British writers and educators, the answer increasingly lay in the superior character and exemplary virtues that they believed members of the ruling class should possess, if they did not already. Such characteristics would give upper and upper-middle-class elite the moral authority to maintain their hold on the reins of power. Nowhere was the idea of the virtuous, exemplary elite more compellingly embodied than in the ethos of the gentleman.

By the latter half of the nineteenth century, being a gentleman meant conforming to a code of masculine behaviour that was seldom clearly or consistently defined, but was usually well understood by its adherents. Although individuals who did not hail from backgrounds of privilege could learn the code, many Victorian and Edwardian Britons believed that it came naturally only to those who could claim an aristocratic lineage. This stands to reason, since the code of the gentleman, to a large degree, was an edifice whose foundations rested on a celebration and application of certain ideals that many nineteenth-century Britons associated with the aristocratic warrior culture of mediaeval knights. These ideals might be encompassed under the broad heading of 'chivalry.'[31]

The exact principles of modern chivalry are difficult to pinpoint, since its tenets were never decisively standardized, and often only vaguely articulated. More often than not, chivalric ideals were conveyed through the language and imagery employed to celebrate national icons. A biographer of Sir James Outram, one of the military heroes of the Indian Rebellion, praised him as being 'ever actuated by the chivalrous spirit of a true knight errant, and would redress wrongs and help the weak.'[32] The inscription on Outram's monument in Calcutta praised him as a 'faithful servant of England; large minded and kindly ruler of her subjects; in all the true knight; the Bayard of the East.'[33] Another soldier who saw action during the Rebellion expressed his impression of the conflict in similar terms when he described the valour of British officers:

> even the Enfield rifle has not reduced all men to a dead level, but there is still a place to be found for individual prowess, for the lion heart, and the iron will. One seems transported back from the prosaic nineteenth century to the ages of romance and chivalry, and to catch a glimpse, now of a Paladin of old, now of a knightly hero *san peur et sans reproche* ... [34]

While thorough, in-depth discussions of nineteenth-century chivalric ideals were not particularly common, there were a number of notable Victorian men of letters whose influential and popular writings and lectures had an enormous influence on how this code of conduct came to be understood and applied within society. One of these works was Kenelm Digby's *The Broad Stone of Honour*, published in 1822. In this book, which was subtitled 'Rules for the Gentlemen of England' and 'The True Sense and Practice of Chivalry,' Digby defined the concept of chivalry and presented it as a code of behaviour that could guide the conduct of modern gentlemen just as well as it had shaped the ideals of the virtuous mediaeval knight. Digby was a contemporary of Sir Walter Scott, the prolific author of immensely popular novels and poems such as *Ivanhoe* (1820), and 'The Lady of the Lake' (1809), which romanticized the Middle Ages and glorified the figure of the heroic, chivalrous knight. But while Scott consciously implied chivalry was a thing of the past, the phenomenon of a vanished and not-necessarily superior age, Digby explicitly argued that the best ideals of that code should serve as a blueprint for the construction of a moral ethos suitable for the contemporary governing class.[35]

Such sentiments were later echoed and expanded upon by other thinkers, most notably Thomas Carlyle. In *Past and Present* (1843), Carlyle articulated his ideal of a ruling class whose mandate to govern rested in their heroic character and willingness to rise above self-interest. To earn their right to lead society, such a class was duty-bound to embrace struggle and self-sacrifice. He attacked the industrialists and aristocrats who ruled England at the time, the former because they exploited their workers in the pursuit of profits, the latter because they ignored their obligation to serve the greater society. 'A High Class without duties is like a tree planted on precipices,' Carlyle wrote. 'In a valiant suffering for others, not in a slothful making others suffer for us, did nobleness ever lie.' Furthermore, according to the author, the privileged position of the aristocracy compelled them to accept the role of martyrs under certain circumstances. Carlyle asserts:

> Every noble crown is … a crown of thorns … In modern, as in ancient and all societies, the Aristocracy, they that assume the functions of an Aristocracy … have taken the post of honour; which is the post of difficulty, the post of danger, – of death, if the difficulty be not overcome.[36]

For Carlyle, the ideal of an England governed by heroes could not be realized unless the country's leading classes jettisoned self-interest for a more sublime ethos. He felt that modern rulers should look to the ancient codes of mediaeval chivalry for a model of appropriately 'noble' behaviour, not just on the battlefield, but in the metaphorically brutal struggles of the political and industrial realms. 'Man is created to fight,' according to Carlyle, but society's heroic natural leaders are those who fight with chivalry. He compared greedy, exploitative capitalists to the 'ignoble godless Bucanier [*sic*] and Chactaw [*sic*] Indian,' and reminded the reader that, while such men may appear to succeed in the short-term, to achieve glory in the eyes of 'Mankind and the Maker of Men':

> thou shalt be strong of heart, noble of soul; thou shalt dread no pain or death, thou shalt not love ease or life; in rage, thou shalt remember mercy, justice; – thou shalt be a Knight and not a Chactaw, if thou wouldst prevail![37]

In his discussion of heroic qualities, Carlyle praised 'toughness of muscle,' but reserved his strongest admiration for 'toughness of heart,' which he defined as 'persistence … desperate, unsubduable patience, composed candid openness, clearness of mind.'[38] By the mid-nineteenth century, other British thinkers were drawing upon Carlyle's ideas and applying them to their own discourses on the nature of manliness and the ethos of the gentleman. However, for some of the most popular and influential of these thinkers, toughness of heart was an attribute inextricably linked with toughness of muscle; one simply could not possess the former without the latter.

The two foremost advocates of this ideal of masculinity were Charles Kingsley and Thomas Hughes. Both men began their public lives as crusaders for the downtrodden; in their youth they helped to organize the Christian Socialist movement in England. Carlyle influenced both men, and both men were avid sportsmen. From

Carlyle's metaphorically pugilistic dictum that man was born to fight, be it on the battlefield, or against ignorance, disease and the forces of nature, Kingsley and Hughes fashioned a philosophy of manliness that celebrated literal physical tough-ness and athletic prowess, in conjunction with Christian purity, self-sacrifice and chivalry, as the essential components of ideal masculinity. This doctrine, derisively labelled 'Muscular Christianity' by its critics, was preached from the pulpit by the nationally renowned clergyman Kingsley, and articulated in the widely read essays and literary works of both men. However, in all likelihood it was Hughes' 1857 novel *Tom Brown's Schooldays* that disseminated the ideal of 'Muscular Christianity' to the widest audience, and consequently can be credited more than any other single artefact with establishing the doctrine as a major force in British culture. By the end of the nineteenth century, Hughes' novel had gone into at least 50 different editions and reprints, and was canonical reading for schoolboys throughout the English-speaking world.[39]

Tom Brown's Schooldays tells the story of the title character's coming-of-age at Rugby, the English public school Hughes actually attended as a youth. Tom is de-picted as a tough, courageous boy with an innately chivalrous tendency to take the side of the underdog in a scrap. He hails from a family of stalwart country gentry with a long tradition of service to the nation and empire. 'Wherever the fleets and armies of England have won renown, there stalwart sons of Browns have done yeomen's work,' writes Hughes. 'With the yew bow and cloth-yard shaft at Cressy and Agincourt ... with hand-grenade and sabre, and musket and bayonet, under Rodney and St. Vincent, Wolfe and Moore, Nelson and Wellington, they have car-ried their lives in their hands.' This is because, first and foremost, 'the Browns are a fighting family,' of whom 'one may question their wisdom, or wit, or beauty, but about their fight there can be no question.'[40] The theme of the novel concerns Tom's evolution, under the firm but benevolent tutelage of Thomas Arnold, the headmaster at Rugby, from a good-hearted but undisciplined young ruffian into the ideal of a manly Christian gentleman consecrated to battle for God, the empire and his fellow man. For Tom's father, Squire Brown, this is, after all, the primary object of a public school education, more so than intellectual development. 'Shall I tell [Tom] to mind his work, and say that he's sent to school to make himself a good scholar?' He asks at one point. 'Well, but he isn't sent to school for that – at any rate, not for that mainly,' he concludes. 'If only he'll turn out a brave, helpful, truth-telling Englishman, and a gentleman, and a Christian, that's all I want.'[41]

Tom Brown's outlook might have been echoed by many a public school pupil in the decades before the First World War, for it was in the public schools that an ideal of manhood based on physical fitness and chivalry came to be most actively promulgated, particularly once the institutions began to open their doors to an increasing number of middle-class boys in the mid nineteenth century. With the greater social mobility resulting from the Industrial Revolution, Britain's landed gentry found that by the mid 1800s they had to share their once-exclusive status as the nation's elite class with members of the well-to-do bourgeoisie whose wealth put them on a par with their traditional 'betters.' Greater access to the highest social rank meant that institutions once closed to all but the aristocracy opened up to the well-off middle class as well. For the male offspring of these bourgeois elite, that often meant the opportunity to attend one of the nation's prestigious public schools.

Between 1870 and 1914, England's public schools enjoyed their heyday as the social training ground for the nation's young gentlemen-to-be. Despite being ostensibly academic institutions, the primary mission of the public schools in these years was to inculcate elite youth with the values and attributes essential to their future role as leaders of British society.[42] The education received by the student at Eton, Harrow, Marlborough, Charterhouse, Rugby, or any one of the dozens of expensive, boarding-house institutions scattered throughout England was aimed less at improving the intellect than at instilling Christian morality and developing certain manly virtues. For aristocrats witnessing the increasing number of upper-middle-class boys enrolling in the once-exclusive public schools, it was particularly important that these institutions work to transform those youngsters who were not well born into men who would exemplify all that was best in the nation's character. In other words, into men thoroughly indoctrinated with the ethos of the gentleman. By the last decades of Queen Victoria's reign, this goal was pursued primarily through the promotion of athletic competition, particularly the playing of team sports like cricket, football and rugby.[43]

Team games were first organized at several public schools in the 1850s as a way of controlling the leisure time of pupils, many of whom filled their free hours with rather brutal mischief – shooting rabbits, robbing local hen houses, and bludgeoning frogs, for instance.[44] When the first pilot sports programs proved to be a success, public schools throughout the nation, especially those whose enrolment was swelling with upwardly mobile middle-class students, adopted organized games as a way to maintain discipline and order outside of the classroom. However, by the last two decades of the nineteenth century, team sports were more than just diversionary in nature. In many ways they now dominated the public school experience, relegating academics to a subordinate role. Behind this development lurked a belief, firmly held by many educators, parents and students, that games best taught the values and virtues vital to the moulding of the young gentleman-to-be. Advocates of the primacy of organized sports in public schools claimed the games imparted chivalric attributes such as physical and moral courage, loyalty and team spirit, a respect for fair play, the capacity to accept defeat graciously, and the ability to both command and obey. As one writer put it, even the 'lad who leaves an English public school disgracefully ignorant of the rudiments of useful knowledge, who can speak no language but his own, and ... who has devoted a great part of his time and nearly all of his thoughts to athletic sports,' still carried away something useful from his experience, namely 'a manly straightforward character, a scorn of lying and meanness ... and fearless courage.' The writer goes on to say that 'This type of citizen ... with all his defects, has done yeoman's service to the Empire; and for much that is best in him our public schools may fairly take credit.'[45]

For those who believed sports should dominate the public school experience, the virtues and attributes gained by young elites on the playing field prepared them for any type of manly endeavour, including being a warrior. For decades there had been a connection between public school training and martial proficiency. After all, it was following Napoleon's final defeat that Wellington allegedly declared Waterloo was won 'on the playing fields of Eton.' However, as the century drew to a close, the link between war and the public school ethos was more explicit than ever before. By the 1880s and 1890s, it was already a cliché in Britain to employ sporting jargon when speaking or writing of war. By the same token, war was often treated as a metaphor for sports. One of the most famous examples of this late-nineteenth-century tendency to draw analogies between the playing field and the battlefield is Henry Newbolt's 1898 poem 'Vitai Lampada':

> There's a breathless hush in the Close tonight
> Ten to make and the match to win-
> A bumping pitch and a blinding light,
> An hour to play and the last man in.
> And it's not for the sake of a ribboned coat,
> Or the selfish hope of a season's fame,
> But his Captain's hand on his shoulder smote-
> "Play up! play up! and play the game!"

Years later, the former cricket brave finds himself in a different, more desperate contest in a savage, faraway outpost of Empire.

> The sand of the desert is sodden red-
> Red with the wreck of a square that broke;
> The Gatling's jammed and the Colonel dead,
> And the regiment blind with dust and smoke;
> The river of death has brimmed his banks,
> And England's far and Honor a name;
> But the voice of a schoolboy rallies the ranks:
> "Play up! play up! and play the game!"[46]

The imagery and language of Newbolt's poem is especially symbolic of the cultural moment in which it was written. The zenith of the cult of games at the public schools coincided with a particularly aggressive phase of imperial expansion and heightened tensions between Europe's Great Powers. During the 1880s and 1890s, and particularly during the decade immediately preceding the First World War, the arms race and contest for colonial spoils among European rivals helped create an increasingly militarized atmosphere in Britain. At the same time, Charles Darwin's theory of evolution, popularized after the mid nineteenth century and inappropriately applied to social development, seemed to provide a 'scientific' foundation for the idea that the fate of nations and races, no less than that of natural species, was determined by the iron laws of 'survival of the fittest.'[47]

For the young men learning how to be gentlemen on the public school playing fields, the stakes of the 'game' were becoming higher and higher in late Victorian and Edwardian Britain. Many of the qualities associated with being a 'proper gentleman' had long been conflated with the attributes of the good military officer. Thus, not surprisingly, it was the public schools that traditionally provided the men who filled the ranks of the British officer corps. If, as many believed, there was to be a general European war, a struggle that would determine global supremacy or perhaps even the fate of the British nation and 'race', then the leading class would have to be prepared when duty called.

In the wake of the British Army's rather lacklustre performance in the South African War, and amid worries about the effect of urbanization on the manpower pool in Britain that would be tapped in any major war, the War Office decided to bolster the readiness of the nation's officer class for a future conflict by establishing Officer Training Corps at most of the country's public schools. By the early 1900s, most young men at England's elite institutions received at least some basic military training, but the OTC programs at many schools were often mediocre at best. In general, OTC students spent their time drilling, firing rifles and studying tactics that were outdated during the Crimean War. Nor was there a great deal of interest among most boys in what the corps had to teach. While some regarded OTC as yet another arena in which to cultivate the manly virtues of their class, many others felt the program was a boring waste of valuable time that could be spent more usefully on the playing field. In addition, a number of boys absorbed almost nothing of what they supposedly learned in OTC. However, as one man who would go on to serve as a junior officer in the Great War discovered, this did not necessarily lead to low grades on the program's proficiency tests:

Twenty questions I was asked, and I looked sheepish and I said "Don't know" to each one. Then he said, "Is there anything you do know?" and I gave him the two pieces of knowledge I had come armed with – the weight of a rifle and the episodes in the life of a bullet from the time it leaves the breech till it hits its man. Then I saluted really smartly, and the gentleman gave me 60 out of a hundred. Company Drill came next which merely consisted in drilling a Company (as you might think) of most alarmingly smart regulars. For this I got 70 (every one got 70) – and then I went off to Tactical. Tactical was equally a farce. I was told to send out an advance-guard, lost my head, sent out a flank guard, scored 70 per cent.[48]

If the purpose of OTC was to provide young men with the practical skills they would need as officers in a modern war, then the achievements of the program were dubious at best. What the OTC did accomplish, by its mere presence in the public schools, was to reinforce continually the idea among students at these institutions that they were members of the leading class, and could expect to serve as the vanguard of any British military force in the next martial crisis.

It might have been much better for these potential future officers if there had been some way to acquaint them with the lethal implications of modern military technology. The skills learned on the playing field would not increase their chances of survival when facing a nest of Maxim machine guns or a battery of 77mm field pieces. And the values and virtues taught by team sports, while helping to motivate the conspicuous, almost suicidal, bravery traditionally displayed by British officers, were not in and of themselves enough to carry the day against the deadly weaponry that ruled the modern battlefield.

A major factor contributing to the widespread ignorance among British civilians about twentieth-century warfare was the fact that Europe had been relatively strife-free for most of the nineteenth century. There had not been a Great Power conflict since 1871, and Great Britain had not been involved in one since 1856. However, between these years and 1914, technology utterly transformed the battlefield.[49] Unfortunately, the overwhelming majority of elite-class youth who would enlist in the Great War were relatively unaware of this development. In the public schools and universities where they obtained their education, the emphasis of the curriculum was almost exclusively on liberal arts, an area where technological advances were unlikely to be discussed. Most public schools emphasized the teaching of Greek and Latin, and universities tended to steer students toward the liberal arts. This is reflected in enrolment statistics at Oxford University in 1900. A mere eight per cent of the student body was enrolled in Natural Sciences, and six per cent in Mathematics, compared to 34 per cent in Classics and 33 per cent in History. Similarly, at Eton in 1884 there were 28 Classics masters but no scientists.[50] The dearth of scientific and technological knowledge among the young elite had serious consequences in terms of how they imagined any future conflict would be fought.

At the outbreak of the Great War, a great many of the youthful volunteers commissioned as junior officers in Britain's armed forces believed that the war in Europe would resemble the martial clashes of the nineteenth century, with massive armies moving swiftly across the Continent and clashing in a few great, decisive battles that would quickly decide the outcome.

So it was that on the eve of the First World War, many of the young men of Britain's privileged classes were no less ignorant and naive about the nature of modern war than J. F. C. Fuller had been when he embarked for South Africa as a youthful subaltern. But they were just as certain as he had been about how they would respond when faced with the test of battle, and they owed that security to the same fundamental illusions that underpinned his convictions. Young gentlemen were never allowed to forget a pantheon of noble heroes, some real, some fictional, with a lineage stretching unbroken from ancient Troy to modern England, who fought bravely, lived chivalrously, and died gloriously; who were, consequently, perfect romantic role models for youths who aspired to the virtuous manhood befitting their class. When war came in 1914, the sons of privilege volunteered for service in droves. The enthusiasm with which some members of this cohort greeted the opportunity to fight is nowhere better expressed than in the soldier poet Rupert Brooke's 'Peace,' written shortly after the outbreak of the war:

Now, God be thanked who has matched us with his hour,
And caught our youth, and wakened us from sleeping,
With hand made sure, clear eye, and sharpened power,
To turn, as swimmers into cleanness leaping,
Glad from a world grown old and cold and weary,
Leave the sick hearts that honour could not move,
And half-men, and their dirty songs and dreary,
And all the little emptiness of love!

Similarly, in 'The Dead,' Brooke celebrates the rewards of ultimate sacrifice:

Blow out, you bugles, over the rich Dead!
There's none of these so lonely and poor of old,
But, dying, has made us rarer gifts than gold ...
Blow, bugles, blow! They brought us, for our dearth,
Holiness, lacked so long, and Love, and Pain,
Honour has come back, as a king, to earth,
And paid his subjects with a royal wage;
And Nobleness walks in our ways again;
And we have come into our heritage.[51]

There was very little about the social and cultural context in which Britain's young men of privilege were steeped that might have provided them with a better understanding of war, or prepared them for the shock of a modern one. Rather, much of what they absorbed from that context helped fortify the value system and code of conduct that would drive them as young subalterns in the Great War over the top and into the teeth of decimating firepower. How losing so many sons of privilege affected Britain's public imagination will be dealt with in a subsequent chapter, as will the spiritual and psychological consequences for some of the members of this social cohort whose pre-war illusions were shattered by wartime realities. Suffice it to say that these two issues lie at the heart of the emergence of Britain's post-war 'Lost Generation' myth. There can be little doubt that for many of the country's young elite, the nature of the conflict they encountered between 1914 and 1918 significantly altered how they viewed war, forcing them to scrutinize, perhaps for the first time, the values and convictions that impelled them toward martyrdom.

The 'Lost Generation'

Much of the power of the 'Lost Generation' narrative in Great Britain derives not so much from reality, which was bad enough, but from the perception – widespread throughout society during and after the Great War, but particularly so among the elite – that the conflict was an unmitigated demographic disaster for the country's leading class. Out of this assumption emerged the related idea that the loss of so many potential worthies dealt a mortal blow to the nation's future. Decades after the war, J. B. Priestley would declare that 'nobody, nothing will shift me from the belief which I shall take to the grave that the generation to which I belonged, destroyed between 1914 and 1918, was a great generation, marvellous in its promise.'[52]

It is relatively easy for historians to prove that Britain's war generation, even the cohort comprised by young men from the upper and upper-middle-class was not 'destroyed' as Priestley asserts. The simple fact is that the majority of the elite who served returned home alive. Among British and Irish peers or sons of peers who went to war, one in five died.[53] While this is an indicator of high casualties among the privileged class, the fact that four-fifths of those same men survived shows how important it is to differentiate decimation from extermination.

However, casualty figures from a variety of sources seem to suggest that the war, while not wiping out the larger part of England's young elite, did slay them in numbers disproportionate to those of other classes. For instance, the one in five peers killed is noticeably higher than the overall wartime average for the British fighting services of one death per every eight men enlisted.[54] Also, the universities of Oxford and Cambridge, traditionally England's bastions of elite higher education, together sent a total of 26,529 men into the services between 1914 and 1918. More than 19 per cent of the enlistees from Oxford, and about 18 per cent of those from Cambridge, did not survive the war. Similarly, most public schools lost about one in five of their 'old boys' who fought. By comparison, the overall proportion of all men mobilized in Britain who did not survive the war was 12 per cent.[55]

The reason for the uneven distribution of death among Britain's classes is simple. The majority of those from the elite who served in the British Army during the war did so as junior officers, and the possibility that a subaltern would be killed or wounded during his tour was far greater for him than for enlisted men. In the first year of the war, for instance, over 14 per cent of Britain's army officers were killed in combat, as opposed to 5.8 per cent of lower-ranking soldiers. Over the course of the conflict this disparity would decrease only slightly.[56]

It is important to understand that, for England during the war, the death of so many junior officers represented a tragedy far greater than just the untimely loss of a great many wealthy, privileged young men. Within the caste system of English society, it was members of the elite who traditionally dominated positions of leadership, responsibility or authority within the nation. Most of the country's politicians, diplomats, colonial administrators, judges, lawyers, poets and philosophers sprang from their ranks. The public schools and universities that supplied young officers to lead in battle were training grounds for boys destined to one day steer the ship of state or mould tomorrow's culture.

During the war, the impression that the future was being mortgaged on the fields of France and Belgium was exacerbated by the poignant deaths and public mourning of young members of the elite who had achieved some degree of acclaim before the war. The widely acknowledged talent of poets such as Percy Wyndham and Julian Grenfell was deemed irreplaceable, and the un-realized potential that they and others took with them to the grave haunted the living. Perhaps Rupert Brooke provides the most famous example of a promising future tragically abbreviated by the war. Only days after his poem 'The Soldier' was praised and read aloud in the pulpit by the dean of St. Paul's Cathedral, Brooke died of blood poisoning en route to Gallipoli. The young poet was eulogized by the First Lord of the Admiralty, Winston Churchill, who described him as 'joyous, fearless, versatile, deeply instructed, with classical symmetry of mind and body … all that one would wish England's noblest sons to be in days when no sacrifice but the most precious is acceptable, and the most precious is that which is freely proffered.'[57]

Of course, just as the generation of privileged youth whose ranks were ravaged by war was not entirely destroyed, many of its survivors played major roles in the post-war affairs of the country. Two former junior officers, Harold Macmillan and Anthony Eden, became prime ministers. Other upper-class veterans of the trenches, including Edward Wood, Oliver Lyttelton and Oswald Mosley, became important inter-war politicians. In fact, ex-officers ranked second only to lawyers as an occupational category in the House of Commons in the 1920s.[58] Politics was not the only field where the war generation made its mark after 1918. Former subalterns were significant, talented players in the arts, law, the civil services and the military, as well.

Be that as it may, the idea that the Great War liquidated almost an entire generation of young elites persisted in England, even as veterans of that class rose and
made their reputations. Reports estimating the number of British war dead were
published by a number of government agencies and private researchers soon after
the Armistice, but they did little to confirm or refute public perceptions. Their figures on overall losses varied wildly, ranging anywhere from 500,000 to 1 million,
and they seldom provided data broken down by class or rank.[59] But certainly many
in the country might have brooded over the 2,200 patrician names listed on the
Great War Roll of Honour in Debrett's *Peerage* of 1918.

Furthermore, many in post-war Britain did not need accurate casualty statistics
to know that their country and their class had paid a terrible price in blood for victory. They remembered the long lists of names on the Rolls of Honour in school
chapels, the photographs of fallen soldiers in local newspapers, and, most significantly, the friends and relatives that they had lost. Lord Asquith, referring to the
death of his son Raymond in the war, expressed the feelings of many of his contemporaries in Britain toward what they saw as an entirely lost generation of young
men. 'Whatever pride I had in the past and whatever hope I had for the future,' he
wrote, 'by much the largest part was vested in Raymond. Now all that is gone.'[60]

2

New World Sons of Empire

New World Paragons

Charles Edwin Woodrow Bean, the Australian journalist whose accounts and descriptions of the nation's soldiers in the First World War would play a pre-eminent role in enshrining the ideal of the 'digger' within the country's culture, was struck during his assignment as a correspondent at Gallipoli in 1915 by what he saw as a stark contrast between the physical and mental attributes of the average British soldier and those of the typical Australian fighting man. Like many commentators, colonial and British, in an era when the cultural landscape of the Western world was awash in Social Darwinist ideas, Bean articulated his impressions of this contrast in terms of 'racial' differences between the men of the Motherland and of the Dominion. His encounters with British 'Tommies' on the Peninsula convinced him that the Anglo-Saxon race in Great Britain had degenerated virtually beyond hope of restoration. 'The truth is that after 100 years of breeding in slums, the British race is not the same, and can't be expected to be the same, as in the days of Waterloo,' he wrote in his diary. Bean believed that the future survival of the British people rested with the superior racial stock evolving in the 'White Dominions' of the British Empire. 'The only hope is that those puny, narrow-chested little [Tommies] may, if they come out to Australia, [New Zealand] or Canada, within two generations breed men again. England herself, unless she does something heroic, cannot hope to.'[1]

For Bean, the underlying explanation for the inferior state of the British race lay with the adverse affects of the Motherland's class system. He believed that only the British elite enjoyed the kind of healthy living conditions and lifestyle, and developed the kind of martial ethos, that made for superior soldiers. 'England is breeding one fine class at the expense of all the rest,' he lamented. Social and political relationships in Australia, which he saw as being more egalitarian than those of Britain, produced an army in which the ability and the opportunity to lead and to make decisions on the battlefield was not limited or restricted to men hailing from the elite. Bean argued that the average Australian, because of the environment and society in which he had been nurtured, could be turned into a soldier with a year's training. This was not the case with the average Tommy of Kitchener's Army because, as a result of the 'British social formula,' the only non-professionals in that force who possessed attributes of nerve, physique, spirit and self-control comparable to those that were evident among the amateurs of the Australian Imperial Force were the junior officers. The ideal of the English gentleman that helped to motivate their exemplary battlefield performance was an admirable ethos, in Bean's view, but it was not an outlook that could transcend its class-specific identifications. In fact it only served to highlight the barriers of class and ideology that characterized the British Army, as well as British society.[2]

Bean's belief that the environments and societies of the Dominions were producing a superior specimen of manhood than that which was being bred in the over-urbanized, class-ridden Motherland was not a new idea at the time of the First World War, though this line of argument perhaps achieved its apotheosis during the 1914–18 conflict. Rather, it was consistent with certain conceptions of collective identity that had emerged and developed in the Dominions over the course of the late nineteenth and early twentieth centuries. As the white populations of Britain's settlement colonies became increasingly composed of men and women who were born in these lands, rather than in the Motherland, many Dominion citizens, particularly among artists, intellectuals and media commentators, endeavoured to define for themselves and for their countries distinctly 'Australian', 'Canadian' or 'New Zealand' identities. Often these identities were constructed within the Dominions primarily by comparing and contrasting certain qualities represented as typical of the land and its people with idealized or stereotypical understandings of their British counterparts. Thus, the articulation of Australian, Canadian or New Zealand identity almost always involved coming to terms with or confronting the complex relationship between the Dominions and Great Britain.

The ties that bound the Dominions to Britain – from formal political, economic, and military links to more abstract bonds of heritage and culture – were an inescapable fact of life in the settlement colonies. Prior to the mid-nineteenth century, these ties were usually invoked, by British and colonial commentators alike, to reinforce Britain's status as the benefactor and guardian of the Dominions, a role which granted Britain an undeniably superior position in the imperial relationship. Of course British economic and military superiority to the Dominions was a real and incontrovertible phenomenon, but it was not only in such concrete realms where this hierarchy was manifested. Many in Britain and in the Dominions internalized an understanding of the Metropole as the centre of civilization and of far-flung colonies such as Canada, Australia and New Zealand as the periphery. Surely, the thinking went, in these newly settled lands, with their harsh and inhospitable environments, the quality of civilization (i.e. white political and cultural institutions) that would develop there, if it developed at all, would be significantly inferior to that of the British Isles? It was a view that was at least as prevalent in the Dominions themselves as in the Motherland. Thus the Australian poet who in 1819 celebrated the kangaroo as 'Thou Spirit of Australia,/That redeems from utter failure,/From perfect desolation,/And warrants the creation/Of this fifth part of the Earth.'[3]

However, during the nineteenth and early twentieth centuries, the continued demographic expansion and economic and political development of the Dominions was accompanied by a growing consciousness among the residents of these countries – particularly among the native-born – of their identification with the land in which they lived, and with the types of societies evolving under the Antipodean sun or in the chillier climes of North America. [4] Britain's Dominions experienced their primary phases of development in an era when politics and culture in Europe and other parts of the world were profoundly influenced by the ideals of romantic nationalism. Those in the Dominions who sought to articulate identities as 'Australians', 'Canadians' or 'New Zealanders' drew upon themes and subjects found in similar attempts in Europe and elsewhere to generate nationalist sentiment among populaces. For Australian, New Zealand and Canadian writers and artists with this agenda, those aspects of colonial life that had previously been characterized as unappealing – the harshness of the environment, the vast unsettled tracts, the isolation from Europe, the supposed lack of history, and the absence of a cultivated elite among the inhabitants – were celebrated as virtues. Not quite 100 years after one newcomer to Australia saw the kangaroo as the only redeeming feature of a land of 'failure' and 'desolation,' the Australian poet Dorothea Mackellar would declare:

> I love a sunburnt country,
> A land of sweeping plains,
> Of ragged mountain ranges,
> Of draughts and flooding rains;
> I love her far horizons
> I love her jewel-sea
> Her beauty and her terror –
> The wide brown land for me![5]

Similarly, the Canadian nationalist Charles Mair waxed ecstatic over the virtues of his country in the poem 'Kanata':

> The Eastern and the Western gates
> Are open, and we see her face!
> Between her piney steeps she waits
> The coming of each alien race.

Dear Genius of a virgin land,
Kanata! Sylph of northern skies!
Maid of the tender lip and hand,
And dark, yet hospitable, eyes.[6]

Mackellar established in her poem a contrast between the attributes of her own land and the qualities typically highlighted in celebrations of Britain's landscape. For Mackellar, 'the love of field and coppice, or green and shaded lanes,' did not appeal to her.[7] Mair, for his part, used the Canadian landscape to convey a contrast between the peace and political freedom available in the New World with the strife and tyranny of the Old World. Europe's 'uncouth peasants' journeyed to Canada seeking 'Freedom 'neath the Western Sun,' and it is in North America where the cause of liberty must 'on these fresh fields be lost or won.'[8] The use of landscape and environment as a metaphor to illustrate the divergences between British society and the societies that were emerging in Australia, Canada and New Zealand was a common device employed by nationalist writers and artists in the Dominions. The Australian poet and essayist Marcus Clarke drew in 1876 an explicit connection between the different physical environments that characterized the British Isles and Australia, and between the political and social environment of liberty and egalitarianism that he believed prevailed in Australia, but not in Great Britain. According to Clarke, April in Australia, unlike April in England, 'bears no blossoms, No promises of spring; Her gifts are rain and storm and stain, And surges lash and swing.' However:

Though Scotland has her forests,
Though Erin has her vales,
Though plentiful her harvests,
In England's sunny dales;
Yet foul amidst the fairness,
The factory chimneys smoke,
And the murmurs of the many
In their burdened bosoms choke.

For Australians, the beauty, tranquillity and grandeur that characterized some parts of the British Isles were no substitute for more substantial virtues to be found in their own land, but which were largely absent from Britain:

We've left the land that bore us,
Its castles and its shrines;
We've changed the cornfields and the rye
For the olives and the vines.

Yet still we have our castles,
Yet still we bow the knee;
We each enshrine a saint divine,
And her name is Liberty.[9]

According to many of the artists and commentators in Canada, Australia and New Zealand interested in proclaiming the exemplary attributes of their countries, many of the aspects of Dominion life that earlier critics had forecast would inhibit the development of white civilization were in fact producing political and social institutions superior in their democracy and egalitarianism to those of the Motherland.[10] With the popularization from the mid-nineteenth century onward of Social Darwinist ideas characterizing nations and ethnic groups as 'races' engaged in a perpetual struggle for dominance, where success was determined by a people's fitness for survival, a number of observers further argued that many of the salient qualities of life in the Dominions – including the battle against a hostile environment (and sometimes against hostile indigenous peoples), the struggle to settle and cultivate a frontier, a strenuous life lived out of doors, the lack of a rigid class hierarchy – were responsible for the evolution of a breed of colonial humanity superior to that being produced in Great Britain. The Canadian nationalist scholar Robert Grant Haliburton in 1869 prophesied the future pre-eminence of Canada due to the fact that 'it is a Northern country inhabited by the descendants of Northern races,' including Saxons, Teutons, Scandinavians, Celts and Norman French. The invigorating climate of the North American Dominion would combine with the excellent racial pedigrees of its settlers to produce 'a healthy, hardy, virtuous, dominant race.'[11] Of course, an Antipodean version of the idea that climate equalled destiny existed as well. 'The quality of a race of beings is determined by two things: food and climate,' declared Marcus Clarke in 1877. These two factors would produce in 100 years an Australian described as 'a tall, coarse, strong-jawed, greedy, pushing, talented man, excelling in swimming and horsemanship,' who would, in 500 years 'have changed the face of nature and swallowed up all our contemporary civilisation.'[12] In a slightly less ominous vein, the Dominion poet Bernard O'Dowd hoped in 1900 that Australia would be home in the future to a 'coming Sun-God's race.'[13]

According to one of the primary tenets of Social Darwinism, the destiny of races and nations was largely determined by their victory or defeat in the wars and other contests that characterized the eternal struggle for survival and mastery among the peoples of the earth. Similarly, romantic nationalist ideals often depicted war as a fundamental rite of passage through which would-be nations had to pass in order to achieve full-fledged nationhood. Thus it is perhaps not surprising that many Dominion nationalists pined for the test of battle in order to prove their country's mettle on the world stage. Henry Lawson, one of Australia's most popular and critically acclaimed native-born writers at the turn of the century, penned in 1895 a strident poem celebrating the power of war to forge Australia into a nation. In 'The Star of Australasia' he wrote:

> We boast no more of our bloodless flag, that rose from a nation's slime;
> Better a shred of a deep-dyed rag from the storms of the olden time.
> From grander clouds in our 'peaceful skies' than ever were there before
> I tell you the Star of the South shall rise – in the lurid clouds of war.
> It ever must be while blood is warm and the sons of men increase;
> For ever the nations rose in storm, to rot in a deadly peace.

Lest there be any doubt, Lawson assured his audience that the young men of Australia would make outstanding soldiers in any future conflict:

> There are boys out there by the western creeks, who hurry away from school
> To climb the sides of the breezy peaks or dive in the shaded pool,
> Who'll stick to their guns when the mountains quake to the tread of a mighty war,
> And fight for Right or a Grand Mistake as men never fought before.[14]

Lawson was but one of many observers of Australian society who discerned the military potential of its manhood, particularly of the males hailing from 'the bush,' that is, the rural hinterland of the country. The rugged frontier lifestyle of the cattle-drovers and sheep shearers who inhabited the outback made them natural warriors in the minds of some commentators. Francis Adams, a British journalist who lived in Australia between 1884 and 1890 declared that he 'would not set at a pin's fee the survival of any European army attempting to occupy a fraction of the Australian Interior.' His observations of the Dominion's 'bush people' led him to wonder: 'What foes could be more formidable than these crack-shot mounted infantry men, in their own waterless steppes? They would harry out of existence the best disciplined and best commissariat army in the world.'[15] Along the same lines, a chronicler of Canada's involvement in the South African war of 1899–1902 stated that 'Both because of its climate and because of the conditions of life prevailing, Canada should produce plenty of good fighting men. Over large areas the people are still pioneers...' The writer glossed over the fact that most Canadians at the time resided in cities or towns by declaring that:

> In the older settled regions, too, the pioneer days, with their discipline in adaptability and self-reliance, are not so far distant that their influence has been lost in the milder and more conventional ways of comparative wealth.[16]

Of course, many who idealized the Dominions as incubators of 'natural' frontier warriors represented New Zealand as particularly remarkable in this regard, home as it was to two 'martial races', the Pakeha (a Maori word that, by the late nineteenth century, was commonly used in New Zealand to denote the islands' European – mostly British – settlers and their descendents) and the 'native' Maori.[17] According to the narrative of New Zealand history prevalent before the First World War, European settlers (with considerable military aid from Great Britain) had only subdued the proud, warlike Maori with great difficulty during the series of wars fought between the two peoples in the 1840s and 1860s, with each side winning the respect of the other as a noble and formidable opponent. Since then, Maori and Pakeha had lived in relative harmony, 'two long lines of conquerors fused and blended'[18], culturally, and in some cases, ethnically (though, according to the conventional version of this narrative, the Pakeha strain remained dominant in both cases, destined to absorb the best aspects of the Maori before that people inevitably disappeared). It did not require a great stretch of the romantic imagination to envision the martial prowess of Maori native warriors and bush-savvy Pakeha amalgamated into an invincible fighting force of 'natural' New Zealand soldiers. Such visions could sometimes inspire remarkable flights of fancy. For example, in describing of an assault by New Zealand troops on Turkish trenches during the 1915 Gallipoli campaign, one correspondent depicted a Maori unit leading their Pakeha counterparts in a haka (a Maori ritual of chanting and dancing traditionally performed before battle) as they awaited the signal to go over the top:

> Now [the Maoris'] eyes were rolling and their breath was coming in long rhythmical sobs. The groaning sound of it was quite audible; in another minute they would have been up on their feet, dancing their wild war dance. But then came the signal; and Hell was let loose.[19]

The idea that the men from the rural regions of the Dominions possessed innate martial prowess by virtue of their hardy ways of life, their familiarity with weapons and their knowledge of bush-craft or wilderness survival skills proved one of the more powerful and resonant components of the colonial identities being constructed in the nineteenth and early twentieth centuries. The 'frontiersman' was one of the stock figures associated with New World settlement, in the United States and Canada as well as in Australia and New Zealand. Each country had its standard 'national type' in this regard that often came to be represented as emblematic of the nation as a whole. In Australia, Canada and New Zealand, democracies without long-standing military traditions of their own from which to derive inspiration and pride, and without a leading class that had internalized traditional martial virtues, the natural warriors of the hinterland served an important symbolic function in the military context as symbols or embodiments of martial virtues appropriate to colonial societies idealized as egalitarian, rural and generally close to nature. Significantly, just as in Britain the martial paragons of the upper class maintained a connection to a pre-industrial past by virtue an ethos traditionally associated with the rural gentry, the outdoorsmen-turned-soldiers of Australia, Canada and New Zealand represented, according to their propagandists, specimens of the British race untainted by the degenerative effects of industrialization. Long before Bean made his comparison of British and Dominion soldiers at Gallipoli, commentators were contrasting the athleticism and physical fitness of colonial fighting men to the lack of these attributes among the average enlisted Tommy. Writing about a daylong series of sporting contests in South Africa between troops from various parts of the Empire, one Canadian journalist commented:

> The entire day of sport was a struggle between the Colonials present; the British soldiers had practically no place in the contests, and it is to be feared that the Colonials thought themselves a superior race of beings. But this inferiority of the English soldiers as athletes should be no matter of surprise.[20]

The Bonds of Empire

Attempts to define and celebrate a positive Australian, Canadian or New Zealand identity, so evident within the cultures of each Dominion between the mid-nineteenth century and the eve of the First World War, do not necessarily indicate the emergence during this period of broad-based movements to chart a more nationalist course for any of these Dominions in relation to their status within the British Empire. On the contrary, the writers, artists and scholars who glorified the virtues of their respective Dominions generally constituted a small, but vocal, minority of middle-class English-speaking elites in each country. Their agenda, insofar as it was nationalist, was often complex, and by no means reflected a uniformity of aims. At the cultural level, many of the writers and artists whose projects involved depicting and celebrating the Australian, Canadian or New Zealand landscape and its people struggled against what they saw as the prevailing belief in the Dominions that the civilization of the colonial fringe was inherently inferior to that of the Metropole. In their view, this crippling lack of self-esteem inhibited the development of cultural institutions in the Dominions, and encouraged those that did exist to remain, in the words of Henry Lawson, 'toady to England and all that is English.'[21] At the political level, it was very often the case that those who might in some ways be considered Canadian, Australian or New Zealand 'nationalists' did not, especially by the late nineteenth/early twentieth century, necessarily aspire for independence from the British Empire, but rather for more autonomy, power or respect within the Empire.

For instance, among the English speaking elites in both countries there existed small but influential factions of 'imperial nationalists.' These individuals believed that the continued dominance, if not the future survival, of the British Empire could only be assured if its centre of power shifted away from the Metropole and more toward their respective Dominion. They typically advocated some form of imperial federation, arguing that the formal unification of the colonies with the Motherland would create an Empire that would not only be invincible against its foes, but would also grant Canada, Australia or New Zealand equality of status with Britain within the Empire. This status that would be commensurate with weight and influence that the Dominions would eventually attain in the world, given the growth in population and power that they would inevitably experience in coming decades.

On the one hand, 'imperial nationalism' reflected certain geopolitical realities of the time. Too weak militarily and economically to stand alone, the self-governing Dominions continued to be dependent on the protection and support of Great Britain. Withdrawal from the secure confines of the Empire seemed unthinkable from any rational perspective, particularly in light of the vulnerability many Canadians, Australians and New Zealanders increasingly felt in the face of ever-more powerful and potentially menacing neighbours such as the United States in North America and Japan in the Pacific. The political developments that culminated in Confederation in Canada in 1867 and Federation in Australia in 1901 had to a significant extent been powered by such security concerns. At the same time, the realization that these strategic anxieties were not necessarily a top priority of the British government contributed to a mounting frustration among many Dominion leaders with the Motherland's insensitivity to colonial concerns and interests, and this in turn galvanized drives for increasing political, military and economic autonomy and self-sufficiency within the Empire.

'Imperial nationalism' – particularly before the twentieth century, when demographic trends were less supportive of such forecasts – was sometimes shaped by visions of an Australian, Canadian or New Zealand future in which the Dominions had ascended to the status of great powers, and thus to pre-eminent roles as the leading nations of the Empire. Advocates of 'imperial nationalism' were often keen to demonstrate the national potential of Canada, Australia and New Zealand, and to reveal to the world the sterling qualities of the white races hailing from those lands. They also genuinely revered the bonds of heritage and culture that they believed linked the Dominions and the Motherland. Consequently, they typically supported calls for colonial contributions of men and material to Britain's late-nineteenth century imperial adventures, including, most significantly in terms of scale and cost for the Dominions, the 1899–1902 war in South Africa. Canada contributed 7,368 men to the campaign, of whom 270 were killed or died of disease.[22] Australia sent 16,175 troops to fight the Boers; 588 never returned.[23] New Zealand provided

6,495 soldiers, losing 70 in battle and 158 more to disease or accidents.[24] This sacrifice proved just a small prelude to the infinitely more immense losses of the First World War, but it revealed that, as would be demonstrated even more decisively between 1914 and 1918, desires for a greater voice in imperial policy-making and for more sovereignty in determining the extent and nature of their obligations to the Empire were not necessarily seen by colonial nationalists as incompatible with the most fervent demonstrations of loyalty to the Empire.[25] Indeed, according to the logic of leading colonial policy-makers at the time, extremes of loyal sacrifice could raise the esteem of the Dominions in British eyes, and generate the kind of gratitude and respect that would lead to elevated status within the Empire.[26]

However, Dominion participation in the South African War also revealed, to a greater extent than ever before, that there existed alternative visions of Australian, Canadian and New Zealand nationalism which challenged the idea of the continued development of these countries within an imperial context, and which raised the spectre of divisive future contests over the nature of Dominion nationhood. In Australia there had existed since the mid-nineteenth century a pugnacious, largely working-class strain of nationalism, exemplified at the turn of the century by the irreverent, occasionally republican sentiment expressed in the pages of the Sydney *Bulletin*. This journal, for instance, criticized the new Australian flag, unveiled in 1901, as 'vulgar and ill-fitting, – a staled réchauffé of the British flag, with no artistic virtue, no national significance.' Furthermore, according to the editorial: 'That bastard flag is a true symbol of the bastard state of Australian opinion, still in large part biased by British traditions, British customs, still lacking many years to the sufficiency of manhood which will determine a path of its own ...'[27] Even these strong words paled in comparison to the anti-imperialism of the radical working-class press in Australia, who, to cite just one example, routinely derided Empire Day – the holiday dedicated to celebrating the bonds of Imperial unity and loyalty – as 'Vampire Day.' Such sentiment found its political expression during the South African War in the opposition by a small but vocal wing of the Australian Labor Party to the Dominion's involvement in the campaign.[28]

In Canada, opposition to the imperial loyalty of the dominant English-speaking majority came primarily from French Canadian politicians and men of letters, such as Henri Bourassa, who in 1899 resigned his seat as a Liberal member of Parliament over the plans of the Liberal government of Wilfrid Laurier to send Canadian troops to South Africa. Bourassa and others who shared his views advocated a form of French-Canadian nationalism focused on ensuring the political rights and cultural survival of the French-speaking minority in the Dominion. It was a brand of nationalism centred on the ascendance of Canada as a North American, rather than as a British-imperial, power, and that strongly criticized the idea that Canadian fidelity to the Motherland and the Empire should transcend even the Dominion's own national interests.[29] As was the case with dissenting opinion in Australia, Bourassa and other Canadian critics of the South African War were loud but lonely voices crying in the wilderness at the time. However, the ideals of nationalism that they articulated in this period would provide an important template for the more powerful and influential expressions of dissent that appeared after 1914.

As might be expected, the First World War's impact on nationalist ideals and aspirations of every type was profound. The Great War was arguably the most extraordinary event in the histories of Australia, Canada and New Zealand since they attained self-government. Never before had the physical resources of the Dominions been mobilized on such an epic scale for such a massive undertaking. Never before had these colonies experienced the kind of simultaneous demographic catastrophes and social convulsions that they endured during the war. As a result, the years between 1914 and 1918 witnessed within the Dominions a review and re-evaluation of their political relationship to Britain, and of their status within the Empire, that was unprecedented in its scope and intensity. At the same time, the war encouraged colonial citizens to articulate and celebrate, to an extent that was truly novel in its scale and in its appeal across social boundaries, ideals of Australian, Canadian and New Zealand national character that were defined by their opposition to certain qualities that were associated with 'Old' Britain.

The rest of this chapter will focus exclusively on the experience of Canada, Australia and New Zealand between 1914 and 1916. These first two years of the war were characterized by a remarkable degree of consensus within the Dominions. Not only was there almost universal support for the conflict, few even questioned the conventional view that it was duty and a sense of filial obligation to the Motherland that compelled them to take up Britain's cause. It was also during this period that each Dominion experienced its respective baptism of fire. These tests of battle would prove to be seminal events in the development of nationalist visions within Canada, Australia and New Zealand.

The Test of Faith

On 1 August 1914, as the storm clouds of war gathered ominously in Europe, Australia's Liberal Prime Minister, Joseph Cook, facing defeat in the impending national election, delivered a campaign speech in which he addressed the worsening crisis on the other side of the world and what it meant for the Dominion. 'If it is to be war, if the Armageddon is to come, you and I shall be in it,' declared Cook, to which his audience responded with loud applause. 'It is no use to blink our obligations. If the old country is at war so are we.'[30] The previous day, Cook's opponent, the Labor Party leader, soon to be prime minister, Andrew Fisher had pledged that 'should the worst happen … Australians will stand beside our own to help and defend (Britain) to our last man and our last shilling.'[31]

When the British Empire finally did enter the war on 4 August 1914, the news was greeted with feverish rejoicing in cities throughout the Dominions, in scenes that echoed the wild celebrations observed in belligerent capitals from Berlin to London in response to the outbreak of hostilities on the continent. In the Canadian city of Toronto, Ontario, for example, Britain's declaration of war brought thousands of jubilant citizens into the city streets, where they 'jammed every available inch of space, vibrating with unrestrained enthusiasm.' Many in the throng waved Union Jacks or, more rarely, Canadian flags, and hundreds of voices filled the air with rousing choruses of 'Rule Britannia' and 'God Save the King.' Near the offices of *The Globe*, one of Toronto's leading newspapers, a huge crowd gathered to hear the latest bulletins from Europe. As each dispatch was read, the people 'cheered and swayed as if possessed. Hats shot aloft, ten thousand throats boomed out a concerted roar...'[32]

That same day, north of Toronto, in the little town of Pembroke, Ontario, on the banks of the Ottawa River, Grace Morris was sitting on the veranda of her home with her 20-year-old brother, Ramsey, and several friends, when her 18-year-old brother, Basil, returned from the telegraph office and reported that Canada was at war. Breaking the stunned silence that followed this announcement, one of the young adults in the group exclaimed, 'But this is *our* war.'[33]

For Canada, Australia and New Zealand, as well as for the Morris family and millions like them in all three countries, those words would prove accurate and prophetic. When Britain went to war that fateful August, Canada, Australia and New Zealand, as Dominions of the Empire, automatically became belligerents as well. There was no consultation between the Motherland and her colonial subjects on this matter, and in 1914, few in any of these countries objected to this. Dominion autonomy in this case was basically limited to the authority to determine the nature and extent of their nation's contribution to the imperial war effort. The governments in these dominions used this power as an opportunity to demonstrate their enthusiasm for the Empire's cause. Canada quickly raised and financed an expeditionary force of more than 30,000 volunteers that arrived in England in October 1914. Not wishing to be outdone, Australia offered to raise and pay for its own expeditionary force of 20,000 men that it was prepared to send to 'any destination required of the Home Government.'[34] New Zealand, smallest of the three Dominions in population, nevertheless rapidly mobilized and dispatched an expeditionary force numbering 8,574 men.[35]

In the first delirious days following the outbreak of war, few in the Dominions could have foreseen that by the time the conflict finally ended four years later, 619,636 Canadians, 416,809 Australians and 128,525 New Zealanders would have served in their nation's armed forces. Nor could anyone have imagined that Canada, with a pre-war population of slightly more than 7 million, would suffer approximately 60,000 war dead between 1914 and 1918. Australia's losses would be even more startling: 60,000 men killed from a country with a total population that stood at about 4 million in 1914. New Zealand's sacrifice was equally shocking, with more than 16,000 fatalities from a country with a 1914 population of somewhat more than 1 million. [36]

There can be little doubt that had the citizens of Canada, Australia and New Zealand been gifted with prescience, there would not have been such a stunning dearth in those countries of publicly expressed opposition to the war at its outset. Politicians, clergy and members of the press, regardless of their ideological persuasion or religious affiliation, were nearly unanimous in their support for Dominion involvement in the conflict. Most justified their stance with rhetoric that reminded colonial citizens of their duty to the Empire. In Canada, it was the French-Canadian statesman Wilfrid Laurier, from his position as the leader of the Liberal opposition, who eloquently voiced what would become his country's most famous pledge of loyalty to the Motherland. 'It will be seen by the world,' he declared, 'that Canada, a daughter of old England, intends to stand by her in this great conflict. When the call goes out, our answer goes at once, and it goes in the classical language of the British answer to the call to duty: "Ready, Aye Ready."'[37] In Australia, the Labor Party was similarly strident in its call for fidelity to Britain in its time of need. 'Australia is as much a part of the British Empire as England is,' asserted a 6 August 1914 editorial in the *Worker*, 'and while we remain so any attempt to evade responsibilities under present conditions would not only be courting eventual disaster as a people, but would be altogether unworthy of us.'[38]

Dissent, in the rare instances where it appeared in public, was generally relegated to the most extreme fringes of Dominion society. In Australia, several radical socialist newspapers published editorials that were virulently anti-war (significantly, however, they avoided directly criticizing Great Britain or the Empire, an omission which is remarkable given the antipathy to these entities routinely expressed prior to 1914). For instance, *Direct Action*, the journal of the Industrial Workers of the World in Australia, called in a 22 August 1914 editorial for the working class to fight the real enemy, not each other. 'When we fight … we must have some definite purpose in view, some interest at stake,' the writer stated.

> Let the emancipation of all our kind be the prize for which we fight. Let us band ourselves together, soldiers, civilians and all workers. Let us remonstrate by every means in our power, against this willful wastage of lives. Let us combine to crush this mere handful of autocrats and plutocrats; these devilish engineers of war; these betrayers of our souls, these barterers of human lives for a few baubles of their blood-tainted, sweat-wrung wealth![39]

Similar sentiments were echoed in Canada among a tiny minority of leftist radicals and pacifists. These included Francis Benyon, the women's editor of the *Grain*

Grower's Guide, who suggested that mothers refuse to send their sons to be shot down in order to gratify the greed of gun-making corporations.[40]

However, these dissidents were lonely voices crying in the wilderness, at least at first. The initial environment of overwhelming pro-war consensus encompassed even many of the groups and individuals that had been in the past, and would be in the future, the most intractable and compelling critics of the established order. For example, Henri Bourassa, the Quebecois nationalist, conferred his stamp of approval on Canadian involvement in this war – a remarkable development given his long-standing anti-imperialism and vehement opposition to the Dominion's participation in the South African War. However, his support was notably subdued considering the general mood of the hour, and it was justified on grounds that were consistent with the French-Canadian *nationaliste* position. In a 1914 editorial, Bourassa urged Canadians not to lose sight of their own national interests (which were not necessarily identical to those of Great Britain or France) when determining the nature and extent of the Dominion's war effort:

> Canada must begin by resolutely envisaging its real situation, to take exact account of what it can do, and to ensure our own internal security before starting or pursuing an effort that it will perhaps not be in a state to sustain until the end.[41]

In Australia, Daniel Mannix, the Coadjutor Archbishop of Melbourne, refrained from openly opposing the war, but he nevertheless raised some hackles across the Dominion by implying that Britain's intervention in the European war provided a convenient justification for delaying a final resolution of the recent troubles in Ireland. On the whole, however, Australia's Irish Catholic leaders, even those who identified themselves as Irish Nationalists, were less ambivalent in their declarations of support. One Australian bishop advised his countrymen to look to the Nationalists in Ireland for an example of loyalty to the Empire in its hour of need. 'Such an example, coming from a people who have more reason than anyone else at such a time, to nurse a grievance, shows what an enormous wave of devotion and enthusiasm will sweep over the whole Empire,' he declared.[42]

Even the Sydney *Bulletin*, under the leadership of a new editor, had by 1915 abandoned its pugnacious anti-imperialism and radical nationalist socialism, and, in the words of one observer, 'turned patriotic.'[43] A year into the war, it was possible to find an editorial expressing the following sentiments concerning the dire possible consequences of Britain's defeat:

> No one will pretend that the British Empire can be wiped out. Such things do not happen. The enemy may gain a sort of a win, and yet be as poor by comparison with Britain, a decade hence, as he was before the war. But if

that happens no Australian or Scotsman or South African or other white in-
habitant of the Empire will be able again to hold his head high in the company of a German. Our drama, our poetry, our songs, and our proverbs will
need to be recast as a prophylactic against the justifiable derision of the for-
eigner. The racial pride which has become a part of all but the utter degener-
ates amongst us will have to be laid aside … The avoidance of the possibility
of such a horror … is worth every sacrifice and effort that a people can
make.[44]

So it was in the Dominions in 1914–15 that even the most traditionally discord-
ant voices within these societies did not rise to challenge the harmonious chorus
proclaiming fidelity to the Imperial cause. A poem in the Brisbane *Courier* declared
the colonies to be 'One with Britain, heart and soul/One life, one flag, one fleet,
one Throne.'[45] Such were the affirmations of faith that would launch this crusade.
However, after 1915, as the conflict dragged on beyond all expectation, with
mounting human and material costs in exchange for diminishing returns on the
battlefield, and as the Dominion contribution escalated from a token commitment
to a full-scale mobilization of national manpower and resources, the idea of enduring such dramatic sacrifices solely in the name of duty to the Motherland faced
escalating challenges. This became increasingly the case as the fallibility of British
arms was demonstrated time and again in battle. There were still deep reservoirs of
conviction and sentiment that could be tapped by those in the Dominions seeking
to inspire their countrymen to bleed for the allied cause, but the images and concepts that would tap these wellsprings had to be adapted to reflect the unfolding
events and changing circumstances of the war.

Natural Soldiers?

At the war's outset, many in the Dominions expressed the concern that the issue in
Europe might be decided before colonial troops had the opportunity to prove their
mettle. As we have seen earlier in the chapter, citizens of Australia, Canada and
New Zealand often could not help but feel (especially when confronted by the
smug condescension of the Metropole), that colonial status carried with it a badge
of inferiority. Such perceptions had not been decisively dispelled by recent Dominion victories in cricket test matches or by participation in the South African War.
However, as one Australian commentator remarked in 1914, the conflict raging in
Europe was 'an infinitely more serious enterprise than the South African campaign.'[46] The fitness of colonial manhood would face the ultimate test, at least according to the vulgarized notions of social Darwinism and romantic nationalism so
prevalent around the turn of the century: Battle alongside and against the finest
military forces produced by European civilization.

Within the Dominions at the start of the war, optimism and high expectations prevailed among those who speculated about how colonial troops were likely to perform in combat. Such opinions, not surprisingly, ran counter to much of the conventional wisdom in British military circles about the quality of Dominion troops, despite the lauded performance of Canadian units at Paardeberg in South Africa, and the useful role Australian mounted infantry played in the counter-insurgency phase of that same war. Viewing the untested colonial recruits in 1914 and 1915, British commanders tended to dismiss them, not entirely without reason, as fine physical specimens who were ill-trained, ill-disciplined and badly led compared to the fighting men of the Motherland. After helping the Canadian Contingent disembark upon their arrival in England in the autumn of 1915, Captain J. F. C. Fuller commented that the Canadians would make fine soldiers with six months training, as long as all their officers were shot.[47]

Dominion pundits sought to refute such negative assessments, often countering these initial judgments with claims grounded in their own dubious myths. For example, Harry Gullet, the Australian correspondent who pronounced the European conflict a far more serious affair than the South African War, in the course of the same article, speculated at length about how Australian soldiers might perform on the battlefields of France and Belgium. Dismissing as 'groundless' the fears of British officers that colonials would not tolerate the severe discipline necessary in 'orthodox European warfare,' Gullet acknowledged that Australians bred to the bush might find Europe a more foreign environment than South Africa. He wrote:

Men in their element upon the veldt will be a little at sea upon the cultivated fields of the Continent. But if the Colonial is anything he is adaptable, and he won't be long a stranger to his new surroundings.

Furthermore, unlike in South Africa, the Australian trooper in Europe would be a paragon of discipline.[48] 'In South Africa he may have resented orders at times because they came from officers who had a very limited knowledge of the open country,' Gullet explains.

In Europe it will be different. The Colonials, quick to appreciate that they are a little strange to the work in hand, will cheerfully accept all orders. They should display all the best qualities of the British soldier, and be distinguished by individual resource and a sense of locality which will be invaluable even upon the congested battlefields of Europe.[49]

Thus, in the early days of the conflict, before anyone knew just how unorthodox would be the ghastly war that devastated the 'cultivated fields of the Continent,' Gullet strove mightily to adapt the legend of Australian martial prowess formed in the South African War, a legend revolving around the supposed 'natural' facility of the Australian bushman for the irregular warfare of the veldt, to the expectations of what would be required of ideal soldiers in the 'civilized' warfare practiced on the Continent. Not that Gullet's image of the typical Australian soldier in 1914 as a scion of the bush had much basis in reality. Australia was one of the most urbanized countries on earth at this time, and the overwhelming majority of recruits to the Australian Imperial Force came from the cities and towns. Furthermore, 21 per cent of enlistees were British-born, and so were not likely to find themselves 'at sea' in the un-bush-like environment of Europe (New Zealand fielded a similar percentage – 20 percent – of British-born enlistees in its Expeditionary Force).[50]

Regardless, the myth of the frontier warrior, of the Australian or New Zealand male as a 'natural' soldier by virtue of his rugged lifestyle and pioneer heritage would continue to appeal to the imaginations of men and women in and outside of these Dominions for quite some time. This despite the fact that even New Zealand, the Dominion that since the earliest days of large-scale European settlement had conformed most in reality to the stereotype of a primarily rural, agrarian colonial society, was, by 1911, a nation with a predominately urban population.[51] Nevertheless, one observer, celebrating the accomplishments of the Australians and New Zealanders at Gallipoli, attributed their fine performance to the fact that over time, in the course of battling to conquer a hostile continent, they had come to possess as a people certain qualities, such as strength of character and physique, as well as certain skills, which made them inherently superior fighting men. 'Nature, as well as the deliberate plan of the Australasians themselves, has ensured that an army of Australasians must necessarily compose a very fine fighting force,' he declared.[52]

Canadians too recast pre-existing stereotypical images of the national type to create an ideal of the 'natural' warrior who would excel on the battlefields of Europe. One Canadian journalist described his country's soldiers as:

Men from the prairies, from the wheat fields and the lumberyards of the West; men accustomed to the saddle and to sport of all kinds; men who can wield an ax more deftly than I can hold a pen; men accustomed to face death twenty times a year or more, and who have waged war with Nature or with wild beasts all their lives – what wonder that they sprang to the call of war as surely never men sprang before.

The author goes on to explain that Canadian soldiers posses all the attributes and interests of the trained sportsman and backwoodsman. These elements, which include 'decision, initiative, resource [sic], endless courage and the capacity for endurance,' are crucial to the formation of good fighting men, and 'are hardly to be found in the men of towns and cities.'[53] This notwithstanding the fact that in reality, most of the Canadian volunteers recruited during the war came from cities – Toronto, Montreal and Winnipeg each supplied enough men for two battalions in 1914; Vancouver and Edmonton were not far behind in their contributions. Also, as in Australia and New Zealand, the British-born comprised a disproportionate percentage of Canada's initial contingents: two-thirds of the 1914 recruits originally hailed from the Motherland.[54]

At any rate, regardless of the social and demographic realities within the Australian Imperial Force, the New Zealand Expeditionary Force or the Canadian Expeditionary Force at the time, Australians, New Zealanders and Canadians began the war with an established ideal of the typical fighting man they were sending to take part in the conflict overseas. In all three countries the popular image was of hardy, athletic, resourceful warriors gifted with a natural talent for soldiering thanks to the biological influences and formative experiences of a frontier lifestyle. It did not matter a great deal whether that frontier was the frigid wilderness of Canada, the arid Australian outback, or the temperate New Zealand bush, the martial attributes supposedly produced were essentially the same. Such reassuring myths inspired confidence among Dominion citizens acutely aware that their nations lacked any military traditions comparable to those of European powers. In the winter of 1914, as the CEF, NZEF and AIF underwent their final phase of training before being sent into action, neither the Canadian soldiers enduring the mud and misery of Salisbury Plain in England, nor the Australians and New Zealanders sweltering in Egypt had anything equivalent to the reservoir of proud martial history that was available to their British counterparts as a source of inspiration and self-assurance. Meanwhile, men and women on the home front in the Dominions waited anxiously to see whether their fighting men would pass the test of battle.

"Birth Pangs of Our Nationality"

Canadian, Australian and New Zealand troops would receive their baptisms of fire within days of one another, on battlefields thousands of miles apart. The men of the CEF were tested first. On 22 April 1915, the Germans launched the first poison gas attack of the war against a sector of the Allied line in the Ypres salient on the Western Front that was held by a French Algerian division on the left and the 1st Canadian Division on the right. The German chlorine gas, in the form of a greenish-yellow cloud borne on the wind across no-man's land, reached the French-Algerian position first. Within minutes, the unprotected colonial troops were pouring from their trenches, choking and gasping as they tried to escape the asphyxiating gas. French and British artillery gunners to the rear of the Algerians were also stricken, and abandoned their guns as they fled before the terrible new weapon. Suddenly four miles of Allied defences lay unmanned, and the British flank was completely exposed. The crucial task of filling this breach fell to the Canadians. For five days they held their portion of the line against repeated assaults by the Germans, withstanding a gas attack against their positions on 24 April. Equipped only with cotton bandoleers to protect their mouths, the Canadian defenders, coughing and collapsing, eyes and throats burning, battled furiously to repel waves of advancing Germans. Somehow, the men of the North American Dominion prevailed. They had lost two miles of ground, 208 officers and 5,828 men. But the Germans had not been able to exploit the success of their new weapon and achieve a breakthrough on the Western Front.[55]

In the greater scheme of the war as a whole, the battle known as Second Ypres was a sharply fought engagement, but rather small-scale, particularly when compared to the epic set-piece battles of 1914 or to the massive campaigns that would unfold in the west between 1916 and 1918. For Britain, France and Germany, the battle was simply another in the series of bloody, indecisive encounters that characterized 1915, distinguished only by the introduction of poison gas to the battlefield. However, for Canada, Second Ypres proved a far more meaningful event.

The men of the CEF had been the first Dominion troops tested in a major battle, and they had, in the words of one Canadian commentator, 'proved the mettle of their pasture.'[56] Men and women on the home front in Canada received the news of their troops' heroic stand at Ypres with unabashed pride, often mingled, at least privately, with shock and sorrow at the high casualties.[57] Newspapers across the Dominion published the official communiqué from the British War Office praising the Canadians' performance in the battle. 'The Canadians had many casualties, but their gallantry and determination undoubtedly saved the situation. Their conduct has been magnificent throughout,' concluded the statement. Many Canadian publications also reported the words of Sir John French, the general commanding the Empire's troops on the Western Front. French expressed his 'admiration of the gallant stand and fight of the CEF at Ypres. They have performed a most brilliant and valuable service.'[58]

The accomplishments of their soldiers stirred the imaginations of many Canadians, some of whom were moved to try and immortalize the events on canvas. Paintings like Richard Jacks' *The Second Battle of Ypres* portrayed the battle in the traditional late-nineteenth-century romantic style of Lady Butler and her imitators. Except for the presence of machine guns, the scenes depicted might as well have been from Wellington's Peninsula campaign or the Crimean War. Poison gas was not even represented in these paintings, a surprising omission given the fact that the appearance of the weapon was most dramatic and novel feature of Second Ypres. In any case, these compositions were well received by the Canadian public, and advertisements hawking reproductions appeared in a number of journals and newspapers.[59]

For a country that had gone to war in 1914 very conscious of its lack of military experience and martial reputation, Second Ypres provided Canada with instant respect and credibility as a people to be reckoned with. Furthermore, many in the young Dominion saw the battle as a watershed in the evolution of the Canadian nation. For example, a 1915 post-Ypres recruiting poster listed the names of several Flanders villages newly familiar to the Canadian public from accounts of the battle, and described them as 'new names in Canadian history.' The poster went on to declare: 'More are coming. Will you be there? Enlist!'[60]

Talbot Papineau (a descendent of Louis Joseph Papineau, the Patriote leader of 1837), who was serving as a subaltern in a Canadian unit in the Ypres sector, predicted that there would be 'many sad hearts' when people on the home front learned of the casualties suffered by the CEF in the fighting that April. 'Some reports are appalling,' he continued. 'I should feel dreadfully if they are true, yet what a glorious history they will have made for Canada. These may be the birth pangs of our nationality.'[61]

Already in 1915 Papineau and others in the Dominion were articulating the broad outlines of the narrative that would largely come to represent Canada's war experience: The rise of a nation as a result of the sad but sublime blood sacrifice of its fighting men. The pain and shock many Canadians felt once they learned of the high casualties suffered at Ypres could be somewhat mollified by the gratitude of the imperial patron. However, for many of these same Canadians, the names of certain villages and fields in Flanders, hitherto obscure, could now evoke in them the kind of deeply emotional responses that a religious shrine might stir in the faithful. Since 1914, much of northern France and Belgium had already become sacred ground, for French, Germans and British. Now Canada had its own patch; a legion of martyred countrymen had ensured it. Perhaps there is no better testament to the inspirational power of this martyrdom than the last verse of John McCrae's well-known poem, 'In Flanders Fields.' McCrae, a medical officer with the CEF, wrote his composition shortly after a long session spent treating casualties from the battle of Ypres. His elegy, which assumes the voice of the Canadian dead buried under the soil of Flanders, concludes with these lines:

Take up our quarrel with the foe:
To you from failing hands we throw
The torch; be yours to hold it high.
If ye break faith with us who die
We shall not sleep, though poppies grow
In Flanders fields.[62]

Australia and New Zealand's baptism of fire came within days of Canada's, not in France or Flanders, but in the Mediterranean, on the Gallipoli Peninsula in Turkey.[63] For Australia and New Zealand, the legends and traditions born at Gallipoli would fundamentally shape the way people in the Pacific Dominions perceived and remembered their nations' war experience. The long and ultimately futile campaign would inspire many in Australia and New Zealand to express sentiments very similar to those articulated by Canadians after Second Ypres. However, Gallipoli would prove far more important to emerging visions of the Australian and New Zealand nations, and to developing conceptions of Australian and New Zealand national identity, than any single battle or event of the Great War, including Vimy Ridge, would prove for Canada.

For an operation that came to be known as a 'splendid failure,' the strategic thinking behind the Gallipoli campaign was sound enough. Allied leaders, frustrated by the stalemate in the West, turned their attention to the southern theatre and to Turkey, which had just entered the war on the side of the Central Powers. The Allies believed that an attack against the 'sick man of Europe' might stand a greater chance of success than they had so far achieved by battering themselves against Germany's defences on the Western Front. Britain's First Lord of the Admiralty, Winston Churchill, proposed an assault on the strategically important Dardanelles, the straits held by Turkey that controlled passage between the Black Sea and the Mediterranean. Allied planners hoped that the capture of the straits (and eventually, Constantinople) might force Turkey out of the war, or at the very least, open up a way to supply Russia, which would put more pressure on the Germans in the East.[64]

After a naval attack on the Turkish forts guarding the straits failed, British planners decided to stage an amphibious landing on Gallipoli, the narrow peninsula forming the north-western side of the Dardanelles. The bulk of the Allied landing force would be composed of British, French and Indian troops, but there would also be a sizable contingent of Australians and New Zealanders involved (their forces would come to be known by their acronymic designation, ANZAC), thereby ensuring that troops from the Pacific Dominions would see their first major military action of the war. Thus far, the only reputation these soldiers had won for themselves was for ill-discipline, thanks to their disorderly conduct in the brothels, bars and bazaars of Cairo, where they had been stationed as they waited to be sent to Europe. Now at last they would have the chance to prove themselves, but in a different theatre, and against a different enemy, than they had expected.[65]

No better site than Gallipoli could have been chosen for what many Australians and New Zealanders would come to regard as a rite of passage into nationhood. The Dardanelles was in fact the fabled Hellespont. As one commentator at the time wrote:

All the country thereabouts has been dedicated to war and Romance from time immemorial ... Here it was, nearly 500 years before Christ, that Xerxes threw a bridge of boats across for his conquering army to pass over ... On the eastern shore, near the mouth of the Dardanelles, and within sight and sound of the thunderous battles of today, is the site of that ancient Troy whose long siege rages for ever in Homer's Iliad; but the Greek and Trojan heroes he has immortalised knew no such terrific fighting, did no such deeds of mighty valour as have fallen to the share of the incomparable heroes who are fighting there now.[66]

The Anzacs landed on these storied shores in the early morning hours of 25 April 1915. Despite the fact that the first assaulting force was put ashore over a mile from their intended position, onto a portion of the beach with much more difficult terrain than where they were supposed to land, the initial attack was successful in establishing a narrow beachhead, largely thanks to the incredible bravery and élan of the ANZAC troops. However, Turkish forces under the command of Mustafa Kemal (later known as Kemal Ataturk, the founder of modern Turkey) soon contained the gains of the Anzacs, and literally within 24 hours of the landing the entire campaign bogged down, deteriorating into trench warfare reminiscent of the Western Front. So it would remain for nearly eight months, until the entire Allied force was evacuated from the Peninsula (the most successful single operation of the campaign) in December 1915, leaving behind 46,000 Allied dead, including 7,594 Australians and 2,431 New Zealanders.[67]

The news of the 25 April landing at Gallipoli was greeted in Australia and New Zealand with excitement bordering on euphoria, due in no small part to the stirring reporting of Ellis Ashmead-Bartlett, the British war correspondent assigned to the Dardanelles, whose account of the initial ANZAC assault was printed in most major Australian and New Zealand newspapers. Ashmead-Bartlett confirmed the preconceptions many colonials had of themselves, describing the Anzacs as a 'race of athletes.' His praise of their courage and high spirits in battle allayed Australian and New Zealand apprehensions about how their soldiers would perform under fire. 'They had been tried for the first time and had not been found wanting,' wrote Ashmead-Bartlett. 'These raw colonial troops in these desperate hours proved worthy to fight side by side with the heroes of Mons, the Aisne, Ypres and Neuve Chapelle.'[68] Just as had been the case for the Canadians after Second Ypres, the Anzacs were showered with praise from all quarters of the Empire. The Archbishop of Canterbury declared that 'the feat of arms which was achieved on the rocky beach and scrub-grown cliff of the Gallipoli Peninsula ... was a feat, we are assured, whose prowess has never been outshone, has scarcely ever been rivalled, in military annals.'[69] Australians and New Zealanders responded to such sentiment with elegies of their own. One Australian poet penned these lines in tribute to her fallen countrymen at Gallipoli:

Clean aims, rare faculties, strength and youth,
They have poured them freely forth

For the sake of the sun-steeped land they left
And the far green isle in the North.
What can we do to be worthy of them
Now hearts are breaking for pride?
Give comfort at least to the wounded men
And the kin of the men that died.[70]

For the duration of the operation, very little appeared in the Australian and New Zealand press, or in any other cultural forum, that might have deflated the Dominions' burgeoning sense of pride in the performance of their soldiers and of their countries. At the same time, despite the best efforts of British and Dominion officials to keep the extent of the debacle hidden from the general public, it became increasingly obvious to men and women on the home fronts in the weeks and months after the landing that the campaign was mired in stalemate. The censors could not hide from ordinary Australians and New Zealanders the alarming casualties the Anzacs were suffering on the Peninsula, as every week the long rolls of honour that appeared in newspapers in both countries presented the grim reality in stark terms. Nor could the strenuous efforts of correspondents to depict the events of Gallipoli in a way that instilled hope for victory in the domestic population conceal how little progress Allied forces had actually made beyond the ground that they had seized in the initial landing.

For the most part, Australians and New Zealanders seeking to assign blame for the operation's lack of success placed the fault at the feet of the British. Australian and New Zealand soldiers on the Peninsula, in their letters back home, often expressed the opinion that the course of the campaign might have been different were it not for the poor performance of British troops, particularly the men of Kitchener's New Army and the Territorials. 'I don't' think much of the Tommies and there are great tales told of their bravery??' wrote one New Zealand trooper in a letter home. 'I can't stand them myself; that is the class we have fighting with us.'[71] An Australian serviceman who observed the British at Gallipoli recorded in his diary his contempt for the Tommy and his 'helpless imbecility, sluggishness and chicken-heartedness.' He went on to state that 'for me the British soldier is ever branded as all that is incompetent, useless, lazy and good for nothing … Once I used to worship the British soldier as a hero and was proud to be a Briton, but jigger me if I am now … for we see nothing but British blundering, boasting, bullying, bluff and blasting failure and doing nothing.'[72] Some Australian and New Zealand senior commanders shared the disparaging view of the British held by their men. John Monash, who would later command the AIF on the Western Front, as a colonel at Gallipoli lamented the poor quality of British troops:

> Over and over again they have allowed themselves to be driven out of positions which have been hardly (*sic*) won by Austr. and N. Z. troops ... altho' some are better than others, they can't soldier for sour apples. They have no grit, stamina or endurance, poor physique, no gumption, and they muddle along and allow themselves to be shot down because they don't even know how to take cover ... They have a willing enough spirit, and plenty of dull stupid courage, but they simply don't know enough to come in out of the wet.[73]

In the case of Australia, the tendency to blame the British for the fiasco on Gallipoli also characterized attitudes within the Dominion's higher civilian circles of power as well. Keith Murdoch, an Australian journalist and newspaper entrepreneur, visited Gallipoli shortly after the failure of the Suvla Bay offensive, the last and largest attempt by the Allies to break out of the Peninsula. After consulting there with Ashmead-Bartlett, who was also highly disillusioned with the British conduct of the campaign, Murdoch wrote a scathing indictment of the British military leadership on the Peninsula, particularly of the commanding British general, Sir Ian Hamilton. Murdoch's missive, though never published for public consumption in Australia, ultimately came to be circulated not only among Australian government officials, but also within the British establishment, where it provided ammunition to the critics of the Gallipoli campaign (chief among them, David Lloyd George, who was at that time the Minister of Munitions). The letter eventually helped bring about the removal of Hamilton and the abandonment of the operation.[74]

It is difficult to know to what extent the general public in Australia and New Zealand was aware of the aspersions being cast upon the British by their countrymen at Gallipoli. Almost all of the comments cited above were set down in private, or intended for a very limited, privileged audience. With the dismissal of Hamilton, Gallipoli became a public scandal in Great Britain, but the recriminations and government in-fighting that ensued there only received spotty coverage in the Dominions.[75] Even when the campaign was officially deemed a failure, and Allied troops withdrawn from the Peninsula, public criticism of the British and their conduct of the operation was generally muted in Australia and New Zealand. Most commentary struck a note similar to that sounded by an editorial appearing in the *West Australian* shortly after the evacuation:

> We cannot comment upon tactics, nor offer expert opinion upon strategy; yet we are able to measure results and appraise the cost. For eight months our men with their British brothers and French Allies have done all that men could do ... but [the campaign] was not a strategical success ... The fault did not lie with the soldiers, it rested with those in command. No one person can

be singled out and made a scapegoat, nor, perhaps with justice any group of persons. There were errors of diplomacy, errors of tactics, mistakes of administration ... against which it was impossible to cope ... No loss of prestige will ensue from the evacuation of the peninsula. The Allies have already paid the full penalty on this account ... The steps now taken are not an indication of a weakening of our resolution, but are a recognition of the non-success in one quarter, and evidence of a determination to prosecute the war elsewhere more vigorously, and upon principles more in consonance with approved strategy.[76]

Certainly much of the Dominion criticism of British decision-making at Gallipoli was justified. The operation was largely conceived and planned by British leaders, and as such, it was ill-conceived and poorly planned in many respects. For instance, the medical facilities in the theatre were appallingly inadequate. Officials in charge of the medical services had severely underestimated the number of casualties that the fighting would produce, and had not made sufficient arrangements for the transport and accommodation of the wounded. As a result, injured men often lay for days on the beaches of the Peninsula, exposed to shellfire as they waited for evacuation. On the overcrowded, understaffed transports themselves, conditions were seldom better: One ship carried between 400 and 500 wounded with only one bedpan between them.[77]

On the battlefield, poor planning resulted in the Allied forces, particularly the Anzacs, being unprepared for the trench warfare that ensued once the invasion stalled after the initial landing. Australian and New Zealand troops at first completely lacked sufficient trench and engineering stores, including barbed wire, timber and entrenching tools. They also had no howitzers, a crucial artillery piece in a trench warfare setting. Furthermore, ammunition was often in short supply, and much of what they possessed was of poor quality; men frequently resorted to manufacturing grenades from ration tins, old iron and rifle ammunition. Poor British staff work also can be blamed for breakdowns in the system of reinforcement that left many colonial units on the Peninsula dangerously undermanned for much of the campaign.[78]

Still, it is important to remember that the Australian and New Zealand performance at Gallipoli is far from immune to criticism. The Australian and New Zealand officers who comprised the middle and lower echelons of command were often as inexperienced in warfare as the men they led. This could have disastrous results in combat. For example, the infamous suicidal charge of the 8th and 10th Australian Light Horse Regiments at the Nek (it is this attack which is depicted in the harrowing climax of Peter Weir's 1981 film, 'Gallipoli') was the result of a breakdown in communication between the frontline and the brigade staff. Contrary to legend, it was an *Australian*, Colonel J. M. Antill, who ordered that the futile attack continue even after the first two waves of light-horsemen had been mowed down.[79] It is debatable whether such a tactical blunder would have occurred later in the war, when more experienced Australian officers generally exercised better judgment on the battlefield.

Of course, the failings of Australians and New Zealanders at Gallipoli was the last thing that men and women in the Dominions would have been aware of, fed as they were on a steady diet of reports glorifying their country's fighting men. To be sure, Dominion troops deserved a great deal of the praise lavished upon them. Few who observed them in and out of the line at Gallipoli failed to be impressed by their dash and composure in battle, their general competence in the skills of sol-diering, and their cheery dispositions even under the most adverse circumstances. Monash recorded this assessment of Australians under his command in a private letter written from the Peninsula:

> I am convinced that there are no troops in the world to equal the Australians in cool daring, courage and endurance ... our boys, capably led, can give the British regulars points and a beating at *any* part of the game, whether it be in digging a trench, or in bayonet assault, or in steadiness under fire ... or in ambulance work, or in cheerfully suffering fatigue and privations, or in marching, or in personal bravery.[80]

A New Zealand soldier, in the diary that he kept during the campaign, expressed similar sentiments. 'When the final word is said of this desperate attempt, I think New Zealand will be placed on the roll of honour along with Australia, as a coun-try that breeds men who are not afraid to die,' he wrote.[81]

Lions of War

One of the consequences of the long duration of the Gallipoli campaign was that it allowed some correspondents and commentators to develop a fairly nuanced rep-resentation of the Australian and New Zealand soldier, one that built upon, refined and eventually transcended the standard romantic clichés of the warrior from the bush. Perhaps no single individual did more in this regard than the Australian jour-nalist C. E. W. Bean, whose idealized depiction of the Australian 'digger', which began to take shape at Gallipoli, would be established by the end of the war as the standard image of the nation's fighting man. [82]

Bean's observations on the Peninsula were distinguished by the fact that he, unlike other correspondents, such as Ashmead-Bartlett, actually lived in the trenches alongside the Australian soldiers he covered. His descriptions of the An-zacs, in and out of battle, did not simply reproduce the pre-existing stereotype of the Australian outback fighting man, though his analysis was heavily informed by this myth and by other misconceptions about the regional composition and social background that characterized the majority of the AIF. At the same time, Bean's perspective was generally more realistic and perceptive than that of most of his contemporaries. His representation of the Australian soldier, though largely positive, was by no means the most flattering portrait of this figure to emerge during the war. Its resonance as a key element in the myth of the nation's war experience was due mainly to how successfully it incorporated a number of the most popular and culturally prevalent notions about Australian character into a single coherent and compelling ideal of the national type. Significantly, some of the notions about Australian character which Bean appropriated into his ideal had originally been articulated by proponents of ideological agendas that might seem diametrically opposed to Bean's own goal of promoting unified and loyal support of the Empire's war effort.

Bean would articulate his vision of the Australian soldier most thoroughly and comprehensively in the correspondence he filed from the Western Front between 1916 and 1918. His writing from this period will be discussed in detail in the next chapter. The analysis below will focus on Bean's observations at Gallipoli where, like his country, he experienced his baptism of fire. What he witnessed on the Peninsula would play a crucial role in the development of his ideas about the Australian fighting man as a paragon of the emerging nation.

Bean had accompanied the AIF to the Dardanelles as the official representative of the Australian press. At the time of this assignment he was already a well-known journalist in Australia, having written for the *Sydney Morning Herald* since 1908. However, Bean's notoriety did not prevent him from becoming ensnared in administrative red tape that severely hindered his effectiveness as a reporter during the initial phase of the Gallipoli campaign. The problems he experienced in obtaining proper press credentials meant that he was prevented from filing articles from the Peninsula until several days after the landing. Even after he was permitted to report, rivalry between colonial and British authorities resulted in his stories being published in Australia a day later than those of his British colleagues. As a result, Bean's dispatches from Gallipoli might not have had as wide a readership in Australia as those of Ashmead-Bartlett, for example. Regardless, Bean's observations during this period would form the nucleus of the legend that he, more than any other figure, would work to create and propagate. [83]

Like most of his fellow correspondents, Bean was impressed by the martial prowess of the Australian soldier. He devoted a great deal of analysis toward trying to explain what lay behind the well-documented élan, ferocity and intelligence of the Australian trooper in battle. Even before the war Bean had expressed the not-uncommon view that the Australian 'national spirit' was a product of the bush, 'that mysterious half-desert country where men have to live the lives of strong men.'[84] So it is not surprising that he, as others had before him, ascribed much of the credit for the fighting abilities of the Australians at Gallipoli to the attitudes, attributes and skills acquired through exposure to the hardy lifestyle of the outback. 'The wild, pastoral independent life of Australia, if it makes rather wild men, makes superb soldiers,' Bean asserted in the diary he kept on the Peninsula.[85] Bean was well aware that not every member of the AIF had experienced the bush, but he believed that the values of the frontier played a dominant role in shaping the outlook of even city-dwelling Australians.

As discussed at the beginning of this chapter, Bean expressed disdain for the British soldier and for the class system that characterized both the British Army and British society in general. By contrast, the AIF, as Bean saw it, was not an army of rank-and-file sheep led by the aristocratic adherents of an exclusionary warrior code. Rather, Australian fighting men were inspired and guided by a standard of conduct that transcended class, as well as other social differences, and united them behind a single nationally distinct ideal. Bean would label this code 'mateship,' after the practice of Australian soldiers referring to one another as 'mate' (a habit which derived from an older custom among working-class Australians). Bean divested the term of its traditional radical connotations of working class solidarity, redefining it to signify the bonds of loyalty and camaraderie between *all* Australian soldiers, regardless of class. This was, in fact, a fairly radical transformation of the concept of 'mateship' from an exclusionary, class-identified ideal into a more inclusive standard of behaviour that trumped social antagonisms and encouraged solidarity among Australian fighting men of every background.

Bean had not yet fully developed his conception of 'mateship' by the time of the Gallipoli campaign. That would only come later, after he had further observed the men of the AIF on the Western Front. By way of definition, suffice it to say that 'mateship' was a code of camaraderie and loyalty among Australian soldiers, born of their shared immersion in the intense and peculiar experience of waging war, that encouraged them to downplay (for the duration of the conflict, at least) class, ethnicity or religion as defining identities, and to instead define themselves first and foremost on the basis of national, regional and/or military unit identities. In and of itself, this phenomenon was certainly not unique to the AIF; it was observed within the armies of almost every belligerent nation, and anyone today familiar with the social and psychological dynamics that operate within small groups such as combat units would recognize it as a standard behavioural tactic to ensure unity and harmony among individual members. What was novel about the ideal of 'mateship' as it came to be understood and articulated in relation to the AIF, was the degree to which it was interpreted and depicted, by Bean and others, less as an informal behavioural phenomenon than as a distinctively Australian code of conduct that was central to definitions of national identity.

The place of class within the ideal of 'mateship' was crucial to Bean's interpretation of the concept. Even before the war, Bean had described Australia as a land in which the feudal class distinctions that characterized the Motherland were all but absent. Throughout his career his consistently mythologized the Dominion as a country distinguished by a degree of social mobility and equality of opportunity that made the formation of rigid caste hierarchies and uncompromising class consciousness along the lines of what prevailed in England practically impossible.[86] In many ways, Bean's was a simplistic, some would say naive, understanding of social relations in Australia, but it was fundamental to how he perceived and interpreted what he witnessed on the battlefields of Gallipoli, and later, on the Western Front.

Bean arrived in the Dardanelles in 1915 with a belief that Australian social and political relationships had, like the country's manhood, evolved to a state of decided superiority over their British antecedents. What he observed during the long, futile campaign on the Peninsula only confirmed this view. At one point Bean recorded the following in his diary:

> Well, the problem of Gallipoli reduces itself to – why can't the British fight? … in a year's training [the Tommy] can't be turned into a soldier because to tell the truth he's a very feeble specimen of a man – and it seems to be the British social formula to make sure he sticks there. In a nation with only one class [Australia], it's in nobody's interest to keep anyone else in "his place" – and his place is, from his birth, the best place he can get and keep. To my mind this war… is just Britain's tomahawks coming home to roost.[87]

Significantly, Bean's scathing criticism of British troops and British society did not mean that he was anti-imperialist. Quite the contrary – Bean, Australian by birth, had received his education at an English public school and at Oxford University. Like his father before him, he had taken advantage of the career opportunities available in the outposts of Empire, returning to Australia in 1904. Bean may have excoriated (privately) the incompetence of British commanders, the inadequacies of British troops, and the flaws of British social structure, but he remained devoted to the Empire that he believed he (and Australia) was duty-bound to serve.

At the same time, Bean was an Australian nationalist, and became more so as the war went on. For Bean, this position was not irreconcilable with his imperialism. As he saw it, Australia was bound to Britain by unbreakable ties – of economic and military dependence, to be sure – but also, and more profoundly, of heritage, culture and, to use Bean's own language, race. These bonds commanded the loyalty (though not the subordination) of the Dominion to the Motherland, even if the price of that loyalty was sometimes painfully high. In his writings before the war, Bean had linked the ideal of 'mateship' with his expectation of Australian devotion to the Motherland in the event of a crisis. He described the average Australian as the most loyal man on earth, and declared that if Britain were ever in danger, the citizens of the Dominion, regardless of ideological affiliation, would stand beside their 'old mate,' the Motherland.[88]

Bean's brand of pro-imperial nationalism was, in many ways, broadly consistent with the nationalism promoted around the turn of the century by certain members of the middle-class, English-descended, native-born elite in Australia. What was new was Bean's appropriation and use of language and terminology customarily associated with the virulently anti-imperialist nationalism of Australian working-class radicals. The historian K. S. Inglis has said that there have been two main streams of Australian nationalist tradition, one radical and the other patriotic.[89] Bean's accomplishment was to harness the former tradition in the service of the latter.[90]

While Bean's newspaper correspondence from Gallipoli may have been less widely read than that of some of his contemporaries, he nevertheless found other ways to make fundamental contributions to how Australians perceived both the war they were fighting in the Dardanelles, and the Australian soldiers who were fighting it. His most important and successful early expression of his Anzac ideal appeared in *The Anzac Book*, a commemorative annual of the Gallipoli campaign that was commissioned in November of 1915, and published in January 1916, shortly after the evacuation of the Peninsula. Though the book was ostensibly 'written and illustrated in Gallipoli by the men of Anzac,' it was fundamentally the creation of its editor, Bean. He had solicited contributions from all Dominion soldiers on the Peninsula, but of the 36,000 troops stationed in the Anzac zone, only about 150 (mostly Australian) men responded. From this narrow sample Bean selected for publication only the material that met his aesthetic standards, avoided expressing horror, bitterness or disloyalty, and most importantly, conformed to his vision of the Australian (and secondarily, New Zealand) soldier.[91]

The image of the AIF fighting man that emerges through the poems and illustrations in *The Anzac Book* is of a brave, independent, resilient warrior who endures the danger and discomfort of his situation with sardonic good humour. He is irreverent toward authority (particularly that which has not earned his respect)[92], disdainful of military spit and polish, and nonchalant about the possibility of being killed or wounded. But he is a fierce, skilful and resourceful fighter, tough as nails when facing adversity, and ice cool in the heat of battle. A great many of the cartoons selected by Bean contrast British officers, and their obsession with style, to Australian soldiers, who are the epitome of substance. Other poems and cartoons portray the AIF as an egalitarian institution, the ultimate exemplar of meritocracy and social levelling. One drawing places the 'before' picture of a buffoonish, obviously affluent, monocle-wearing civilian beside the image of the same man in uniform, now looking confident, serene, worthy of admiration. The caption reads: 'It's not what you were, but what you are today.'[93]

The Anzac Book was a huge success in Australia and New Zealand, selling over 100,000 copies by September 1916. The fact that it sold so well indicates the degree to which the image of the country's fighting men that it presented appealed to the general public. Australian soldiers also seemed to like the way they were portrayed: By November 1916 AIF members had bought more than 53,000 copies.[94] Certainly it is probably not the literary merits of *The Anzac Book* that most explain why it became a best seller. Brian Lewis remembers receiving a copy of the book as an adolescent in Melbourne. He found that 'some of it was of about the same standard as a school magazine and some of it of very high quality. There were some good drawings and some good verse, some pathetic and some comic.' Overall, *The Anzac Book* was 'presentable, but it was like any obituary.'[95]

Lewis' characterization of *The Anzac Book* as an 'obituary' is fitting, given that Bean intended the annual to be, at least in part, a commemorative souvenir of the Gallipoli campaign. The memorial aspect of the book probably goes a long way toward helping to explain its success in the Pacific Dominions. In the months following the evacuation of the Peninsula, men and women in Australia and New Zealand demonstrated an intense desire to commemorate in some fashion the campaign which had achieved almost unprecedented importance as an event in the lives of many citizens, as well as in the history of the young nations. The language and imagery associated with these early efforts to memorialize Gallipoli would foreshadow many of the themes and tropes that would appear in connection with later and larger attempts to commemorate the Australian and New Zealand experience in the Great War as a whole.

The form that commemoration took in the immediate aftermath of the Gallipoli campaign was largely rhetorical. The stone or bronze monuments and memorials, soon to be nearly ubiquitous edifices in town squares, schools and churches throughout Australia and New Zealand would, for the most part, only come later. The end of the operation spawned a wave of speeches, newspaper commentaries, editorial cartoons and poems celebrating and eulogizing Gallipoli and the Anzacs who fought and died there. 'Lions of war, our noblest and our best,' begins one verse honouring the men of Anzac. 'Who won the desperate beach and death-lash'd crest/ And looked on Fate's most awful face unhid/ Poorly our praise may match the thing you did.'[96]

The wave of tributes peaked around 25 April 1916, the first anniversary of the landing at Anzac Cove, and the first observance throughout Australia and New Zealand of what would eventually become in both countries the national holiday known as Anzac Day. The anniversary of the landing provided an opportunity for politicians, journalists, poets and other artists to interpret the meaning for Australia and New Zealand of the Gallipoli campaign and its sacrifices. Employing rhetoric that often echoed sentiments widely expressed in Canada in the wake of Second Ypres, many Australians and New Zealanders characterized Gallipoli as a 'rite of passage' or a blood sacrifice that earned their country the status of nationhood. An Anzac Day book of remembrance published by the New South Wales Returned Soldiers Association contains numerous poems that reflect this perspective. 'Lo, Australia holds her place/ bought with her blood for price,' reads one stanza in a typical verse. Another poet declares Gallipoli to be a 'New Altar' among the Empire's shrines of patriotic devotion. 'We of the British blood would ever turn,/ Pilgrims from these Dominions oversea,/ Fain to salute the altars where did burn/ The sacrifices immense that hold us free;' she declares. 'Now, holy places – if new-consecrate,/ Dear as of old devotion – we claim today.'[97]

For Australians and New Zealanders, the new found national pride they felt at their accomplishments on Gallipoli provided them, much as Second Ypres had for Canadians, with a fresh source of inspiration for the struggle in which they were engaged. However, the Australian and New Zealand experience at Gallipoli differed from the Canadian experience at Second Ypres in a number of important ways. First of all, the prolonged duration of the Dardanelles campaign, its perceived importance to the overall Allied war effort, and the prominent role played by Australasian forces in the operation granted it a much more exalted status in the eyes of Australians and New Zealanders than Second Ypres ever achieved for Canadians. Also, Gallipoli was a failure[98], and moreover, it was a failure that many Australians and New Zealanders, particularly those with a firsthand experience of the campaign or firsthand knowledge about its management, blamed, at least privately, on the British. Among those Australians and New Zealanders whose vision was relatively un-obscured by the fog of censorship and propaganda, Gallipoli had been a disillusioning revelation of British fallibility. For Canadians, this disenchantment still lay in the future.

Still, even for enlightened citizens of the Pacific Dominions in the spring of 1916, doubts about the British had not hardened into conviction, and whatever trepidation they felt seldom found its way into mainstream public discussion of the war. It was still possible a year after the landings at Anzac for Australians and New Zealanders to be at least as inspired by the idea of fighting and dying in the service of the Motherland and Empire as they were by the thought that they were consecrating their own national traditions. For every testimonial in the New South Wales Anzac Memorial that praises how the Australian and New Zealand soldiers have earned for the Dominions 'the right to be considered real world-citizens with a share in shaping the future destiny of the World,' there is a line of verse that invokes the emotional bonds of Empire. 'What have we done for England?' asks one poem. 'Now you know: By those green graves that shall for ever be/ The richest colour in man's memory.'[99] These words echo the lines of J. D. Burns' 'For England,' an extremely popular poem that was published in Australia shortly after the landings at Anzac Cove in 1915. The opening stanza reads:

The Bugles of England were blowing o'er the sea,
As they had called a thousand years, calling now to me;
They woke me from dreaming in the dawning of the day,
The Bugles of England – and how could I stay?[100]

In a similar vein, poignant, and far from unique, evidence of the continuing power of imperial identity as an emotional force is offered by the simple lines of poetry included in a 25 April 1916 'In Memoriam' notice for an Australian lance-corporal killed at Gallipoli. They read:

Never the lotus closes,
Never the wild fowl wake;
But a soul goes out on the east wind,
That died for England's sake. [101]

As the First World War unfolded, events on the battlefield and on the high seas nourished among an ever-increasing number of Australians, Canadians and New Zealanders a growing loss of confidence in the inherent superiority of British leaders and institutions. This was especially true of those with an intimate knowledge of the conduct of the war, and the idea that the Dominions should no longer be relegated to a subordinate status in the imperial family gained a wider currency in the circles of power. Furthermore, as a consequence of the war, aspects of Australian, New Zealand or Canadian identity 'discovered' and celebrated by pre-war promoters of national self-awareness achieved a heightened cachet within mainstream culture, as traits or attributes associated with the 'national type' in these Dominions were modified and adapted to construct a new, wartime paradigm of the Australian, Canadian or New Zealand male.

All the same, the impact of the war on feelings of identity in the Dominions was ambivalent to say the least. Evidence of the weakening hold of the British mystique on popular imagination, and of the growing sense of a distinct identity accompanied by rising assertiveness, was counterbalanced by the fact that expressions of loyalty to the Empire, and of pride in the British heritage, were never more prominent in the Dominions than during the war years, and indeed this upsurge of pro-imperial sentiment would survive as a defining cultural characteristic at least until the end of the Second World War. Furthermore, as evidenced by the fierce domestic debates over the issue of conscription – particularly in Canada and Australia – even as the war helped crystallize ideas of uniquely Canadian, Australian or New Zealand identities, such developments were not always accompanied in these countries by a genuine sense of coalescing national unity. On the contrary, the war years often divided citizens within the Dominions as never before.

3

The Lords of Battle

The Anzacs: From Gallipoli to the Western Front

For Canadians, Australians and New Zealanders the bloody baptisms of 1915 were mere prelude to the ordeal that awaited them on the Western Front. Beginning in the summer of 1916, first the Australians, and then the Canadians and New Zealanders, would be fed into the meat grinder that was the Somme campaign. From this point forward, more Canadians, Australians and New Zealanders would fight and die on the fields of France and Belgium than in any other theatre of the Great War. For Australia and New Zealand, Gallipoli would always loom larger in the national consciousness, but for all of the Dominions, the Western Front would prove to be a powerful crucible for shaping emerging conceptions of national identity, and for fundamentally altering how they perceived themselves and their countries in relation to the Motherland.

As we have seen, the Canadians had been stationed on the Western Front since 1915, but it would be the Australians who would first take part in the British Army's enormous offensive on the Somme. In some ways the Australian Imperial Force was lucky, having arrived in the line too late to participate in the dreadful slaughter at the start of the campaign on 1 July, when British forces suffered more than 60,000 casualties (including 20,000 killed) in a single day.[1] The Australian initiation into the Somme would be traumatic enough, however. In just 24 hours on 19 July, the AIF's 5th Division lost 5,533 dead and wounded in an ill-conceived feint attack near the village of Fromelles.[2] This frightening toll was fairly typical by the standards of Western Front battles, but came as a shock to many Australian observers: In one day a single division had suffered 68 per cent of the total casualties endured in nine months on Gallipoli. Nor did the operation achieve the desired result of preventing the Germans from moving troops to other parts of the Somme. As C. E. W. Bean later remarked in his Official History, the value of the attack at Fromelles, if any, 'was tragically disproportionate to the cost.'[3]

Bean and others attributed much of the blame for the futility and carnage of Fromelles to poor planning and preparation by the British commander in charge of the operation, General Sir Richard Haking. The assault was conceived in confusion, with ill-defined and contradictory objectives, and conducted in an appallingly slip-shod fashion. British artillery coverage was far from adequate, and the preliminary bombardment only served to alert the Germans to the impending attack. The Australian troops went over the top in the still-bright early evening light, and so made easy targets for German artillery and machine guns. After the operation had failed at such alarming cost, the British High Command added insult to injury in the view of many Australians who knew better by characterizing the battle in an official communiqué as 'some important raids … in which Australian troops took part.'[4] Furthermore, Australian criticism of the British performance at Fromelles was not limited to the commanders of the operation. Bean asserted in the official history that the alleged failure of a British division, the 61st, to adequately support the Australians' flanks reinforced the perception, already prevalent in the AIF after Gallipoli, that 'the new British armies lacked something in fighting capacity.'[5]

Fromelles was only the beginning of the Australian trial on the Somme. On 23 July, the 1st, 2nd and 4th divisions of I Anzac Corps launched a major assault against the German defences near the village of Pozières. Thanks to better preparation and coordination between the artillery and infantry than occurred at Fromelles, the initial attack was remarkably successful, with the Australians overrunning the German defences and capturing most of the village of Pozières with relatively light casualties. Unfortunately, the commander of the operation, General Sir Hubert Gough, was encouraged by success to press for more ground, with the consequence that the Australians were funnelled into a narrow salient where they were subjected to a systematic and unbelievably intense artillery bombardment by the Germans. For seven weeks the units of I Anzac, beginning with the 1st division – which was relieved by the 2nd division on 26 July, which was relieved by the 4th division on 5 August – endured an almost continuous rain of shells as they clung to the ground they had won around Pozières.[6] Incredibly the Australians maintained their offensive throughout the never-ending barrage, launching major attacks on 29 July and in mid-August. The assaults achieved limited gains, but always at an extremely high cost, confined as they were to a frontage of a mile or less, which enabled the Germans to concentrate their artillery against the attackers. Moreover, the ground won was seldom held strongly enough to resist determined German counterattacks. By the time the Australians were withdrawn from the Pozières sector of the battlefield, they had suffered 23,000 casualties, including 6,741 dead, and gained in the end only a few yards of earth.[7]

From an overall operational standpoint, the Pozières campaign was just as much an exercise in futility for the AIF as Gallipoli, and nearly as costly. However, the fighting at Pozières – particularly the violence and prolonged duration of the enemy's artillery barrages – was far more intense than had generally been the case at Gallipoli. The letters written by Australian fighting men who experienced this bat-

tle often convey a sense of unremitting horror and desperation that is largely lacking in the accounts produced by soldiers on the Peninsula. One sergeant jotted
down the scene he witnessed in the midst of a bombardment: 'Heavy firing all
morning – simply murder. Men falling everywhere ... Expecting death every second. 23 men smothered in one trench. Dead and dying everywhere. Some simply
blown to pieces. Shells falling like hail during a storm.' Another soldier recounted
an artillery barrage that drove many men 'stark staring mad and more than one of
them rushed out of the trench over towards the Germans. Any amount of them
could be seen crying and sobbing like children their nerves completely gone ...'[8]

According to Bean, for many men in the AIF, Pozières reinforced, at least temporarily, their growing disillusion with the British High Command. 'Some of the
more thoughtful soldiers wondered (and could not be blamed for wondering)
whether any sufficient object was being gained by this excessive strain and loss,' he
wrote in the Official History. 'It is not surprising if the effect on some intelligent
men was a bitter conviction that they were being uselessly sacrificed.'[9] Several of
the high-ranking Australian officers who had been instrumental in the planning of
the fiascos at Fromelles and Pozières were replaced shortly after the failure of these
operations.[10] By contrast, senior British commanders, such as Gough, seemed to be
immune from the consequences of their ineptitude. This led to feelings of resentment among some Australian observers over what seemed to be a policy of making
scapegoats of Dominion commanders for the failures of their British superiors.

However, if after the Somme battles there increasingly existed among Australian
soldiers the degree of bitterness toward the British that is alluded to by Bean, the
country's fighting men generally avoided expressing such sentiments in public. The
complaints and criticisms of highly placed Australian military officials were almost
always aired only in private. Ordinary fighting men, whose options were more limited in this regard, occasionally vented their anger in letters or in their diaries. For
example, one Australian junior officer, in a last letter written before his death at
Pozières, decried the 'murder' of his friends 'through the incompetence, callousness, and personal vanity of those high in authority.'[11] Far more typically, however,
writings by the men of the AIF expressed a general disillusion with war, rather than
specific ill will toward their commanders. One infantryman wrote after Pozières:
'God I have seen the most gruesome sights the most awful tragic scenes it has been
my cruel lot to witness ... take it from me, none of mine will ever tackle this job
again ... if men refuse to fight all the world over war will cease.' Just as at Gallipoli,
Australian attitudes in the trenches on the Somme were frequently characterized by
a fatalistic sense of duty, laced with pride at the mettle of their countrymen. One
sergeant who had been a logger in civilian life wrote:

The Australians have been in the thick of it at last and ... have actually ex-
celled themselves. What a reputation we will have if we keep on going. But I

am sure I have no desire to keep at this game much longer. I'd sooner be slicing hunks off a tough old Gray Box, than poking holes in a Prussian, any day. But I suppose that will have to wait till the other job is finished.

Evidence of devotion to the Motherland and Empire, so pervasive in the first two years of the war, did not altogether die out as a result of the experience on the Somme. An Australian captain sought to console his wife by asking her to 'remember it is better to die for you & Country than to be a cheat of the empire.' However, the Australian sense of their superior martial prowess – particularly over that of the British – which had developed at Gallipoli, was only augmented by their performance at Fromelles and Pozières. 'The Australians ... took a village ... the English had 3 goes at,' wrote one lance corporal during the latter battle. 'And [the Australians] stop in a trench while 15 inch shells are landing and very few of them show any fear.'[12]

However, pride in Australian capabilities, and dissatisfaction with Britain's leadership and battlefield performance – which was evident, though perhaps not to the degree suggested by Bean – did not combine in the wake of Fromelles and Pozières to produce any significant impetus for redefining the status of the AIF within the British and Allied forces. As we will see later in this chapter, this contrasts sharply to the reaction of Canadian leaders in response to their country's initial experiences on the Western Front. The Canadian Expeditionary Force's tour in the Somme slaughterhouse, which coincided with that of the New Zealand Division, while slightly more successful than that of the AIF, resulted in casualties on a comparable scale to those suffered by the Australians. For many Canadian policy makers, the Somme merely confirmed the conviction, growing since Second Ypres, that the extent of Canadian sacrifice and British ineptitude made it imperative that the Dominion attained greater administrative and operational control over its forces in the field. Among Australian leaders, the momentum for such changes took far longer to generate.

New Zealand represented a different case altogether. The comparatively small population of the island nation meant that for the duration of the war it could contribute manpower sufficient for no more than a single division. This division, though commanded by a New Zealander, Andrew Russell, for the entire conflict would never achieve the same level of tactical autonomy as a 'national' force enjoyed by the divisions that would eventually comprise the Australian and Canadian corps. In fact, such autonomy was never really sought by New Zealand's military and civilian leaders. They remained less concerned about where and how British commanders employed New Zealand troops on the battlefield than about ensuring that the loyalty of the small island Dominion was not exploited to burden them with a disproportionate share of the colonies' manpower contributions.

To return to the example of Australia, of the many possible explanations for the Dominion's delay, when compared to Canada, in attempting to win for its forces increasing operational and administrative independence from Britain, perhaps the most significant factor was the prevailing outlook among the AIF's senior commanders. In 1916, the upper echelon of the AIF was still dominated by British and Anglophile officers. The commander of the AIF until 1918, General Sir William Birdwood, hailed from the ranks of that most imperial of British institutions, the Indian Army. During the war, despite his innumerable professions of identification with Australia and its people, he consistently showed himself to be more inclined to favour the interests of the Empire over those of his adopted Dominion, or perhaps to see those interests as indistinguishable. Even many Australian-born senior officers, such as Brudenell White, the commander immediately below Birdwood in the AIF hierarchy, tended to emphasize the Imperial identity of the AIF, rather than its status as an Australian 'national' army. Such men had very little motivation to push for the 'Australianization' of the AIF's officer corps, or for the creation of an autonomous, independent Australian Corps, preferably under the command of an Australian.[13] For Australia, the lack of initiative in this area, from both military and civilian officials, is in notable contrast to the Canadian experience. The largest Pacific Dominion produced no counterpart to Sam Hughes, Canada's fiercely nationalistic Minister of War between 1914 and 1916. Nor was there an Australian equivalent to George Perley and his Canadian Overseas Ministry, which replaced Hughes and provided the CEF with an effective administrative infrastructure for the rest of the war. The AIF's administration in London, while nominally independent from the British High Command, remained under the control of Birdwood, rather than an Australian, and so never really attained much genuine autonomy.

For Australians on the home front in 1916, the Somme battles that summer, despite a scale, intensity and loss of life comparable to or even exceeding that of Gallipoli, did not have the kind of impact on the popular imagination that had been generated by the earlier campaign. Despite the fact that British forces comprised the bulk of the Allied contingent at Gallipoli, the prominent and widely celebrated role played by the Anzacs in the events on the Peninsula ensured that men and women in the Dominion would regard Gallipoli as an Australian (and New Zealand) battle. By contrast, Fromelles and Pozières were, by the standards of the titanic struggles being waged on the Western Front in 1916, relatively minor episodes. The AIF was, at this time, just another cog in the tremendous wheel that was the British Army, and that army was engaged in the incredibly massive exercise in bloody futility that was the Somme offensive. Over a period of four months, a total of 51 British divisions, of which the Australians contributed four, battered unsuccessfully at the German defences, suffering in the process more than 600,000 casualties. At the Somme, the Australian soldiers were, in the words of Brian Lewis, 'now in a big amorphous sort of war, not their own Anzac.'[14]

In Australia, coverage of the AIF in France seemed to confirm this view. Fromelles was almost completely ignored by the press, while Pozières received piecemeal coverage that was heavily censored and highly distorted. Australians were left to glean the truth about the operations from the lengthening casualty lists that summer and fall, and from the way that minuscule gains in ground were hailed as significant victories. 'The casualty lists in the papers made it all clear to us,' recalls Brian Lewis. 'Every day we saw men and women wearing bits of black, and we knew of others wearing no sign at all. The pattern of the war was set.' After the Somme, Australians reacted to press reports of allied success on the Western Front with increasing scepticism and decreasing enthusiasm. According to Lewis:

> At home, there was no rush for the paper before breakfast to read of the new victory; there were victories in the paper but we did not believe in them any longer. There might be some new place-name, but it soon fell back amongst the other place-names as somewhere where thousands had been killed.[15]

If the reaction of Australian leaders and of citizens on the home-front to events at Fromelles and Pozières seemed muted and low-key, particularly compared to the response inspired by Gallipoli, it was nevertheless the case that the Somme battles affected Australian wartime society in a number of concrete and significant ways. The most important of these was undoubtedly the enormous strain that the battles placed on the all-volunteer AIF's ability to meet its manpower needs. The ramifications of this problem proved to be profound, as it led directly to the crisis over conscription that would disrupt the domestic front in Australia for the rest of the war. The development of this crisis will be addressed in detail in the next chapter. Once again, Australia's experience provides an interesting contrast to that of Canada and New Zealand (whose Parliament had approved conscription even before its forces saw service on the Somme). For the North American Dominion, the battles that the CEF fought on the Somme in the fall and early winter of 1916 would lead to a manpower crisis comparable to that of Australia's. Many Canadian leaders, like their counterparts in the Antipodes, would view conscription as the solution to this problem. The issue of compulsory service would prove to be no less controversial within Canadian society than it would within that of Australia. However, the debate would ultimately be resolved very differently in Canada and Australia, and the fault lines that the crisis revealed in each Dominion would illuminate that country's own particular social cleavages.

Canada: Toward a 'National' Army

Still, conscription in Canada loomed only as a distant possibility in September 1916 when CEF troops took over trenches on the Somme not far from those recently vacated by the Australians. 'Instructions have been received that we are to move today to the slaughter grounds of the Somme,' wrote one Canadian private in his diary before shipping out for the battlefield.[16] That soldier's sense of dread would prove justified. Beginning on September 15, Canadian troops, alongside the newly arrived New Zealand Division, would fight and die for virtually the same ground that had recently cost the lives of so many of their colonial brethren. The Dominion troops were participating in the same general offensive, a second attempt to smash the German lines on the Somme that would last from September to November 1916. Like the Australians, the Canadians and New Zealanders suffered horrendous casualties to achieve limited gains. The Canadians' most notable successes were the capture on 15 September of Courcelette, a German-held village not far from Pozières[17], and the taking of Regina Trench, a strong German defensive position that held out through nearly two months of ferocious and bloody Canadian attacks. The New Zealanders were instrumental in the capture of the hamlet of Gueudecourt on 26 September, but were unable to achieve a breakthrough beyond that. In the end, three months on the Somme cost the CEF 24,029 casualties, and two months in the same sector for the New Zealanders left them with more than 7,000 dead and wounded.[18]

For Canada, from a military standpoint, their experience on the Somme was almost identical to that of Australia. However, the reaction of Canadian citizens on the home front to the success of their troops at Courcelette, if not to the terrible price that they paid for it, contrasted notably to the low-key reaction of Australians to the results of Pozières a few months earlier. A Canadian film documenting 'The Battle of Courcelette' enjoyed considerable popularity. Also, newspapers throughout the Dominion trumpeted the victory. The *Globe* of Toronto quoted the British correspondent Philip Gibbs, who said: 'The Canadians have gained great glory by their attack. The full story of the Canadian victory will thrill the great Dominion like a heroic song.' A reporter with the same newspaper praised the troops of the CEF using a metaphor drawn from a popular national sport: '[At Courcelette] No home run was expected from them, but only a sacrifice fly, to use baseball language, but they made a home run and brought in all the men on the bases.'[19] However, for many Canadians, like their Australian counterparts, 1916 was the year when, in the words of Sandra Gwyn, 'the war stopped being an aberration and turned into a constant, a nightmare of which people could no longer foresee the end even while still clinging to the assumption that surely, somehow, it must eventually end.'[20]

For many Canadian decision-makers, the Somme seemed to confirm their belief that the Dominion deserved a greater degree of autonomy on the battlefield and more control over the disposition of its troops. That Canada by 1916 was closer to achieving these goals than Australia was due largely to the determined agitation on the part of several powerful and influential members of the North American Dominion's military and civilian leadership. For example, Canada's colourful and controversial Minister of War between 1914 and 1916, General Sam Hughes, was an ardent nationalist who had exercised an astounding degree of personal control over the organization and administration of the Canadian contingent since the start of the war. On the one-hand, Hughes' arbitrary and idiosyncratic brand of micro management had resulted in an appalling degree of administrative chaos within the overseas support services of the CEF (a situation which would shortly lead to his dismissal and replacement by the Overseas Ministry under George Perley). On the other hand, Hughes had held a low opinion of British military commanders ever since his service in the South African War, and this prejudice, combined with his Canadian patriotism, ensured that he strove to fill the ranks of the CEF's senior command with Canadians. This state of affairs stands in stark contrast to that which prevailed for Australia at the time, where appointments to the higher echelons of command in the AIF were generally at the discretion of the British General Birdwood. Moreover, after battlefield setbacks for the CEF (such as the fiasco at St. Eloi in March-April 1916), Hughes, together with his ally Max Aitken (the future Lord Beaverbrook) – a Canadian-born financier who owned the mass-circulation British newspaper *Daily Express* and held a seat in England's Parliament as the Conservative member for Ashton-under-Lyme – made sure that British officers, rather than Canadians, suffered the consequences. After St. Eloi, for instance, it was the British commander of the Canadian Corps, Lt.-General Sir Edmund Alderson, who was removed, and not two lower-ranking Canadian officers more directly responsible for the failure of the operation.[21]

Ironically, whatever the extent to which Sam Hughes' nationalist outlook promoted and safeguarded the 'Canadianization' of the CEF's senior command, it was his organizational ineptitude which actually brought about what proved to be the most profound manifestation of Canadian autonomy over their war effort in the months after the Somme. By 1916, the overseas military administration of the CEF was an unmitigated disaster: England was awash in Canadian officers who owed their appointments more to political influence than to battlefield experience, and who were consequently not assigned to units fighting in France, but were instead allowed to swell the ranks of the bloated but largely ineffectual Canadian military bureaucracy in the mother country. There was thus a surplus of desk-bound captains, majors and colonels shuffling papers in England, and a shortage of officers at the front where they were sorely needed. Furthermore, many of the logistical and support services of the CEF, including the Army Service Corps, the Veterinary Corps and, most seriously, the Canadian Army Medical Corps, were highly disorganized and corrupt. [22] To a significant extent, the administrative crisis overseas could be blamed directly on Sam Hughes. Not only had the Minister of War and his cronies been personally responsible for appointing some of the unqualified officers languishing in Britain, but in a broader sense, neither he nor his underlings demonstrated any gift for bureaucratic organization, and his decision-making was often based less on objective, rational judgment than on political interest or personal whim. Hughes' managerial style perpetuated a highly inefficient system of support for the CEF, and this situation threatened to undermine the country's entire war effort.

By the end of November 1916 Hughes was gone, fired by Prime Minister Borden. To replace Hughes' autocratic regime, Borden designated Sir George Perley as the Minister of the Overseas Military Forces of Canada (OMFC). Perley's Overseas Ministry was basically a Canadian government department based in London that was charged with responsibility for the personnel, property and expenditures of the Canadian forces in Britain and on the continent. On the one hand, the new ministry effectively extended the reach of Ottawa across the Atlantic. At the same time, Borden granted Perley and his department a great deal of authority to formulate policies and make decisions on the spot that did not always have to be cleared with Ottawa.[23] Shortly after his appointment to head the new ministry, Perley articulated the new conception of Canada's belligerent status in relation to Great Britain that was emerging as a result of the Dominion's war effort, and which the creation of his department symbolized. 'The Dominion is no mere auxiliary,' he wrote.

> The Dominion is at war, a partner in all things with the other members of the Alliance ... The Dominion has, in truth, put her all into the fray. She has, with no stint, with no reservations, given her blood, her toil, her possessions. No less than the British forces ... no less than the heroic armies of France, Russia and Italy ...[24]

In its relative independence from home front control, and in the resulting initiative with which it carried out its task, Canada's Overseas Ministry proved to be quite distinct from the London-based organization dedicated to the administration of Australia's forces overseas. Like its Canadian counterpart, the AIF administration was formally independent from the British High Command, but all policy decisions made by the Australian organization had to be cleared through Melbourne. Furthermore Birdwood, in addition to being in charge of Australia's forces in the field, retained command of the AIF administration as well. The day-to-day operations of the administrative headquarters at Horseferry Road were run by a commandant, Brigadier-General R. M. McC. Anderson, who, like Perley, had been a successful colonial businessman before the war, but who, unlike Perley, showed little facility for the duties of his wartime position and proved to be unpopular with British and Australian officials alike. Nevertheless, the AIF bureaucracy under

Birdwood and Anderson was never marked by any degree of chaos or corruption comparable to that which prevailed during Hughes' tenure at the head of the CEF's administration. Nor, however, did the AIF administration ever become a force for projecting and protecting the national aspirations and interests of Australia in the same way that the Overseas Ministry did for Canada.[25]

By 1916, it seemed evident to many Canadians that the Dominion's war effort had transcended the response that could be expected of a loyal colonial subject. So far, the country had provided thousands of men to the Allied cause, and had financed that contribution completely on its own. That these sacrifices had not resulted in any appreciable gains on the battlefield was frustrating to Dominion leaders. Even more frustrating, however, was the condescension with which the British rebuffed Canadian efforts to play a more direct role in the Empire's decision-making about the war. Borden had visited England in 1915, and had been stymied in his efforts to obtain information about the true state of affairs on the battlefield and in the British government, until he threatened to withdraw Canada's support from the war. He subsequently received a frank and highly disturbing status report from then-Minister-of-Munitions David Lloyd George, who painted a lurid picture of an Imperial war effort sabotaged by the incompetence of British political leadership.[26]

Once back in Ottawa, Borden soon found that he was isolated once again, and cut off from any information about what was happening overseas, except for what the censors allowed to be published in the press. His repeated entreaties to members of Britain's War Cabinet to establish some system whereby the Dominions could be informed and consulted about the progress of the war met with a dismissive response from Andrew Bonar Law. In November 1915, the British statesman wrote Borden that 'as regards the question of consultation … I am … not able to see any way in which this could be practically done.' Furthermore, Bonar Law continued, 'if no scheme is practicable then it is very undesirable that the question should be raised.' Borden was infuriated by the attitude displayed in this note, and fired off a passionate letter to George Perley, which he was instructed to show to British cabinet ministers. Few statements made at the time better illustrate the direct relationship between Canada's contribution to the war effort and the emerging belief that this contribution entitled the Dominion to something more than subordinate status in the eyes of the Motherland. Thus it deserves to be quoted at length. Borden wrote:

> During the past four months since my return from Great Britain, the Canadian government … have had just what information could be gleaned from the daily Press and no more. As to consultation, plans of campaign have been made and unmade, measures adopted and apparently abandoned and generally speaking steps of the most important and even vital character have been

taken and postponed without the slightest consultation with the authorities of this Dominion. It can hardly be expected that we shall put 400,000 or 500,000 men in the field and willingly accept the position of having no more voice and receiving no more consideration than if we were toy automata ... Is this war being waged by the United Kingdom alone, or is it a war waged by the whole Empire? If I am correct in supposing that the second hypothesis must be accepted then why do the statesmen of the British Isles arrogate to themselves solely the methods by which it shall be carried on in the various spheres of warlike activity and the steps which shall be taken to assure victory and a lasting peace? It is for them to suggest the method and not for us. If there is no available method and if we are expected to continue in the role of automata, the whole situation must be reconsidered. [27]

Toward the end of 1916, British leaders announced that they would summon the Dominion premiers to London in 1917 for an Imperial War Conference to 'consider urgent questions affecting prosecution of the War, the possible conditions on which in agreement with our Allies we could assent to its termination, and the problems which will then immediately arise.'

The call for an Imperial War Conference culminated attempts by Canadian leaders in the months after the Somme to ensure that the Dominion controlled more and more of its own war effort. The staggering cost in blood and treasure of the war thus far, and the impression that British mismanagement was to blame for much of the futility on the battlefield, led Canadian decision-makers to press for an increasingly vocal and autonomous role in the conduct of their military affairs, but it generally did not lead these men, particularly the English-Canadians among them, to waver in their support for the Allied cause. On the contrary, Canada's commitment to the conflict only deepened after the carnage of September-November 1916. In this sense, the North American Dominion was no different from any other of the belligerents engaged in the orgy of self-destruction that was the Great War: For every country, the long line of slaughtered martyrs which lengthened with each bloody battle only stiffened the resolve of many men and women to demand that more fodder be fed into the maw of 'victory,' if only to justify the horrendous sacrifices that had already been made.

The establishment by Canadian political leaders of autonomous control over the Dominion's overseas war administration was paralleled on the battlefield by the CEF's attainment after 1917 of an increasing amount of independence from the authority of British commanders. Not only was the CEF after June of that year under the command of a Canadian, General Sir Arthur Currie, the forces of the Canadian Corps, even though they remained under the operational control of the British Army, could not be committed by the British High Command unless they first obtained Currie's approval. Furthermore, the CEF on the Western Front was a permanently self-contained formation: Its divisions could not be detached and shifted to other corps at the discretion of the High Command, as had been the practice in the past. The fact that the relationship of the CEF to the rest of the British Army changed when it did was no coincidence. Perhaps more than any other event the CEF's remarkable victory at Vimy Ridge in April 1917 ensured its elevation to a new status.

At Vimy, Canadian troops captured a strategic German position that since 1915 had withstood repeated assaults by the cream of the British and French armies. The operation, conducted primarily by Canadian troops supported by a relatively small number of British forces, resulted in the capture of more ground, more prisoners and more guns than any previous British offensive on the Western Front. More-over, the attack was a masterpiece of tactical execution, largely because it was one of the most competently planned and thoroughly prepared operations of the war to that point. At a cost of 3,598 killed and 7,004 wounded, the CEF scored what was perhaps the most impressive Allied offensive victory on the Western Front since 1914.[28]

Canadian commentators were naturally exuberant about the achievement of their countrymen. The *Globe* of Toronto called the capture of Vimy Ridge 'a red-letter day' for the Dominion. 'Canada has reason to be proud of the distinction conferred upon their country by Canadian troops,' the newspaper declared. 'To the glorious defense of the Ypres salient is added the magical name of Arras …'[29] The Manitoba *Free Press* was even more effusive in its language:

> There is no Canadian, worthy of the land of his birth, whose heart does not beat high, whose spirit does not mount at this achievement of our young Ca-nadian manhood, who does not feel that everything that is Canadian is finer and nobler by the glory won for us all on those steep slopes.[30]

The British general who commanded the operation, Sir Julian Byng, was re-warded for his success with a promotion. The Canadian Corps was rewarded for its achievement by the appointment in June of General Sir Arthur Currie as its first Canadian commander. Currie had played a prominent role in helping Byng plan and carry out the assault at Vimy. With a Canadian in command of its overseas forces, many in the Dominion believed that the martial prowess and elite status of Canada's soldiers were confirmed.

The Apotheosis of the Dominion Armies

By 1918, the British High Command would acknowledge its respect for the fight-ing abilities of the Canadian, Australian and New Zealand divisions on the Western Front by employing these units as, in the words of one latter-day historian describing the role of the CEF in this period, the 'shock army of the British Empire.'[31] Between August and November 1918, troops from Australia,[32] alongside those of Canada and New Zealand, would spearhead the British Army's contribution to the Allies' final victorious offensive against Germany, a campaign that was labelled by commentators at the time as The Hundred Days.

For its part, The AIF of 1918 that played such a prominent role in the final Allied offensive was a sharp-edged instrument of war, forged in the crucible of its bloody experiences on the Somme and in subsequent debacles. It had also become, as of June 1918, an autonomous corps, with its five divisions unified under the command of a native-born Australian, Lt.-General John Monash. This development echoed the creation of the Canadian Corps under Currie the previous year, and resulted in the same form and degree of independence on the battlefield that was enjoyed by the forces of the North American Dominion. Thus by 1918 the two colonial corps, for the first time in the war, enjoyed the status of small 'national' armies fighting in a sovereign, if junior, partnership with other Allied forces on the Western Front.

The creation of a unified and independent Australian Corps had come about gradually, with unification coming first. After nearly two years of intense political pressure from Prime Minister Hughes, as well as from influential journalists such as Keith Murdoch and C. E. W. Bean, among others, British Government officials and General Haig in November 1917 agreed to group Australia's five divisions within a single corps under the command of the British general Birdwood. Monash later assumed command of the Corps after Birdwood was promoted to take over the Fifth Army from Gough, who had been sacked after the unit's collapse during the massive German offensive in March 1918. Along with the ascendancy of an Australian to lead the Dominion's forces in the field came an autonomous status for those forces comparable to that which was enjoyed by the Canadians. This development had been strongly advocated by Hughes and other Australian leaders, many of whom often justified their positions by pointing to the beneficial effect that the independence of the Canadian Corps' had on the morale and combat effectiveness of the North American Dominion's fighting men.[33] Furthermore, by 1918, many Australians, for a number of reasons, increasingly felt that it would be better if they, and not Great Britain, controlled their Dominion's destiny on the battlefield.

Australian disillusion with the British command perhaps reached its pinnacle in April 1917, when, at the same time (and in the same region, Arras) that the Canadians at Vimy Ridge were experiencing their greatest triumph of the war thus far, the AIF was suffering through yet another costly fiasco, this time at Bullecourt. There, as had been the case at Fromelles and Pozières, the Australians were victimized by poor planning and preparation, for which many in the AIF held their British commanders primarily responsible. Throughout the operations at Bullecourt – which consisted of two major battles, the first in mid-April and the second in early May – the Australian infantry often lacked adequate artillery support, and the tanks which the British commander, General Gough, hastily committed to the enterprise proved almost completely useless. Nevertheless, Australian troops fought bravely, as usual, even managing to take some of their objectives before being forced to withdraw in the face of fierce German counterattacks. A total of nine days of fighting at First and Second Bullecourt cost the AIF 10,000 casualties, and represented a daily casualty rate that was ten times higher than at Gallipoli.[34]

According to Bean, 'Bullecourt, more than any other battle, shook the confidence of Australian soldiers in the capacity of the British command.' Indeed, the remarkable fact that the Australians had, at least temporarily, won some of the objectives set before them by their commanders, despite being handicapped by an ill-conceived battle-plan and insufficient fire support, seemed to confirm Bean's characterization of the AIF at Bullecourt as 'a magnificent instrument recklessly shattered in the performance of an impractical task.' For Bean and other Australian observers in the Spring of 1917, that metaphor might just as well have described the entire experience of the AIF on the Western Front to that point. 'Never yet since their arrival in France had any of the Australian divisions been employed in large operations in which the ultimate objective was really attainable with the means used for attaining it,' Bean wrote. 'Such success as they had achieved had been won by troops persisting, through the sheer quality of their mettle, in the face of errors.'[35]

Bean's assessment expressed a point of view that was increasingly prevalent among Australians on the Western Front by 1917. Bullecourt only deepened the contempt toward British commanders that some soldiers in the AIF had felt as early as Gallipoli, but that had become far more prevalent in the wake of the Somme battles. One Australian officer declared in December 1917:

Everyone here is 'fed-up' of the war, but not with the Hun. The British staff, British methods, and British bungling have sickened us. We are 'military socialists' and all overseas troops have had enough of the English. How I wish we were with our own people instead of under the English all the time!

Australians and other Dominion troops occasionally extended their disparagement of British fighting abilities to the Other Ranks, with such criticism particularly evident during the German offensives of March-April 1918, as Australian and New Zealand soldiers rushing to meet the enemy's onslaught passed hordes of panic-stricken Tommies streaming to the rear in ignominious retreat.[36] One New Zealand trooper crowed at the time: '…wasn't it wonderful and glorious when Tommies were fleeing down one side of the road with all their guns, tanks, etc., New Zealand should march up and stop the hordes and well they did it too.'[37]

However, at the same time that their faith in the martial capabilities of the British continued to erode as the war progressed, many Australians and New Zealanders experienced a corresponding surge of pride and confidence in the battlefield prowess of their own soldiers. One correspondent wrote of them in 1918:

These diggers (as they call themselves) in a fight never lose their heads, they never lose an opportunity, they do their damnedest at any job they are at. They are unafraid of odds against them. Once involved in a fight, they fight like corsairs, like desperadoes of the old-time stories.[38]

This sentiment was sometimes echoed in the letters of the 'diggers'[39] themselves. As one wrote:

Its funny, when they want something dashing or dangerous accomplished, they always pick on the Australians or New Zealanders. They do it too, and later one reads ... that 'the British did so and so' ... Never mind, it will be done, and done well by these hard-living, hard-swearing, fighting kangaroos who don't give a damn for anyone; but who are men ... good in every way.[40]

The Australians and New Zealanders solidified their reputations as superior combat formations during the summer and fall of 1917, spearheading together the Allied capture of Messines ridge in June, and then playing central roles in some of the most notable British Army successes at Ypres that autumn. Given that the Third Battle of Ypres is popularly regarded as perhaps the epitome of mud-drenched bloody futility on the Western Front, the achievements of the Anzac divisions during the campaign seem particularly noteworthy. With the exception of the disastrous attempt by the 3rd Australian Division and the New Zealand Division to capture Passchendaele village on 12 October (the village was captured by the Canadians three weeks later), the Anzac troops, at the battles of Menin Road, Polygon Wood and Broodseinde Ridge, among others, turned what thus far had been a story of appalling slaughter for limited gains into a tale of triumph that would remain unmarred by significant defeat for the rest of the war. Crucially, the late-1917 operations involving Australian and New Zealand troops benefited from far more competent British leadership than had prevailed at the Somme and Bullecourt, and seemed to answer Bean's bitter question following the AIF's tragic experience in the latter battle: 'What might not these troops have achieved if prudently employed?'[41]

However it was in 1918 during the final two phases of the war that the AIF and the New Zealand Division truly enshrined their status as some of the most celebrated units on the Western Front. First, during the dark days of the German offensive between 21 March and 5 April 1918, the Australians' tenacious defence of

Amiens, Villers-Bretonneux and Hazebrouck, and the important part played by the New Zealanders in plugging the gap between the British 3rd and 5th Armies on the Ancre River were crucial in preventing the enemy from splitting the British and French armies at their junction and achieving a decisive breakthrough on the Western Front. Then, when in the summer of 1918 the Allies were ready to launch their counteroffensive against the exhausted Germans, it would be the Australians and New Zealanders, along with the Canadians, that would spearhead the British effort during the Allies' last war-winning offensive (The Hundred Days) between August and November of that year. On 8 August, the Australian and Canadian Corps fought side by side, smashing the German positions south of the Somme in what would later be known as 'the Black Day of the German army.' This great victory was followed at the end of August by the Australian capture of Mont St. Quentin, a strongly fortified commanding height – widely believed to be impregnable -that guarded the approaches to Péronne. Three days later, they took Péronne itself. Finally on 29 September, in their last significant action of the war on the Western Front, troops from the AIF, with the help of two American divisions, breached the Hindenburg Line, Germany's last line of defence west of the Fatherland. By 5 October, all of the Australian divisions were out of the line, having been withdrawn for a well-deserved rest.[42]

In light of its impressive achievements between the summer of 1917 and the autumn of 1918, the Australian Corps by the war's end came to be recognized by friend and foe alike as one of the most formidable fighting units on the Western Front. One Australian observer immortalized them with these words:

> They left home in fresh-hatched formations, knowing very little of the outside world, though confident that it was their oyster all the same; they will return, having fought at both ends of Europe and with a military reputation like the soldiers of Cromwell and Marlborough. From the battlefields where men of all races have fought since the beginnings of wars they will bring Australia back the foundations of her national history.[43]

Even some of the Germans who opposed the Australians at various times during this period expressed admiration for the fighting abilities of their adversaries. One German officer described the diggers as 'exceptionally daring, tough, and enterprising soldiery,' while another called them 'great strong figures with dash and enterprise.'[44]

The performance of the New Zealand Division during the Hundred Days was no less stellar than that of the other colonial formations, one of its most remarkable feats being the capture of the fortress city of Le Quesnoy only days before the Armistice. For the Official Historian of New Zealand's war, writing three years after the close of hostilities, the reasons for the martial prowess of New Zealand's manhood were not hard to discern. He wrote:

> From a young and virile people, predominately agricultural, highly Intelligent, of unusually fine physique, a race of horsemen farmers, musterers, athletes and Rugby footballers, it was only to be expected that its manhood, already subject to a compulsory system of military training, should yield sterling material for the purpose of war.[45]

For their part, the Canadian divisions, like those of Australia and New Zealand, enjoyed by 1918 a celebrated reputation as some of the most reliable and effective Imperial formations on the Western Front. The Canadians' secured and solidified their prestigious status, much as the Australians had, through a string of battlefield successes throughout 1917 and 1918. The Canadian triumph at Vimy Ridge was followed quickly by smaller, but no less impressive, victories in Arras that summer at Lens and Hill 70. More significantly, these battles were won by a CEF that for the first time in the war was under the command and control of a Canadian general, Arthur Currie. Loyalty to the British High Command compelled Currie to allow his troops to take part in Haig's ill-fated Ypres offensive in 1917, but the Canadian general's relative autonomy ensured that he would (privately) voice his displeasure at doing so. At Ypres, the Canadians, like the Australians, scored a number of victories, including the capture of Passchendaele Ridge in November, that were outstanding in an operation which otherwise came to be widely regarded by historians and the general public as the nadir of the British Army's offensive frustrations on the Western Front.

The CEF spent the first half of 1918 out of the line, and so played no role in halting the German offensives of that spring. However, as has already been mentioned, the Canadians joined their fellow Dominion troops in spearheading the British effort in the final Allied drive to crush the German Army on the Western Front. After delivering with the Australians the near-mortal blow against Ludendorff's forces at Amiens in early August, the Canadian Corps went on to achieve costly triumphs on its own at Drocourt-Queant and the Canal Du Nord in late August and September. The high casualties suffered by the CEF in these operations – 30,000 dead and wounded between August and October of 1918 – were mitigated significantly by the fact that such sacrifices no longer seemed to be in vain: By the fall of 1918, the Allies were advancing everywhere on the Western Front and movement, which had already returned to the battlefield for the Germans that spring, was a reality for the Entente forces as well. On 10 November, Canadian troops pursuing the fleeing enemy entered the city of Mons, scene of the storied retreat in 1914 by the 'Old Contemptibles' of the original British Expeditionary Force. The Armistice was declared on the following day. Thus, it seemed to many observers and commentators that no more fitting culmination to the chronicle of the CEF on the Western Front could have been devised than to have them end the war in triumphant control of the city where the mettle of British manhood had first been tested (and bested, though only in the face of superior numbers). Of the Canadian capture of Mons, General Currie said: 'It was a proud thing for our race that we were able to finish the war where we began it, and that we, the young whelps of the old lion, were able to take the ground lost in 1914.'[46]

Like their Australian counterpart, the Canadian Corps came to enjoy one of the most celebrated reputations of any Allied combat formation on the Western Front. It was a testament to the high-regard in which they were held by many of their fellow Imperial fighting men that the commander of the Australian Corps, General Monash, doubted the feasibility of the High Command's ambitious objectives at Amiens in 1918 until it was suggested that the Canadians should fight beside his troops.[47] Furthermore, the Canadian Corps garnered respect beyond Imperial family. For instance, King Albert of the Belgians praised their battlefield achievements as being 'unsurpassed by any corps in Europe.'[48]

If anything, the stature of the Canadian and Australian Corps, and the New Zealand division as elite units within the British Army has only grown in the years since the end of the Great War. A number of historians – Denis Winter being perhaps the most influential example – have promoted the idea that Dominion formations by 1918 were significantly superior to their British counterparts, and that these colonial units 'carried' the British Army to victory during the Hundred Days.[49] Recently however, several scholars have conducted detailed analyses of the Dominion divisions' battlefield performances compared to those of British units, and concluded that the colonial formations, while remarkably successful and certainly deserving to be honoured, were not solely or even primarily responsible for the British Army's battlefield triumphs in 1918. For example, Peter Simkins asserts that there were at least 10 divisions originating in the British Isles (out of a total of 50 employed during the Hundred Days) that performed as well or better than the leading six or seven Dominion divisions. Furthermore, many of the best British formations spent an amount of time in the line comparable to or greater than that endured by the workhorse colonials, since one of the consequences of demonstrating talent on the battlefield was to be employed in combat more often, and to be given more dangerous assignments, than other less-capable units (with the predictable result that elite divisions suffered proportionally higher casualties than those with lesser reputations). Of course, none of this necessarily refutes General Monash's somewhat disparaging comment that had there been 20 British divisions as effective on the battlefield as the 10 Dominion divisions, the story of the war might have been different.[50]

Latter-day historians, in explaining the success of the Dominion contingents in the First World War very often emphasize the fact that the Australian and Cana-

dian Corps managed to establish themselves as permanently self-contained formations. Thus, they were spared the usual BEF practice of shifting divisions in and
out of corps almost at random (as happened with New Zealand's forces, given that
they comprised no more than a single division). As a result, the order of battle in
the CEF by 1917 and the AIF by 1918 generally remained permanently fixed at the
same four or five divisions, which ensured an advantageous continuity of leadership from their corps headquarters on down. Additionally, both the Canadian and
Australian Corps were fortunate to be led by two of the Western Front's more
talented commanders, Arthur Currie and John Monash, respectively. The New
Zealand Division was equally lucky in its commanding general, the New Zealander
Andrew Russell. All three commanders were distinguished by their meticulous attention to operational detail, their emphasis on rigorous tactical training for the
soldiers sent into combat, and their insistence on thoroughly prepared plans of
battle that were less likely to squander the lives of their men.[51] Whether these
command traits shared by all three generals were shaped by a common sense of
obligation to preserve the most valuable military asset and precious resource en-
trusted to their care by their governments – the finite manpower of their respective
Dominions – is difficult to ascertain from the available evidence. However, in the
case of Canada and Australia at least, the fact that their contingents were eventually
granted a separate status from the British formations allowed them somewhat more
freedom than most British Isles units to pursue tactical innovation, and encouraged
at the subordinate command level of the Dominion divisions the growth of a spirit
of criticism and independence that was often lacking from their British counterparts.[52]

For many of the observers and commentators, particularly but not exclusively
those from Dominions, who during the Great War attributed the battlefield
achievements of Dominion troops to their independence, innovation and initiative,
these phenomena exemplified essential qualities of national character. Of the Australians, one writer declared: 'The free and independent Colonial life, which makes
men adaptable and self-reliant, breeds the germs of many military virtues and
stands the Australians in good stead in this struggle of endurance.'[53] For many who
sought to explain what made the Dominion fighting men superior, the answer usually rested with the supposed egalitarian nature of colonial society and the strenuous lifestyle stereotypically characteristic of the Dominions. As we have seen,
Australia's C. E. W. Bean assiduously promoted this interpretation of the diggers'
martial prowess. Describing the men who endured the devastating bombardments
at Pozieres, Bean wrote:

There they were in their dusty ditch in that blasted brown Sahara of a country
– Sydney boys, country fellows from New South Wales … heavy eyed, tired
to death as after a long fight with a bush fire or heavy work in drought time,

but simply doing their ordinary Australian work in their ordinary Australian way.[54]

In Bean's view, the rugged struggle against the environment in Australia had prepared these men for the hard work of war. Furthermore, this, and the equality of society, had ensured that in Australia the qualities that made excellent warriors were not to be found exclusively within a single privileged class. Bean often emphasized the degree to which the typical Australian enlisted man exhibited in combat the martial virtues of cool courageousness, leadership and initiative that, among the British, were the exclusive battlefield domain of junior officers hailing from the social elite. According to Bean, the diggers were the 'fresh, gay, modern counterpart to the old Stuart cavalier.'[55] Democracy and the frontier had 'naturally' provided them with the attributes of warriors without necessitating that they internalize a feudal ethos associated with the exaltation of a leading class. At one point in the official history, Bean makes this case explicitly by quoting an observer of the Pozieres battle who described the Australian soldiers as 'walking … erect, not hurrying, each man carrying himself as proudly and carelessly as a British officer does.'[56]

It is not hard to find a similar sentiment rationalizing the battlefield success of Canadian troops as well. One commentator explained the CEF's achievements as resulting from the egalitarianism of the relationship between officers and enlisted men, and from the general lack of a class division between the former and the latter. According to this writer, the Canadian Corps' first officers had been chosen primarily because of their local influence. However:

later on it became the rule at the front that officers were selected from men who had served in the ranks and had distinguished themselves there. In [certain battalions] there were wealthy business men serving as noncommissioned officers, young professional men as corporals, and sons of leading citizens as private soldiers.[57]

The experience of Canada, Australia and New Zealand on the battlefields of the Western Front, and the way in which this record of sacrifice and achievement was interpreted and rendered within the cultures of the Dominions during the war, would be one of the most fundamental elements shaping the memory of the Great War that would emerge in the years following the Armistice. During the war itself, however, the events on the battlefields of France and Belgium, and especially the horrendous casualties endured by the Dominions as they played an increasingly significant role in the Allied war effort, would lead in two of them to unprecedented domestic turmoil as they grappled with the socially divisive affects of trying to mobilize the manpower and resources of their countries to a degree never before attempted in their history. For Canada and Australia, the domestic conflicts of the war years, and the social cleavages that they revealed in each nation, would in many ways establish the terms and define the parameters of the subsequent inter-war debate within each society over the meaning of the 1914–18 conflict. New Zealand, by contrast, though not entirely lacking in domestic anti-war dissent and resistance to the more coercive aspects of mobilization, would provide a model of comparative home-front consensus regarding the nature, if not the extent, of their war effort. Thus, the next chapter will focus primarily on Canada and Australia, where figurative war at home paralleled the literal war they were fighting overseas.

4

The Wars at Home

The domestic battles that rocked Canadian and Australian society in the latter years of the Great War were primarily fought in both countries over the issue of conscription. There were other serious conflicts on the home front in each Dominion: For instance, industrial strife spiked in both countries as the war progressed, as a result of government efforts to harness industry to the war effort, and of organized labour's attempts to ensure that this process benefited (or at least did not exploit) the workers that they represented. However, no single issue generated the same intensity of conflict in these two Dominions as conscription, and almost all other issues were inextricably linked in some way with the debate over compulsory service. Furthermore, the conscription debate in Canada and Australia, more than any other wartime development, defined for the establishment in both countries – that is, those who enjoyed political, social and cultural hegemony within each society – the elements constituting 'legitimate' and 'illegitimate' interpretations of the meaning of the war. Much of the language and imagery employed during the conscription battles to represent certain interpretations of the war's meaning would reappear in post-war debates over the correct understanding of the conflict. Also, conscriptionist and anti-conscriptionist factions in each country often employed in the service of their causes opposing visions of Canadian or Australian nationalism that ended up significantly influencing post-war attitudes in the Dominions toward their relationship with the Motherland and toward their evolving status within the Empire.

In New Zealand, by contrast, conscription as an issue did not divide the country in the way that it did in Canada and Australia. Though the matter was never put to a referendum, as it was in Australia, available evidence indicates that the majority of New Zealanders favoured conscription when it was introduced in August 1916. Opposition to it certainly was neither as widespread nor as intense as in Canada and Australia, and the debate over its introduction thus never achieved the levels of vitriol that characterized the controversy in those Dominions. However, as we will see when New Zealand's experience is explored in greater depth later in this chapter, the *implementation* of the draft in that country did spark significant dissent and resistance, particularly from those who felt excluded from, or rejected, a power structure dominated by those of British heritage and traditional middle-class Protestant affiliations. In this way, conscription – if not the idea of it, then the reality – did reveal social cleavages in New Zealand not unlike those laid bare by the debate over the draft in Canada and Australia. For example, criticism of those, such as Catholic clergy or pacifists, whose vocations or principles led them to reject compulsory military service in any war often emphasized the sectarian or political 'otherness' of these dissenters. Similarly, from the particular rigor and severity with which the state in New Zealand pursued and punished, for example, those conscientious objectors whose religious affiliations did not exempt them from service and Maori who dodged or resisted the draft (most of whom belonged to tribes excluded from the benefits of national citizenship), it is clear that the country's authorities viewed conscription not only as a means of filling military manpower needs, but also as a method of controlling ethnic, religious or political 'outliers' within the nation. Thus, while the focus of this chapter will primarily be on the conscription controversies in Canada and Australia, New Zealand's experience with compulsory service offers an interesting and important comparison and contrast with that of the other Dominions.

Canadian National Identity and the Conscription Crisis

By the winter of 1916, Canada was in the throes of a serious recruiting crisis. The casualties suffered at the Somme, combined with a general slowdown in enlistment between the spring and summer of that year, threatened to deplete the Canadian Expeditionary Force's manpower reserves. By the end of 1916, there were about 100,000 Canadians serving in France, and another 100,000 in the United Kingdom (40,000 of whom were unfit from wounds or other reasons). Casualties thus far numbered 67,890, with 16,466 dead and 2,970 missing. Yet, enlistment had begun to tail off markedly after March 1916, when 34,000 men joined the colours. By July, that number was down to 7,961, and from August to December, between 5,000 and 6,500 men enlisted each month.[1]

One can only speculate on the reasons for this, but there are several possibilities. For instance, by the summer of 1916, even the most strenuous efforts of the press to put a positive spin on events overseas could not hide the fact that the shocking carnage of the war thus far had not brought the Empire and its allies any closer to victory. It would hardly be surprising if the downturn in recruiting reflected a general waning of enthusiasm for the war as people realized, particularly after the Somme offensive failed to break the stalemate in the West, that the conflict would probably be a long and grinding test of the nation's resources and fortitude. At the same time, the reservoir of manpower that had supplied the bulk of the CEF in 1914 and 1915, immigrants born in Britain, were largely tapped out by 1916. Native

Canadians, particularly French Canadians, but English Canadians as well, displayed far less enthusiasm for enlisting than did Canadians who had been born in the United Kingdom. By the end of 1915, the latter group had produced 63 percent of all enlistments, despite the fact that there were three times as many Canadian-born men of military age as British-born.[2]

Military and civilian authorities in the Dominion were well aware of the disparity between the number of native-born Canadian enlistees and British-born recruits. The rhetoric and images that Canadian leaders and shapers of public opinion increasingly employed after 1916 to represent the meaning of the war for Canada emerged, at least in part, from a desire to appeal to native Canadians who were not inspired by the idea of fighting for King and Empire. The substance of this narrative, which encouraged Canadians to view their war less as a demonstration of imperial fealty than as an assertion of nationhood through which men and women in the Dominion could see themselves as part of an international crusade to preserve 'civilization', will be examined later in the chapter. For now, this discussion will concentrate on the domestic political ramifications of the efforts by Canadian authorities to address the looming manpower crisis in 1916.

Canada had easily raised 100,000 men for overseas service by the summer of 1915, and when the ceiling for the authorized strength of the CEF was increased to 250,000 in October of that year, few in the Dominion expressed doubts that this goal could be met as well. The initial success of recruiting in Canada was aided not only by the euphoria and surging British-imperial patriotism of the war's early days, but also by a severe economic recession, ongoing since 1913, that had produced significant unemployment throughout Canada, particularly in the western parts of the country. With these factors helping to drive men to the colours, enlistment totals for the CEF by the winter of 1915 were indeed approaching the desired quota of 250,000.[3]

Even so, certain observers in the Dominion wondered whether the voluntary system would ultimately be able to meet the demands of a war that was already consuming such unprecedented amounts of manpower. Major-General W. G. Gwatkin, the Chief of the Canadian General Staff, cautioned shortly after the ceiling of the Canadian forces was raised, that the increased troop levels might put sufficient numbers of men in the field, but they probably would not provide enough soldiers to fill the ranks of the reserve and support units that would be required as well. For every 1,000 infantrymen at the front, Gwatkin claimed, 3,000 soldiers were needed to place and maintain them in the line. Other critics of the voluntary system denounced it as inefficient and inequitable. The country's 'best men' tended to volunteer, these critics argued, and so the Dominion was potentially being deprived of a disproportionate number of its most talented and valuable citizens. Furthermore, the voluntary system indiscriminately drew men from all industries and professions, including those that were essential to the home front war effort. Conscription would spread the burden of service more evenly through-out Canadian society, they argued, and would ensure that factories and farms crucial to the war at home were not depleted of workers.[4]

By 1916, the voices calling for conscription in Canada were not only more numerous than they had been previously, they were also finding a more sympathetic ear in the Borden administration. The Prime Minister had assured Canadians in December 1914 that the Dominion's participation in the conflict would never necessitate compulsory service. The manhood of Canada stood ready to fight overseas 'freely and voluntarily,' according to Borden.[5] Indeed, by the end of 1915, slightly less than 250,000 Canadian men had freely and voluntarily committed themselves to the cause, but that was still not enough for the Prime Minister. Frustrated by what he saw as the uncooperativeness and condescension of British officials that he dealt with during a 1915 fact-finding trip to London, Borden made a public pledge on New Year's Day 1916 to increase the authorized strength of the CEF to 500,000 men. This dramatic gesture was designed to demonstrate once-and-for-all Canada's loyalty to the Empire, and to impress upon the British just how seriously the Dominion took its role in the conflict. It was a bold and somewhat impulsive move, having been made against the advice of some Conservative members of Parliament, and after only minimal consultation with a few of his ministers. Most significantly, Borden made this pledge without investigating whether the promised men could possibly be secured and delivered under the current system of voluntary enlistment.[6]

Of course, after the enormous wastage of the Somme battles, it was obvious that a ceiling of 500,000 men for the CEF was hardly an extravagant projection of the country's likely manpower needs. However, it was equally clear by the second half of 1916 that the voluntary system would be hard-pressed to provide such a huge quantity of recruits. The decline in recruiting during the latter months of the year occurred despite the increasingly vigorous efforts of patriotic leagues, civic organizations and individual citizens in communities throughout Canada to drive their countrymen to the colours, and despite the enormous amount of social pressure that was placed on able-bodied young civilian males in order to compel them to enlist. One Canadian veteran recalled the tactics employed to shame young men into military service.

> Young girls were going along and they would meet what looked Like a pretty good able-bodied man and they'd pin something white on them called them a coward in other words, because they weren't in the army. 'What are you doing in civilian clothes when all my brothers are in the army?' That sort of thing …There was pressure through the press and through the communities to persuade the men to enlist.[7]

As the rush to the ranks of the CEF subsided, many English-Canadian supporters of the country's war effort began to direct an increasing amount of hostility
toward French Canadians, whom they criticized for responding less-than-
enthusiastically to the call to arms thus far. French-Canadian ambivalence toward a
war effort that many characterized as contrary Canada's national interests was reflected in the comparatively low proportion of French-Canadian enlistees. For a
growing number of English Canadians, the disproportionate burden of sacrifice
that they were bearing as a result of French-Canada's lacklustre showing offered a
compelling justification for conscription. Even at the beginning of the conflict,
despite pro-war demonstrations in Montreal in August 1914 that were just as enthusiastic as any in English-speaking Canada, the number of French-Canadians
who enlisted in the CEF was far fewer than might be expected, given the relative
size of their population in the Dominion.[8] Of the 36,267 men who made up the
first contingent of the CEF in 1914, only 1,245 were French-Canadian.[9] The voluntary system of recruiting did little to eliminate this discrepancy. By April 1917 there
were about 14,100 French-Canadians in the CEF, compared to 125,245 English-
Canadians and 155,095 British-born enlistees.[10] Not surprisingly, English Canadian
commentators did not hesitate to point out the recruiting disparity between the
country's two largest communities. The Toronto *Globe* observed: 'The fact cannot
be hid that Quebec, with a population of over 2 million people, has given a scant
[number of] men to fight for freedom, of whom not less than half were contributed by the small English-speaking minority in the Province.' In an interview appearing in the same paper, Sam Hughes as usual put it more bluntly. '[Quebec] has
not done its duty,' he declared. 'It has not done its duty as it should have done, and
I believe it would have done if the young men of that Province had been taken in
hand by the proper people.'[11]

Of course, most English Canadians who reproached their French-speaking fellow citizens for their cool response to the call of duty generally ignored the degree
to which the insensitive and bigoted policies and attitudes of English-Canadian
authorities after 1914 contributed to the alienation of French Canadians from the
war effort. Given the long-standing antipathy between the two communities, and
the fact that relations between English and French Canadians had been unusually
strained since 1912 due to the ongoing controversy over bilingualism in Ontario
and Manitoba schools,[12] convincing members of Canada's French-speaking minority to don British khaki and sacrifice themselves on distant European battlefields
would have been a difficult proposition even for a government highly attuned to
the sensibilities and concerns of Quebec. In any case, the Borden administration
was not such a government. Early in the war, military authorities botched or ignored opportunities to enact policies that might have generated greater French-
Canadian enthusiasm for the war by mitigating the overwhelmingly English-
Canadian/British character of the CEF.

For instance, sufficient numbers of French-speaking recruits volunteered for the first contingent in 1914 to form a French-Canadian battalion, a gesture that might have convinced *Québécois* that Ottawa was prepared to acknowledge their sense of a distinct identity within the nation. Instead, Minister of Militia Hughes assigned the French-speaking recruits to various mixed-language units. Hughes was by no means a francophile, but his attitude toward acknowledging the distinct identity of French-Canadians merely reflected that of the government at the time: When a British politician suggested to George Perley shortly after Canada entered the war that forming a French-Canadian battalion might bolster morale in Quebec, Perley dismissed this suggestion on the grounds that it would be unwise to highlight 'racial' distinctions within the CEF, since all of its soldiers were Canadians first and foremost.[13] Such idealistic sentiments seemed to contrast starkly to what many *Québécois* rightly or wrongly perceived as an overt anti-French bias within Sam Hughes' army. For evidence of such discrimination, critics needed to look no further than the fact that several well-known French-Canadian military figures were relegated to low-profile posts once the war began, and that a number of French-Canadian staff officers were denied commands commensurate with their rank.[14] The impression that English-Canadians sought to dominate the command and character of the CEF quickly fostered resentment among French-Canadians. By the time that the government authorized the creation of French-Canadian battalions for the second contingent, recruiters found that filling the ranks of these units was far more difficult than they had expected.[15]

While many French-Canadian commentators and politicians sought to portray Quebec's unenthusiastic response to recruiting as an understandable consequence of English-Canada's traditional bigotry toward the French-speaking minority, other observers pointed out certain demographic factors that underlay the reluctance of *Québécois* to enlist. For instance, as Wilfrid Laurier reminded Quebec's detractors, the fact that French-Canadian men tended to marry earlier and to have larger families than English Canadians meant that the province might have 28 per cent of the population of the Dominion, but only 23 per cent of the men of military age. Furthermore, only 29 per cent of Quebec's military-age males were single (and thus more likely to volunteer), compared to 36.5 percent of Ontario's military-age men. Also, Quebec was a more rural province than Ontario, and Canada's cities had provided a much higher proportion of recruits than the countryside. Laurier commented on this disparity in a letter written to an acquaintance in 1916:

Recruiting has been chiefly confined all over Canada to urban population, very little in rural population. When we deduct from the figures in Ontario the British-born, the urban population, and compare on the figures in rural districts, the difference will not be very great, though I admit that the preponderance is in favour of Ontario.[16]

However, demographic realities played a far less important role in French-Canada's lacklustre recruiting than did certain political and cultural factors. For one thing, attempts to generate enthusiasm for the war in Quebec were undermined by the fact that the French-Canadian politicians in Borden's cabinet were all *nationalistes* who had denounced Laurier's call in 1911 for a Canadian navy as a drift toward imperial servitude. As a result, they were not about to support the all-out mobilization and sacrifice of Canadian manpower and resources in order to help Great Britain fight a war in Europe. This had a significant impact on recruiting in Quebec due to the fact that the voluntary system primarily depended on politicians, businessmen and other community leaders stepping forward to raise a battalion. For instance, Arthur Mignault, a wealthy Montreal physician, played a decisive role in organizing Quebec's first two French-speaking battalions in late 1914 and early 1915. However, he was exceptional among prominent French-Canadians in his willingness to contribute to the war effort to such a degree. Even as early as the end of 1914, social pressures among *Québécois* generally worked to inhibit such attempts to stimulate recruiting within their community.[17]

Another phenomenon tempering French-Canadian enthusiasm for the war was their oft-expressed sense of identity as not only a distinct ethnic community within Canada, but also as a specifically North-American people whose political interests were not necessarily determined by ties of loyalty to Britain, or by ties of heritage with France. The allegiance that many French-Canadians felt toward Great Britain might have been real, but their bonds with the Metropole were typically far more ambivalent than was usually the case for English-Canadians. Great Britain was not the 'Motherland' for French Canadians, and to be a part of the British Empire, whatever the benefits, was to acquiesce to the domination of a power whose institutions, traditions and even language were unquestionably foreign. However, this did not necessarily mean, as some English-Canadians during the Great War erroneously assumed, that most French-Canadians felt the same degree of emotional attachment to France that many Canadians of British heritage felt toward England. First of all, there had not been any significant immigration to Canada from France since the eighteenth century. Furthermore, both the Roman Catholic Church in Quebec and the British government had endeavoured to quarantine French-speakers in Canada from the contagions of revolution and atheism emanating from France after 1789. French-Canadians thus generally viewed themselves as more isolated from European concerns, French or British, than did many of their English-Canadian countrymen. The historian O. D. Skelton is perhaps not making an unfair generalization when he states that 'The French-Canadian was a Canadian, and a Canadian only, perhaps not always an all-Canada man, but certainly none-but-Canada.'[18]

The Great War resurrected in French Canada the long-standing animosity prevalent within that community toward contributing the Dominion's blood and treasure to prove their fealty to Mother Britain. Anti-war dissent among French-Canadians between 1914 and 1918 was in many ways a more virulent manifestation of the *Québécois* anti-imperialism expressed earlier in the century during the South African War and the debates over the establishment of a Canadian navy. As he had during previous confrontations between Canada's pro and anti-imperialist camps, Henri Bourassa, after initially declaring his qualified support for the war in the summer of 1914, donned the mantle of radical French-Canadian nationalism, becoming the leading opponent of the Dominion's enormous (and enormously costly) war effort. Consequently, he became the bête noire of English-Canadian supporters of the war, and seemed to symbolize, perhaps unfairly, French-Canadian wartime disloyalty.

As early as 1914, Bourassa's criticisms of what he viewed as the hypocrisy of Britain's motives for going to war, and his condemnation of the intolerance and jingoism that the war inspired in the Dominion drew the ire of English-Canadian patriots. On two occasions during the winter of that year, Bourassa was prevented from speaking in Ottawa when riots broke out in the lecture halls where he was scheduled to deliver his address. In both cases, the riots were preceded by the distribution of anti-Bourassa pamphlets throughout the city which gave the time and place of the lectures, and denounced the *nationalistes* leader as a traitor. 'The Bourassa faction have cast contempt and defiance in the faces of the loyal citizens of Ottawa,' declared one of the broadsides.

> They are well aware of his outrageously false and treasonable utterances since the outbreak of the war. They know that his presence in Ottawa is objectionable, offensive and exasperating to loyal citizens ... yet these abettors of treason and rebellion are determined to flaunt before us this arch traitor of Canada ... They are seeking trouble, and they'll find it. Can this nest of traitors overawe and overcome the stalwart loyal men of Ottawa? ... Who then is afraid to turn out and put down this outrage?... The skull of rebellion must be smashed ...[19]

Angered by the attempts to suppress his message in Ottawa, Bourassa expanded upon his planned remarks and published them through *Le Devoir* in a pamphlet entitled *The Duty of Canada at the Present Hour*. In it, he articulated the argument that would become the cornerstone of the brand of (French) Canadian nationalism that he would promote for the duration of the war. 'Everyone speaks of the duties of Canada to Great Britain or France. Who has thought of the duties of Canada to herself?' Bourassa asked. 'Instead of taking towards the Motherland and the Empire the ridiculous attitude of fervid and trembling lovers, we should learn from the British to look after our own interests.'[20]

For Bourassa, the interests of Canada dictated, if not outright neutrality in the overseas conflict, then only as much support for Great Britain as the Dominion could supply without straining its own resources to the breaking point. After all, according to Bourassa, Canada's military obligations to the Empire, as defined by such agreements between the Dominion and Great Britain as the Constitutional Act of 1791, the British North America Act of 1867 and various Militia Acts, were limited to the defence of its own national territory. As long as the imperial Dominions had no formal voice in the conduct of Britain's foreign policy, then they had no formal obligation to participate in Britain's foreign wars.[21] Furthermore, stated Bourassa, the Empire was an authoritarian and exploitative institution that was unworthy of the sacrifices Canadians seemed so willing to offer in its name. In his words:

> All that is good in British ideals, and there is much of it, would be better served by the free action of several independent British communities than by the common action of a monstrous Empire, built up by force and robbery and kept together for no other purpose than allowing one race and one nation to dominate one-fifth of the human race. British nations have to choose between British ideals and British domination. I stand for ideals and against domination. I may be hanged for it, in the name of British liberty, but that does not matter.[22]

Bourassa's intimations of imminent mortality were not entirely groundless. He was routinely reviled as a traitor in the English-Canadian press, and as the war went on there were more than a few demands from English-speaking provinces that he be interned, or worse.[23] For many English-Canadian supporters of the war, the eloquence and the vehemence of Bourassa's dissident rhetoric, and the fact that with *Le Devoir* he had a national forum in which to promulgate it, ensured that the *nationalistes* leader would assume in their eyes an almost diabolical status as the country's chief 'fomenter of strife' and 'breeder of rebellion.'[24] To his enemies, Bourassa's anti-war and anti-British 'propaganda' was the main reason for the low level of recruits in Quebec, and his agitation posed a threat to the Dominion's war effort and to its internal stability.

However, Bourassa's opponents were not to be found exclusively among English-Canadians. Prior to 1917, the *nationaliste's* position was generally more radical than that of most French-Canadian political and religious leaders. Naturally Laurier and his Liberal followers maintained their long-standing antagonism to the nationalist Quebecois agenda. Many Montreal newspapers, including the *Presse, Patrie* and *Gazette* expressed support for the war effort, and did their best to encourage recruiting in Quebec in an attempt to prevent the introduction of conscription. Also, several members of the higher clergy in Quebec, including Abbé D'Amours, editor of the influential *Action catholique*, voiced their disapproval of Bourassa's inflammatory rhetoric.[25]

One of the most eloquent French-Canadian responses came from Bourassa's cousin, Talbot Papineau. Papineau, like Bourassa, was descended from Louis-Joseph Papineau, the *patriote* leader of the 1837 rebellion, and like Bourassa, considered himself a French-Canadian nationalist. However, the two men split sharply over the issue of Canada's participation in the war in Europe. Where Bourassa saw the Dominion's exploitation at the hands of Britain, Papineau saw an opportunity for Canada, including Quebec, to prove itself capable and worthy of nationhood, and to develop the sense of collective consciousness and meritorious shared history with English Canada that would be essential to the forging of a national identity. Papineau had in fact enlisted in the CEF in 1914, and was serving as a captain on the Western Front in 1916 when his public confrontation with Bourassa took place. Throughout 1915 and early 1916, Bourassa's tirades against the Empire and English Canada had grown increasingly vituperative. When the *nationalistes* linked the bilingual schools issue in Canada with the war overseas by characterizing English-Canadian opponents of bilingual education as 'Boches' and 'Prussians', Papineau was moved to respond.[26]

In July 1916, the Montreal *Gazette* and several other newspapers throughout Canada published an open letter from Papineau to Bourassa in which the young infantry captain took the elder statesman to task for not recognizing the war's true significance for Canada. 'If you were a true Nationalist – if you loved our great country and without smallness longed to see her become the home of a good and united people,' Papineau wrote, 'surely you would have recognized this war as her moment of travail and tribulation.' He continued:

> You would have felt that in the agony of her losses in Belgium and France, Canada was suffering the birth pangs of her national life... if without sacrifices of our own we profit from the sacrifices of the English soldiers, we can never hope to become a nation ourselves. How could we ever acquire that Soul or create that Pride without which a nation is a dead thing and doomed to speedy decay and disappearance?[27]

Bourassa's reply to Papineau appeared in *Le Devoir* on 5 August. He rejected his cousin's characterization of the war as the birth of independent Canadian nationhood. 'The Government, the whole of Parliament, the press and politicians of both parties, all applied themselves systematically to obliterate the free and independent character of Canadian intervention,' he asserted. 'Canada, a nation of America, has a nobler mission to fulfill than to bind herself to the fate of the nations of Europe or to any spoliating Empire.' Finally, according to Bourassa:

The backward and essentially Prussian policy of the rulers of Ontario and Manitoba gives us an additional argument against the intervention of Canada in the European conflict. To speak of fighting for the preservation of French civilization in Europe while endeavouring to destroy it in America, appears to us as an absurd piece of inconsistency. To preach Holy War for the liberties of people overseas, and to oppress the national minorities within Canada is, in our opinion, nothing but odious hypocrisy.[28]

The arguments employed by Papineau and Bourassa in their public exchange exemplified the two poles of the wartime debate over what constituted the legitimate 'nationalist' position toward Canada's involvement in the war in Europe. On the one hand, Bourassa and his supporters in and outside of the French-Canadian community contended that Canada's national interests did not lie in continuing to play such a large and costly role in the war effort, and that the imperfect state of political liberty within the Dominion made a self-righteous crusade on behalf of the oppressed overseas seem particularly absurd. Furthermore, the Allies' war was hardly the most pure and virtuous of causes. Finally, Bourassa argued, the British Empire was corrupt and repressive as an institution, and even as a symbol and an ideal, it was not worthy of the kind of loyalty and sacrifice that Canadians had committed to it thus far. To his opponents, Bourassa's point of view symbolized the antithesis of wartime patriotism, and thus was crucial in defining for the political and media establishment, which was dominated outside of Quebec by English-Canadians, what constituted 'true' Canadian nationalism.

Papineau's perspective, despite being that of a French-Canadian, was in many ways an exemplary expression of the ideal of nationalism proffered by the majority of his countrymen who supported the Dominion's full-scale participation in the war. Most, but certainly not all, of those who adhered to this position were English-Canadians. They tended to be non-isolationists who advocated greater Canadian autonomy from Great Britain, but not in order to decrease the Dominion's contribution to the war. Rather, they sought to exercise more direct Canadian control over the disposition and operation of their forces overseas, and over the allocation of the country's resources. To them, the war was a sacred cause, and as the conflict carried on, it was increasingly characterized as nothing less than a crusade to make a better world, one in which Canada would play an important role. And regardless of whether or not Canada continued to be an imperial Dominion in the formal political sense, the Empire remained a cherished ideal, an institution worth preserving, and a political entity with which Canada should always maintain ties of loyalty and devotion.[29]

Papineau's idealistic rhetoric reflected the language by which the war's meaning increasingly came to be represented after 1916. His theme of the Canadian nation forged through the noble sacrifice of its young men would become a cornerstone of what by the end of the war was the prevailing narrative of the Dominion's experience in the conflict. An equally important component of this understanding of the war and its meaning was the idea that Canadians fought and died in the name of the 'civilization,' 'democracy,' 'freedom' or other such abstract principles promoted and exemplified by the Empire and its allies. One Canadian newspaper in 1916 eulogized the Allied cause, albeit a bit prematurely, with just such rhetoric: 'Rarely, if ever, in the history of the world has humanity risen to such a high level of heroism and self-sacrifice as that reached by the Allied nations as they felt the foundations of civilization crumble beneath their feet.'[30] To cite another example, by 1917 it was no longer enough to commemorate a young man who was killed fighting in France as having fallen for 'King and Country'; it was also necessary to honour him as having died so that 'others might live in freedom.'[31]

During the period between the Somme battles and the victory at Vimy Ridge the drive toward instituting conscription gathered momentum in Canada. The Borden administration increasingly viewed compulsory service as necessary and inevitable if the country were to have any hope at all of meeting its manpower needs as the war progressed. The government's outlook was shaped and supported by a vocal and influential body of opinion among (primarily English) Canadian military and political leaders, business and community leaders and members of the press who continually prodded the regime toward compulsion. However, as we will see, the Borden administration had good reason to believe that conscription would be generally unpopular even among most English-Canadians, or at least among the majority who were not busy writing pro-draft editorials for the newspapers. Furthermore, the government correctly assumed that French-Canadian opinion would be nearly unanimous in its vehement opposition to compulsory service. After all, even though the fiery rhetoric of Bourassa and other *nationalistes* often reflected a more radical viewpoint than that held by many French-Canadian leaders, conscription was the one issue on which the 'extremists' found common ground with *Canadiens* who were generally less opposed to the British Empire or to the Dominion's participation in the war.[32]

Throughout 1916 and early 1917, the Borden government had been laying what could be considered the groundwork for conscription. Between January and June of 1917, the National Service Board conducted a national registration campaign: Canadian men were asked to fill out and return to the government cards requesting information about, among other things, their health, dependents, citizenship status and special skills. Compliance with the registration was strictly voluntary, and officials estimated that less than 80 per cent of eligible Canadian males responded to the survey. Furthermore, the scheme met with considerable opposition from French-Canadians, labour leaders and farmers worried that, despite the government's assurances to the contrary, registration was a precursor to imminent conscription. Some union chiefs argued that the conscription of wealth should precede any conscription of manpower, while others called for a referendum on the issue. However, given that only two percent of Canada's work force was unionized, the opposition of organized labour could do little to impede the drive toward conscription. On the other hand, Canadian farmers were a much more powerful constituency, and if the government ever hoped to successfully implement any scheme of compulsory service it would ultimately have to allay their fears that conscription would completely deprive them of rural labour that had already been depleted by urbanization. Nevertheless, despite the resistance and general lack of enthusiasm that hampered the national registration campaign, the survey succeeded in revealing that there remained about 200,000 men in Canada available for service in the armed forces.[33]

By 1917, it was obvious to Canadian government officials that this pool of men would never be tapped by the voluntary system of recruiting. Nothing demonstrated this more definitively than the failure of the efforts to raise volunteers for the Canadian Defence Force. Since the beginning of the war, the government had tried to maintain of force of 50,000 men under arms in Canada for the purpose of home defence (though by 1917 it was questionable whether such a large force was needed to defend Canadian territory – sabotage was always a threat, but Canada's borders seemed increasingly secure given the fact that the United States stood on the brink of war with Germany). However, the insatiable demand for men overseas threatened to devour those CEF troops who had been reserved for home guard duty. In order to free the members of the CEF in Canada for overseas service, the government launched a campaign to recruit 50,000 men for a Canadian Defence Force, to be separate from the CEF, which would assume the task of guarding the Dominion's borders and military installations. For a variety of reasons, the scheme to raise the CDF was a resounding failure. By April 1917, after a month of recruiting, the campaign had secured less than 200 enlistees. To military leaders, government officials and other observers, this was irrefutable proof that relying on volunteers was no longer a viable option for procuring the needed men for military service.[34]

That more and more Canadian men would be needed for the Allied war effort was increasingly apparent by the spring of 1917, and not just because of the appalling casualty figures. Borden and the other Dominion ministers who participated in the Imperial War Conference and War Cabinet held in London between February and May of that year learned to their dismay of the desperate situation facing the Allies at that point: The French Army on the Western Front was exhausted and mutinous after the carnage of Verdun and the Chemin des Dames; Russia was convulsed in revolution; British shipping was being decimated by German u-boats; the Italians remained locked in a bloody stalemate on the Isonzo River. The only bright spot was the entry of the United States into the war on the Allied side on 7 April. The question was, would the United States be able to mobilize its forces rapidly enough to put them in the field before the Central Powers knocked the Allies out of the war? [35]

During the conference, the British reiterated their polite but firm requests for more men from Canada, requests that they had been making since late 1916. Borden, as he had done in the past, refused to make any definite commitment of additional troops. However, the atmosphere of crisis during those months, combined with the emotions stirred by his visits to the site of the Canadian triumph at Vimy Ridge and to the hospitals housing wounded Canadian servicemen, helped to convince Borden that the Dominion was duty-bound to supply more soldiers to the Allied cause. And given the state of recruiting in Canada at the time, Borden reasoned, these soldiers could be obtained only through conscription. For proof, the Prime Minister needed to look no further than the fact that Canadian casualties in May 1917 numbered 13,457, while enlistments for that month totaled 6,407. On 18 May, just four days after his return to Canada from England, Borden announced to Parliament that the government had decided to introduce a bill authorizing the introduction of compulsory military service. The Prime Minister declared:

> I think that no true Canadian realizing all that is at stake in this war, can bring himself to consider with toleration or seriousness any suggestion for the relaxation of our efforts … Hitherto we have depended on voluntary enlistment … But I return to Canada impressed at once with the extreme gravity of the situation, and with a sense of responsibility for our further effort at the most critical period of the war. It is apparent to me that the voluntary system will not yield further substantial results … The Government have made every effort within its power, so far as I can judge … All citizens are liable to military service for the defence of their country, and I conceive that the battle for Canadian liberty and autonomy is being fought today on the plains of France and Belgium.

At no point in his call for conscription did Borden invoke Canada's duty to the Motherland and Empire. On the contrary, the Prime Minister was quick to repudiate the suggestion that the British government had in any way requested or dictated that the Dominion adopt compulsory service. According to Borden:

> The subject was never discussed between myself and any member of the British Government; if there had been any such suggestion from them, I for one would not have tolerated it. The Government, Parliament and people of Canada are the only authorities that can deal with or determine questions such as those which are embodied by the Bill now presented to this House.

Borden justified the grave and dramatic resort to conscription – a move that would almost certainly increase division and heighten social tensions within Canada – on the grounds that citizens of the Dominion had a 'responsibility' to defend, if not their shores, then certain abstract but cherished values such as 'liberty,' 'autonomy,' etc. At the same time, according to the Prime Minister, Canadians were obligated to provide reinforcements to the men at the front because 'thousands of them have made the supreme sacrifice for our liberty and preservation. Common gratitude, apart from all other considerations, should bring the whole force of this nation behind them.' Borden continued:

> Is there not a call to us from those who have passed beyond the shadow into the light of perfect day, from those who have fallen in France and in Belgium, from those who have died that Canada may live – is there not a call to us that their sacrifice shall not be in vain?... God speed the day when the gallant men who are protecting and defending us will return to the land they love so well... If we do not pass this measure, if we do not keep our plighted faith, with what countenance shall we meet them on their return? ... If what are left of 400,000 such men come back to Canada with fierce resentment and even rage in their hearts, conscious that they have been deserted or betrayed, how shall we meet them when they ask the reason?[36]

Central to Borden's argument for conscription were two main themes. First, Canada's contribution to the Allied war effort had not been, and would not be, compelled by subservience or slavish devotion to Great Britain. Whatever its formal political status within the Empire, Canada was autonomous enough to choose the extent and nature of its participation in the conflict. By introducing conscription, the Dominion was choosing to commit itself as totally to the Allied cause as any other nation within that alliance. Such a commitment was justified because the Allied cause was a transcendent one, nothing less than an idealistic crusade to preserve the exemplary values and institutions of Western civilization. Canada's sacrifices earned it the right to be viewed no longer as a squire to the knights of this crusade, but as a full-fledged champion in its own right. And those sacrifices, according to the second major theme of Borden's argument, *should not be in vain*. In other words, the carnage and suffering already endured by Canada's fighting men mandated nothing less than Allied victory.

Borden's argument in favour of conscription hinged on a representation of the war's meaning that justified the tremendous sacrifices asked (and now demanded) of Canadians by idealizing the aims of the Allied cause and the impact of the conflict on Canada's aspirations to nationhood. It was an appealing and inspiring rationalization of the Dominion's continued commitment to a massive war effort, and was representative of the view most widely articulated by mainstream English-

Canadian government officials, media commentators and other shapers of public opinion during the weeks and months of intense political strife following Borden's proposal of compulsory service. The day after his speech to Parliament, the Toronto *Globe* declared: 'For the Allied nations this is a war of defence, the defence of national independence against the immoral ambitions of Germany, and the defence of international peace. It is a conflict between democratic nations and a military autocracy.'[37] The Manitoba *Free Press* had earlier expressed similar ideas, asserting that:

> what is really threatened by the Prussian ideal of military autocracy is the civilization and future progress of all the nations of the world ... The victory of the allies ... must bring greater freedom and open the avenue to international cooperation, or it will have been achieved in vain ... The principle that the nations of the world form a society, governed by laws and conventions, ruled by a respect for each others rights, and guided in their conduct by the desire to promote the common good, is that for which the Allies are striving. If this be not recognized, the struggle has no meaning worthy of its cost and magnitude.[38]

Such pronouncements, evoking the rhetoric of the United States' president, Woodrow Wilson, were not intended solely for the purpose of rallying the faithful, but also to specifically counter the interpretation of the war advanced by critics of Canada's escalating involvement in the conflict, the most vocal of whom were primarily French-Canadian.

Many *Québécois* anti-conscriptionists justified their positions on nationalist grounds as well. Bourassa and others argued that they, and not pro-war English Canadians, were the legitimate nationalists. They argued that French-Canadian loyalty was given wholeheartedly and solely to Canada, while the divided loyalties of English Canadians made them the pawns of British imperialism. Continued political and social cleavage between the French and English in Canada was inevitable 'so long as English Canadians remain more British than Canadian,' Bourassa declared in 1918.[39] Prior to 1917, Bourassa's rhetoric generally positioned him toward the more radical extreme of *Québécois* opinion, but with the advent of conscription, his views were increasingly reflected in the language of more mainstream French-Canadian commentary. As the battle over conscription wore on, more and more Liberal politicians in Quebec condemned compulsion with anti-imperialist rhetoric that echoed criticisms Bourassa had been making since the 1890s of Canadian involvement in Britain's wars.[40]

The debate in Parliament over the Military Service Act – as the bill authorizing the draft was called – was lengthy and emotional. However, the Conservative majority in the House ensured that the Act would eventually pass, and on 28 August

1917 it was signed into law. Even so, whether or not compulsion would ever actually be carried out in Canada was far from certain at this point. Borden's government faced an election at the end of the year, one that they were expected to lose to the Liberals. The election would no doubt amount to a referendum on the issue of conscription, and the Conservatives could only hope to win if enough English-Canadian Liberals chose to eschew loyalty to their chief, the anti-conscriptionist Laurier, and solidarity with their French-Canadian party compatriots, in favour of allegiance to the majority of their fellow English-Canadians who desired conscription.

Shortly after introducing the Military Service Act, Borden, in an effort to forestall the trauma of a war-time election (and perhaps worried that anti-conscription riots in Montreal on 24 May foreshadowed the French-Canadian response to compulsion), invited Laurier to join him in forming a coalition government composed of equal numbers of Conservatives and Liberals. Laurier contemplated the offer, but eventually rejected it on the grounds that he could not serve in any administration that enforced conscription, and that compulsion was so unpopular in Quebec that French-Canadian Liberals could not support the measure without dooming the province to subsequent political domination by Bourassa's *nationalistes*.[41] Laurier's refusal to join with Borden did not kill the movement toward coalition: ultimately, the twin planks of conscription and Union government supported the Prime Minister's campaign platform. It did, however, guarantee that Canada's next governing coalition would be a 'Union' only in the sense that English-Canadian politicians were willing to put aside their differences and unite against French Canada.[42]

Once it was certain that Laurier would not participate in a coalition, Borden and his followers pursued a two-pronged strategy aimed at capturing the backing of Liberals prepared to break ranks with their leader, and at ensuring that support for anti-conscription Liberals would be almost nonexistent outside of Quebec. This strategy resulted in an ugly, bitter election campaign that polarized English and French speakers in Canada to an extent unprecedented since Confederation. The English-Canadian press, especially – but not exclusively – Ontario's major daily newspapers, set the tone. A full-page advertisement appearing in the Toronto *Globe* on 11 December 1917 asked: 'Is a united Quebec to rule all of Canada?' The ad went on to call upon 'all English-speaking men and women to realize that English-Canada, divided by old-time party questions, is at the mercy of a united Quebec. Union government alone can save Canada from the menace of French-Canadian domination.'[43] Even the Manitoba *Free Press*, whose editor J. W. Dafoe had been a long-time supporter of Laurier and the Liberals, published a similar ad which asked English Canadians if they were willing to place themselves 'under the domination of French-Canadians, who, by spurning their duty in this war, made Conscription necessary?'[44] Such sentiments were echoed *ad infinitum* in the speeches of many English-speaking politicians, in the sermons of English-speaking clergymen, and in

innumerable pamphlets printed and distributed by Unionist sympathizers. According to one flier, a Laurier victory would ensure that French-Canadian 'shirkers'
would become the dominant force in Canada's government. Other broadsides in-
accurately and unfairly asserted that Laurier and Bourassa were allied in a conspiracy to end Canadian participation in the war (Bourassa had endorsed Laurier in this
campaign, but they were allied only in their hostility to conscription; Laurier had
consistently pledged to continue Canada's full-scale war effort if elected).[45]

In Quebec, the language of those opposed to conscription and Union government was generally far less vitriolic than that of their English-Canadian rivals.
However, if the opinions appearing in the press, and expressed on various public
platforms were any indication, the French-speaking province was virtually unanimous in its antipathy to compulsory service and coalition. Of the major French
daily newspapers, only the *Evénement* of Quebec City and the *Patrie* of Montreal,
both Conservative organs, sided with the Unionists.[46] Most periodicals agreed with
Bourassa, who warned that:

Apart from the menace to the economic equilibrium of the country, the inevitable outcome of conscription … is three-fold: (1) labour troubles and
class hatred; (2) racial strife; (3) a deep cleavage between East and West. If
wise counsels do not prevail, it may mean, within a very short period, a second Mexico north of the 45th and 49th parallels.[47]

The results of the 1917 election were perhaps not surprising, given the fact that
they reflected the divisive and heavy-handed, albeit successful, Unionist strategy of
ensuring their victory by marginalizing and neutralizing their opponents. The government won 153 seats, of which three were English-speaking Quebec constituencies. The Liberals carried the other 62 Quebec seats, along with 10 of 28 in the
Maritimes, eight of 82 in Ontario, and two of 57 in the west. The government's
popular majority was only 100,000 with the civilian vote, but the ballots of Canada's fighting men added another 200,000 to that total (the Military Voters Act,
passed in September 1917, had enfranchised all members of the armed forces, regardless of length of residence in Canada).[48] It was a decisive victory for Borden
and the Unionists, one that determined that French Canadian dissenters would
remain isolated in Quebec for the rest of the war. Other factions or segments of
society opposed to conscription had been similarly neutralized: The Wartime Elections Act, also passed in September, enfranchised all female relatives (mothers,
wives, sisters and daughters) of servicemen, and disenfranchised all immigrants
from enemy countries who had been naturalized after 1902, as well as all conscientious objectors. In addition, the government appeased anti-conscriptionist farmers
by pledging to exempt their sons from military service.[49] Given the degree to which
the Unionists stacked the deck in their favour, the question remains as to whether

the results of the election actually reflected enthusiasm for conscription even among English Canadians. Laurier, for his part, had long argued that English speakers were averse to compulsory service, but that 'the attitude which is represented as the attitude of Quebec maddens them, and everyone who is in favour of conscription … favours the movement not because he believes that it is necessary, but because Quebec is represented to be against it.'[50]

The home front battles waged in Canada over conscription and Union government, which intensified and further polarized the earlier debate over the nature and extent of the Dominion's contribution to the Allied war effort, profoundly and permanently altered the country's political and cultural landscape, and also established the paradigm for post-war contests over efforts to commemorate and render into narrative the Great War. Politically, lingering bitterness over conscription ensured that the Conservatives were finished as a force at the polls in Quebec for decades to come. At the same time, the *nationaliste* movement in the province would begin to drift away from the broadly Canadian vision of Bourassa and his followers and toward the more narrowly Quebec-centred (and even separatist) ideas of men like Abbé Lionel Groulx. Thus, even as the First World War contributed to the growth among English Canadians of an outwardly directed nationalism, and to a heightened sense of their country's elevated status as a global power, it encouraged among French-Canadians an increasingly introverted and isolationist nationalist movement.

In general, the remainder of the war after the introduction of conscription was characterized by ever-increasing turmoil on the Canadian home front, as all vestiges of the early war unity and consensus collapsed under the strains produced by the demands of the conflict. Not only was there the continuing resistance of French-Canadians to compulsory service (which culminated in the violent street battles between protesters and government troops in Quebec City on Easter weekend in 1918, in which four civilians were killed and more than 50 wounded. Five soldiers were hospitalized as well)[51], but also growing labour agitation, as well as unrest among the country's farmers. Canadian politics would emerge from the war more contentious and sectarian than it had ever been, and it would be within a prevailing atmosphere of strife and polarization that the defining struggles over the memory of the war would take place.

Australian Identity and the Conscription Debate

In Australia, as in Canada, the enormous losses suffered by their forces in the Somme battles of 1916 produced manpower demands that threatened to overwhelm the capacity of the voluntary system. In August of that year, Dominion officials estimated that an average of 16,500 recruits per month would be required in order to keep Australia's forces in the field up to strength. However, enlistments

for June had totalled only 6,375, and for July, 6,170. These figures showed a significant drop from the first quarter of 1916, when enlistments had averaged 18,700
a month. And thus far in August there had been 4,144 recruits, compared to 6,734
casualties.[52]

The decline in volunteers mirrored what was occurring in Canada, and it is likely
that similar factors lay at the root of the problem in both countries. The Australian
Imperial Force, like the CEF, contained a large percentage of British-born recruits.
The British-born averaged between 13 and 15 per cent of Australia's population
during the war, but comprised between 18 and 23 per cent of the AIF for the duration of the conflict. As in Canada, they made up a larger percentage of the early
formations sent overseas, constituting 27 per cent of the first contingent.[53] By late
1916, this manpower pool, which was somewhat smaller in Australian than in Canada,[54] had largely dried up. While native-born Australians seem to have been a bit
more inclined to volunteer for service than native-born Canadians (including even
those of English heritage), the diminishing availability of British-born enlistees
could not help but have an adverse effect on Australian recruiting.

However, the primary explanation for the decline in enlistments by the summer
of 1916 probably had more to do with the fact that many Australians on the home
front experienced a general waning of enthusiasm for the war in the wake of the
shocking carnage and depressing futility of the Somme battles. That the obfusca-
tions of the censors and the exhortations of propaganda could not completely prevent the wilting of martial fervour among the domestic population is supported by
Brian Lewis' recollections of the mood in Australia after the bloodbaths of the
Somme campaign. He writes:

> Now there was no hope of quick victory; It had been unburied bodies on
> Gallipoli, now it was ragged fragments of bodies scattered in the mud ... At
> school the Head still announced that some Old Boy had died gallantly for his
> country, but gallantry was now a word which meant nothing: we were begin-
> ning to think that he had gone uselessly and inevitably to slaughter ...We had
> started and would have to see it through, and if our luck was good, there
> would not be any close friends in the casualty lists.[55]

Whatever the underlying causes of the decline in recruiting, a growing number
of Australian government officials, community leaders and members of the media
by 1916 were expressing the view that only conscription could ensure that the
Dominion would meet its manpower needs for the rest of the war. As early as September 1915, some of Australia's most prominent national figures had formed a
Universal Service League to promote the adoption of compulsory service (this organization had its North American counterpart in the Canadian National Service
League, formed in April 1916). The members of this group and their supporters

could point to the fact that Great Britain had adopted conscription in January 1916, and New Zealand had followed suit in August. Why should Australia be an exception?[56]

By 1916, the single most powerful figure leading the drive to institute conscription in Australia was the Dominion's prime minister, William Morris Hughes. In his stance on this issue, Hughes went against the majority of the other members of his party, the Labor party – a party which he had been instrumental in building and leading to prominence before the war. Since becoming prime minister shortly after the outbreak of the conflict, Hughes had abandoned his initial unequivocal opposition to compulsory service, declaring in 1915 that the circumstances of the war might necessitate the introduction of conscription. However, the true turning point for the Prime Minister occurred as a result of a visit to Britain between February and July 1916. Just as Borden's participation in the Imperial Conference in 1917 (an event in which Hughes was unable to take part) proved decisive in convincing the Canadian prime minister that the Allied war effort required all the help that the Dominion could muster, and that conscription was vital to sustaining the Dominion's manpower contribution, so Hughes' time spent in the Motherland persuaded him that the gravity of the situation in Europe demanded Australia's total commitment to the Allied cause.[57]

Hughes arrived back in Australia at the end of July, just days after some of the bloodiest fighting experienced by the AIF at Pozières. The Prime Minister was well aware of the looming manpower crisis in light of the disparity between the horrendous casualties of the Somme campaign and the low numbers of recruits trickling into the AIF so far that summer. Still, he did not call immediately for the adoption of conscription upon his return to Australia. Hughes was equally aware of how seriously opinion was divided in the Dominion over the issue of compulsion for overseas service. The interests favouring conscription were influential indeed – they included almost the whole of the non-Labor press, the Liberal Party, and the majority of academic and Protestant church leaders. However, the forces against conscription were formidable as well, including as they did many Irish-Catholic leaders and the country's powerful trade unions.[58] The opposition that Hughes and his supporters faced from within Australia's large Irish-Catholic minority was significant and highly vocal. The British government's brutal quashing of the Easter Rebellion in Dublin in April had fanned the flames of the community's traditional anti-Imperialism and resentment of the English. However, in the summer of 1916, it was the trade unions that particularly worried Hughes, as they were the primary constituents of his own political party, and to defy them posed the serious risk of dividing that party, and perhaps of destroying it altogether.

While Hughes was in Britain, the Australian Worker's Union, the largest and most politically influential union in the Dominion, had passed at its annual convention a motion condemning conscription. In May the Melbourne Trades Hall had organized a special interstate congress of unions to discuss the subject, and the attendees had issued a manifesto that charged that conscription was merely a tool that the ruling class would use to 'render null and void all the achievements of Trade Unionism.' The manifesto, which was subsequently suppressed by government authorities, continued:

> In principle [conscription] is an instrument of national defence; in practice it is made an instrument of working class subjugation. It is so under the Kaiser and the Czar. It is so under the Union Jack and the Tricolor of France, and since in Australia we have seen a slavish imitation of the laws, regulations, verbiage and practices of the Imperial Government, it behooves the organised toilers of Australia to speak and act before the clock of trickery is permitted to strike the hour of doom.[59]

In the face of such sentiment, Hughes knew better than to heed articles appearing in the mainstream press that offered overly optimistic predictions about the effect that the introduction of conscription would have on Australian politics. According to one such editorial, 'Mr. Hughes will find that when he speaks with the authority of his special knowledge he will have no difficulty in obtaining the recruits that he needs, and that if he asks Parliament to bring compulsory service in force, the opposition will be negligible.'[60] Hughes considered seeking conscription by an Act of Parliament, but decided that such a tactic would be opposed by many members of his party – including most of his Cabinet – and any draft bill that got through the House of Representatives would most likely be rejected by the Senate, where Labor held a large majority. The Prime Minister did have the option of mandating conscription under the regulations of the War Precautions Act, but such a measure would require the approval of his Cabinet, and of the Senate. Hughes decided that the best hope of bringing conscription to Australia lay in putting the issue directly before the people by holding a referendum in which they could vote for or against the institution of compulsory service. Such a vote would have no legal force, but, if the majority of Australians voted 'yes' to conscription, it would be much more difficult, if not impossible for most legislators to resist its institution.[61]

On 24 August, the War Office in London provided the perfect pretext for holding a referendum on conscription when it cabled to Australia an urgent request for reinforcements to maintain the Dominion's five divisions in France at full strength. The British asked for 31,500 men in September, to be followed by 16,500 over the next three months. Given the state of recruiting in Australia at the time, there was no way such a request could conceivably be met under the voluntary system. On 30 August, Hughes announced that the government would hold a conscription referendum at the earliest possible opportunity.[62]

The weeks between this announcement and the day of the referendum, which was held on 28 October, would see the supporters and the opponents of conscription wage an extraordinarily divisive and rhetorically vicious campaign for the hearts and minds of Australia's citizens. In the end, the men and women of the Dominion rejected compulsory service by a narrow margin of 71,549 votes out of 2,308,603 votes cast.[63] In making their cases for or against conscription, the adversaries in this contest sought to sway opinion by associating their position with various esteemed social groups, including soldiers, mothers and workers, and with certain ideals considered exemplary, including, among many others, duty, liberty, the Empire, loyalty, race pride, Christianity, and social justice. In the process, the debate over compulsory service revealed the political, social and cultural fault lines within Australia as no single issue had done before.

From the standpoint of high politics in the Dominion, the most significant consequence of the 1916 conscription referendum was the fatal blow that it dealt to the unity of the Australian Labor party. A month after the vote on compulsory service, Hughes was expelled from the ALP, along with a number of supporters who were similarly at odds with the anti-conscription position of the party majority. In November, these exiles formed the National Labor Party with Hughes as its leader. This splinter faction was able to retain office thanks to an alliance with members of the pro-conscription Liberal opposition in Parliament. In February 1917, the NLP formally merged with their Liberal supporters to create the Nationalist Party.[64] Thus, in Australia, as in Canada, the issue of conscription resulted in the division of the country's most prominent left-wing political party, as those members of the organization who felt that their support for the total commitment of the Dominion to the Allied war effort was a position that transcended traditional partisan loyalties aligned themselves with like-minded conservative politicians.

In making their respective cases to the Australian people, each side in the conscription debate combined high-minded appeals to the idealism of voters with the crudest attempts to exploit citizens' fears and prejudices. Those advocating conscription often expressed their position in language and imagery that invited Australians to define their identity in ways that transcended the bounds of class, ethnicity and religion. The introduction of compulsory service could only be ensured if Australians were convinced that a war being fought on such distant shores necessitated such a sacrifice on their part. Thus, pro-conscriptionists tried to persuade men and women in the Dominion that their stake in the outcome of the struggle being waged overseas was as great as it would be if the conflict were taking place within sight of Sydney. This could be more easily accomplished if Australian passions were aroused for abstract concepts – such as 'freedom' and 'democracy' – and loyalties – such as the Empire and British 'civilization' – which were not only some of the most cherished ideals associated with Australian society, but which also allowed citizens in the Dominion to see how their way of life could be threatened even beyond the confines of the country's shores. In one of his many proconscription speeches, Hughes tried to present this vision:

> We are part of the British Empire; that is, we are one of the family of free British nations that engirdle the earth ... If the Empire falls we fall with it. The Empire is fighting for its life. Britain has asked us to do our share ... Is Australia going to prove true to herself, to the traditions of our race, to the men of Anzac; or stand before the world as degenerate and unworthy? The greatest war of all time is raging, the fate of the Empire, of Australia, of democracy, is at stake, and the anti-conscriptionists tell us that we have done enough; that we should leave the fighting to Britain and the Allies ... If we turn tail, and, like cravens, desert the Empire, to whom we owe everything, abandon the Allies who have suffered such awful losses and horrors, and made such great sacrifices – but who still fight gallantly on – if we refuse to reinforce the heroic Anzacs, then, indeed, will fall upon us the doom we deserve, and before the tribunal of nations we shall stand condemned.[65]

Opponents of compulsory service countered such appeals with their own brands of idealistic rhetoric. On the one hand, organized labour and conscientious objectors encouraged Australians to imagine themselves as members of transnational communities – the international working class and the brotherhood of man – whose interests were better served by uniting against their oppressors than by killing one another to further the greedy and expansionist aims of the ruling order. 'Civilised men and women, whether English or German, Australian or Turkish, do not want war,' argued one pamphlet produced by the Australian Freedom League, an organization devoted to the principles of conscientious objection. 'War is forced upon them by the ignorance, distrust and suspicion of one another ... they have gone to war because they trust their rulers more than their own conscience, because, unlike the Christians of old, they obey men rather than God.'[66] At the same time, anti-conscriptionists portrayed hallowed 'Australian' ideals such as 'freedom' and 'democracy' as being threatened not by Prussian militarism overseas, but by the heightened authoritarianism and economic injustice at home which would inevitably result from the introduction of compulsory service.[67]

Among anti-conscriptionists, inclusive idealism did not constitute the sole instrument of persuasion. The foes of compulsion also typically employed arguments that were aimed more narrowly at the self-interest of large, but traditionally oppressed constituencies, such as the working class and Irish Catholics. Anti-conscriptionist rhetoric frequently played upon the not unreasonable apprehension of many within these groups that compulsory service would be employed as a means of social control to ensure their continued subjugation. In addition, the propaganda of the anti-conscriptionists often did not hesitate to exploit the bigotry and paranoia of their targeted audience. Organized labour, for instance, was quick to raise the spectre of hordes of 'coloured' immigrants descending on Australia to replace the white workers who would be conscripted from factory and farm into military service. 'Conscription means the importation of labour, from low-wage countries inevitable for Australia,' wrote one labour commentator. 'Every white labourer, who is by conscription made an economic drone, has to replaced by some other sort of labour ...'[68] Another expressed a similar sentiment with this pithy exhortation: 'Australia bids fair to be a white man's paradise: Do not run the risk of turning it into a black man's Hell.'[69]

The contention by anti-conscriptionists that compulsory service would lead to the importation of cheap non-white labour seemed to be supported by the arrival in Australia in September 1916 of a ship carrying 98 immigrants from Malta. Although the timing of their landing was completely coincidental, it could not have been more fortuitous for the opponents of conscription. The unfortunate Maltese were soon shipped back to their homeland, but not before providing considerable ammunition to those who portrayed conscription as a threat to the government's White Australia Policy that had formally banned coloured immigration since 1901.[70]

Of course, pro-conscriptionists were not at all above playing to the fears and prejudices of Australian voters either. Commentators arguing for compulsion often demonized their opponents in the harshest and most crude terms. Anti-conscription labourites were routinely labelled 'anarchists,' and linked to the widely despised (and banned in Australia after August 1917) Industrial Workers of the World, a revolutionary political and trade organization that advocated the violent overthrow of capitalism. 'I. W. W. Responsible for Roping Organized Labor Into Anti-Conscription Camp,' blared a headline in one pro-conscription pamphlet.[71] Similarly, Irish Catholics who voiced opposition to conscription were frequently accused of fellow travelling with Sinn Fein, an Irish-nationalist organization that was not above using terrorism to achieve its aims. Even conscientious objectors did not escape condemnation by conscriptionists for the unsavoury company in which their pacifist stand placed them. According to one 'Protestant YES voter': 'The "conscientious objector" has linked himself up with the vilest section of the community – the rampant anarchist and the degenerate shirker – who for once find themselves in the company of morally better men than themselves.'[72]

Among the anti-conscription forces in Australia, there really was no single national figure who came to embody dissent – or disloyalty, depending on one's perspective – to a degree comparable to Henri Bourassa in Canada. However, Daniel Mannix, the Coadjutor Archbishop of Melbourne in 1916, did achieve a somewhat singular status as Australia's most prominent, influential and effective critic of compulsion. An intelligent and articulate clergyman with a commanding presence and a sharp wit that made him a compelling orator, Mannix used his high-profile pulpit as one of Australia's leading Irish-Catholic officials to argue relentlessly against the imposition of conscription and to condemn Britain's policies in Ireland. He was an avowed Irish nationalist, but he was never as overtly or vehemently anti-imperialist as Bourassa. However, in some of his speeches, Mannix did present an ideal of Australian nationalism in which he asserted, as Bourassa did for Canada, that the Dominion's interests would be better served, and its future welfare better guaranteed, if it avoided lavishing still more of its blood and treasure on a conflict in which such a massive contribution by Australia was neither essential nor sensible. Declared Mannix:

> I have been under the impression, and I still retain the conviction, that Australia has done her full share – I am inclined to say more than her full share – in this war. Her loyalty to the Empire has been lauded to the skies, and the bravery of her sons has won the admiration of friend and foe alike ... There will be differences among Catholics, for Catholics do not think and act in platoons – and on most questions there is room for divergence of opinion. But, for myself, it will take a good deal to convince me that conscription in Australia would not cause more evil than it would avert.[73]

Statements such as this prompted one Melbourne newspaper to declare: 'Should Germany win the war, the Kaiser will certainly be dead to all sense of gratitude if he fails to decorate the Archbishop with an iron cross.'[74] By 1917, and the advent of a second conscription referendum in Australia, Mannix had succeeded the late Dr. T. J. Carr as the Archbishop of Melbourne, thus placing him even more at the forefront of the movement against compulsion. In one of his speeches from this time, Mannix made common cause with anti-conscriptionist allies in organized labour, and also reiterated his ideal of an Australian patriotism that did not countenance the kind of loyalty to the Empire that justified the excessive and irrational national sacrifice that conscription would entail. In the words of the Archbishop:

> I say that this cheap talk about equal sacrifice is galling, absurd and ridiculous. The wealthy classes would be very glad to send the last man, but they have no notion of giving the last shilling, nor even the first ... In reality, the burden in the end will be borne by the toiling masses of Australia ... [By voting against conscription] You will be acting in your own interests, and in the true interests of the Empire, by keeping Australia free ... If you surrender your freedom by accepting conscription, what assurance have you that the rights you give away will be used to the best advantage of Australia?[75]

By this point in 1917, two years of anti-conscriptionist agitation by Mannix led Hughes to privately contemplate having the troublesome priest arrested or deported. In the end, the Prime Minister did neither.[76]

As we have seen, Australians in 1916 rejected conscription by a slim margin. However, the fact that a small majority of men and women in the Dominion voted against compelling their countrymen to serve overseas did not mean that most Australians also opposed their nation's continued involvement in the struggle against the Central Powers. Nothing better illustrates this than the results of Australia's Federal election in May 1917. Hughes' Nationalist Party, campaigning on a 'win the war' platform, won 46 seats in the House of Representatives (a gain of seven), leaving Labor with 19. In the Senate, the Nationalists attained a majority there as well, winning all 18 of the half-Senate vacancies.[77] As Canadians did at the polls in 1917, Australians used the ballot box to demonstrate just how strong support for the war remained in the Dominion, despite the results of the first referendum. However, for a majority of Canadian citizens (at least the English-Canadian ones), their commitment to the war effort also encompassed an acceptance of compulsory service; if it had not, then they could have voted for the Liberals, who had pledged to maintain Canada's involvement in the war without resorting to conscription. One can only speculate as to why Canadians assented to this extreme measure which Australians rejected (and also how a majority of Canadians might have responded if the issue had been put to a separate referendum), but the presence in the North American Dominion of a large and highly visible French-Canadian minority which was perceived by many English Canadians to be contributing less than its fair share of fighting men to the country's military forces can not be discounted as a decisive factor.[78]

The manpower crisis in Australia for which conscription had been proposed as a remedy did not disappear after the first referendum. Rather, the number of recruits continued to fall, bottoming out at 2,617 in December 1916. The Government's immediate solution was to take the responsibility for raising men out of the hands of the overburdened Defense Department, and to create a specific organization dedicated solely to this essential task. In November of 1916, Donald Mackinnon, a barrister from Victoria and member of the State parliament, was appointed Director-General of Recruiting. Below him was established a tightly organized network of regional, state and local committees to oversee recruiting at each level of government. Under Mackinnon's able leadership, the Government's nation-wide recruiting drive of 1917 was perhaps its most well-planned and well-coordinated to date. Nevertheless, the results were disappointing. During the first seven months of 1917, the number of volunteers generally remained steady at around 4,000 a month, but enlistments never reached the target level of 5,500–6,000 a month. By August, the totals were falling again, down to 3,274 for that month, and then to 2,460 for September and 2,761 for October. Once again, it was

obvious to military and Government officials that the voluntary system was inca-
pable of fulfilling the manpower needs of the AIF, despite the Commonwealth
Statistician's estimate that there still remained in Australia 140,000 fit single men
and 280,000 married men, between the ages of 18 and 40, available for military
service.[79]

Stirred by the falling recruiting figures, and by the same grim atmosphere of crisis among the Allies that had prompted Borden in Canada to introduce compulsory
service there, Hughes in November 1917 announced plans to hold a second referendum on conscription. In putting the question before the people, rather than
simply legislating compulsion as he could have done now that his party held a majority in both houses of Parliament, Hughes was fulfilling a campaign promise.
Even so, the second conscription debate was conducted with even less rhetorical
restraint and even more vehemence from both sides than the first contest. If the
first referendum campaign had been a bare-knuckle brawl, then the second was
fought with brass knuckles. Attitudes on either side of the issue had hardened since
1916, particularly in the aftermath of a massive 82-day general strike in the fall of
1917 – the largest in the country's history – that threatened to paralyse Australian
industry. Shortly after Hughes proposed a second referendum, the *Australian
Worker* described conscription as 'the Lottery of Death,' and declared: 'If Australia
accepts the scheme of military compulsion formulated by the Prime Minister ... it
will abandon every pretension to be a democratic nation, and reduce its citizens to
the level of cannibals drawing lots for an obscene feast.'[80] An anti-conscription
leaflet asked the women of Australia: 'Do you want the furnace of war to consume
all your fathers, husbands and brothers? ... Vote "no" and preserve your Home
Land.'[81] Not to be outdone, the Reinforcements Referendum Council distributed a
pro-conscription flyer entitled 'The Anti's Creed', which asserted that those who
believed that conscription was wrong also approved of the sinking of the *Lusitania*,
the massacre of Belgian priests, the murder of Nurse Cavell, the I.W.W., Sinn Fein,
general strikes and baby killing, among other things.[82] The hysteria of the second
referendum campaign culminated on 29 November with the infamous incident of
the 'Warwick Egg,' which involved Prime Minister Hughes being hit with an egg
thrown from a hostile crowd as he tried to deliver a pro-conscription speech in
Warwick, Queensland.[83]

On 20 December 1917, the people of Australia opted once again to reject conscription, this time by a larger margin of 166,588 votes out of 2,196,906 that were
cast.[84] The AIF would remain an all-volunteer army for the rest of the war, making
Australia the only major belligerent whose forces in the field never included conscripts. With enlistment totals that averaged only about 2,500 a month by 1918,
Australia was with great difficulty able to maintain its five divisions at fighting
strength, though depleted, until they were withdrawn from the line in October
1918. A number of AIF battalions were disbanded in 1918 due to a lack of rein-

forcements, much to the dismay of many Australian politicians and military leaders, but this and other similarly judicious tactics were all that prevented the complete break-up of one or more Australian divisions.[85] Perhaps it is ironic then that it was during this period witnessing the Dominion's gravest recruiting difficulties of the war that the AIF emerged as one of the most celebrated and actively engaged Allied combat units on the Western Front.

New Zealand and Conscription

During the First World War there would be no national referendum in New Zealand on the issue of conscription. Shortly after Hughes and his allies failed in late 1916 to obtain popular sanction for compulsory service in Australia, the New Zealand government refused the demands of anti-conscription miners to allow the Dominion's populace to vote on the issue, prompting the Minister of Defence, James Allen, to express his relief to Prime Minister William Massey that New Zealand had avoided Australia's 'blunder' of putting the question before the people.[86] However, there is considerable reason to doubt whether New Zealand voters would have echoed their counterparts across the Tasman and rejected compulsion. As early as May 1915, shortly after the Anzac landings at Gallipoli and the first heavy New Zealand casualty lists from the fighting on the Peninsula, many newspapers began publishing letters-to-the editor calling for conscription. However, as long as voluntary recruiting continued to meet manpower requirements, New Zealand's government felt no real impetus to translate such sentiments into policy. The situation changed considerably in the summer and fall of 1915, as the creation of additional battalions for the New Zealand Division combined with the fact that enlistment did not increase to produce for the first time the frightening prospect of the demand for men exceeding the supply. Such a crisis was narrowly avoided, but afterward, calls for compulsory service became increasingly vociferous on the editorial pages of mainstream newspapers, and in the speeches of many non-labour politicians.

Indeed it was primarily the fear of how organized labour would respond to the introduction of conscription that motivated the caution with which the New Zealand Government, a coalition of the Liberal and Reform parties, moved on the issue. The labour press had promised 'disastrous upheavals and eruption' in New Zealand society if compulsion was enacted, and as the most vocal and powerful opponents of conscription, labour's threats were taken seriously. The Government's nightmare scenario was a repeat of the large-scale industrial unrest that had rocked New Zealand in 1912 and 1913, and political leaders feared that conscription would provide a galvanizing issue for labour militants. This was not an unfounded apprehension: opposition to conscription united moderates and militants within a labour movement whose divisions after the failure of industrial action in the years before 1914 had been exacerbated by the pro-war stance of many moderates. As conscription loomed with growing inevitability on the nation's horizon, particularly after New Zealand faced its first genuine manpower shortage in December 1915 and the British Parliament began debating in January 1916 a bill authorizing compulsory service in that country, labour leaders responded with what seemed to the Government like ominous signs of imminent resistance. In late January 1916, following a conference attended by 18,000 trade unionists, representatives of New Zealand's labour movement issued a manifesto calling for the conscription of wealth, through the state seizure and operation of the means of production, before the conscription of men was even considered. The manifesto did not specify the consequences if the Government ignored labour's demands (which it ultimately did). However, the conference and the statement that it produced were instrumental in convincing the Government to persist several more months with voluntary enlistment at a time when, if the correspondence and opinion pages of most non-labour newspapers are an accurate indication, a rising chorus of public opinion supported the introduction of compulsion. Ultimately, voluntary recruitment failed to make up continuing shortages, and Parliament passed on 1 August 1916 a Military Service Act authorizing conscription.

One month before this development, the impending draft provided the central impetus for the creation of the New Zealand Labour Party, which represented the formal political unification of organized labour's moderate and militant wings. Though opposition to conscription drew them together, radicals and moderates continued to disagree over how best to express their dissent. Militants advocated industrial action – strikes and other forms of active resistance – while moderates favoured symbolic protest and running labour candidates on anti-conscription platforms in local elections (New Zealand held no national elections during the war). In the end, moderation proved more characteristic of the New Zealand labour movement's response to conscription. Strikes, in which opposition to compulsion was declared as the primary justification, did occur in 1916 after the government began implementing the draft, and in 1917–18. They were, however, limited in scope (confined largely to the country's miners' unions), duration and impact, particularly compared to wartime industrial action in Australia. A major reason for this may have been the simple fact that the most militantly anti-conscription workers tended to be concentrated in fields essential to the war effort – mining, seafaring, waterside labour – and so were likely to be exempt from the draft. Another factor was almost certainly the effectiveness of the government's crackdown against anti-war dissent of all kinds, including, but not limited to, opposition to compulsion. As part of a series of War Regulations passed over the course of the conflict, any speech, writing or action that entailed or encouraged resistance to conscription could be defined as 'sedition' and result in a prison sentence or, if the offender was eligible, induction into the military. By early 1918 more than a dozen leading labour opponents of the draft were in prison (including a future Prime Minister, Peter Fraser), and one, P. C. (Paddy) Webb, Labour M.P. for Grey, had been sentenced to two years' hard labour for refusing to don the khaki when drafted.[87] Of course, labour radicals were not the only dissenting elements targeted by the government. For instance, New Zealand's small but vocal and visible community of pacifists and conscientious objectors suffered disproportionately and perhaps more severely than any other group from harsh policies designed to punish and suppress anti-war activism.[88]

Overall, for New Zealand, the debate over conscription, while not lacking in polarising rhetoric and the potential for deeper conflict, did not engender political and social turmoil on a scale comparable to that seen in Australia and Canada. There are several possible explanations for this. Opposition to conscription in both New Zealand and Australia issued primarily from the organized labour movement, however, in New Zealand that movement as a political force (by 1914) was generally more moderate, and represented a smaller proportion of the voting population (one-fifth in New Zealand, compared to about 50 per cent in Australia).[89] Opposition to conscription in Canada issued largely from within the country's large (nearly 30% of the population in 1916) French Canadian minority, a community that typically displayed a strong sense of identity often defined in relation to its separateness from the dominant Anglo-centric conceptions of the Canadian nation. Already ambivalent about Canada's involvement in what many saw as a strictly European war, and generally less motivated to fight out of loyalty to Britain or the Empire than their English-Canadian counterparts, few French Canadians could accept being compelled to serve a cause that so many had already rejected through their unwillingness to volunteer. Within New Zealand's largest and most visible minority communities, opposition to conscription was far less uniform.

For instance, Maori attitudes toward the draft differed significantly among various tribes. Initially, the Government intended to exempt all Maori from conscription, however (and somewhat ironically) leaders from several 'loyal' tribes who had thus far contributed the largest number of Maori volunteers argued in favour of compulsion in the interest of ensuring equality of sacrifice from those tribes that had provided few or no recruits. Among the tribes where recruiting lagged or was absent, the reasons for opposing, or at least not actively supporting, voluntary service were complex, and often grounded specifically in religious and/or cultural beliefs and political grievances (especially regarding Pakeha confiscation of their land in the nineteenth century), and more generally in their alienation from a government that withheld the benefits of citizenship from them, and yet requested what might be their ultimate sacrifice on its behalf. In one case, concerns about the potential subversive impact of a messianic anti-war Maori separatist leader, Te Rua Kenana, had led to his arrest in 1916 on charges of 'sedition' after a brief shootout with police that left two Maori dead and four policemen and several Maori wounded. Conscription, when it was finally applied to the Maori in 1917, was officially restricted to those residing on the North Island. In practice it was restricted even further, to the Waikato tribes, where the separatist King movement remained strong. Opposition there to registration of Maori for military service cohered around the Waikato leader Princess Te Puea Herangi. Unlike Te Rua, she was not arrested, though several of her followers and defaulters under her protection were.[90] By the end of the war, 552 Maori had been conscripted; none of these served overseas. In all, 2,227 Maori, about 4.5 per cent of New Zealand's Maori population, served in the First World War. Most, at least after Gallipoli, served in the non-combat Pioneer Battalion. Of those Maori who served, 336 were killed or died, and 734 were wounded, a casualty rate of nearly 50 per cent.[91]

The most heated wartime controversy related to conscription in New Zealand arose, like the conflicts with certain Maori, out of the ambiguous and contested status of a minority group within the national community, in this case, that of Catholics in the majority-Protestant Dominion. Though, prior to the introduction of conscription, some observers in New Zealand grumbled that Catholics had not sufficiently 'done their bit' by volunteering in numbers proportional to their eligible population (an inaccurate criticism: Catholics composed about 13 per cent of New Zealand's populace in 1914 and about 12 per cent of the volunteers for the First Division)[92], the specific issue that revealed the country's sectarian fault lines, and led some Protestants to accuse Catholics of 'disloyalty', and some Catholics to accuse Protestants of 'persecution', was the question of conscripting clergy for military service. The Military Service Act did not exempt any clergy, regardless of denomination, from conscription, but instead left it up to local Military Service Boards to grant or reject such exemptions on a case-by-case basis. Given the ecclesiastical laws of their faith, Catholics argued that a blanket exemption from the draft should be granted to their priests, religious teachers and theological students. The government was unwilling to do this, though they did issue 'certificates of exemption' to priests and theological students that they hoped and expected local Military Service Boards would honour. However, some Boards refused to recognize the exemptions, and in early 1917 duly called up a small number of seminary students. Not surprisingly, the Roman Catholic hierarchy and press in New Zealand reacted with almost-universal fury, accusing government officials of colluding with Protestant 'bigots' to deny Catholic rights. This was a charge that might have seemed particularly credible to many Catholics by 1917, given the degree to which the size and political power of militantly pro-Protestant, anti-Catholic organizations had burgeoned since the start of the war. Groups like the Orange Lodge's 'Committee of Vigilance', building on sectarian divisions emerging from pre-war conflicts over government funding for Catholic schools and the perennial Irish Question, and buoyed by wartime papal neutrality and Irish Catholic reaction to the 1916 Easter Rising in Dublin, advanced their own conspiracy theories of collusion between the Government and the agents of Rome to obtain special dispensations for the 'disloyal' Catholic faithful.

Adding fuel to the fire, in the wake of the very vocal and vitriolic Catholic outrage over the conscription of their clergy, Howard Elliot, a charismatic Baptist minister and Orange Lodge leader, began haranguing ever larger crowds throughout New Zealand with virulently anti-Catholic rhetoric and lurid accusations both global (the Vatican started the war) and local (a nun found drowned in Taumarunui was pregnant). In July 1917, at an Auckland rally attended by 3,500 people, Elliot announced the formation of the Protestant Political Association (PPA). By 1919 the PPA claimed 225 branches and 200,000 members. Elliot's techniques of mobilization were classic demagoguery and appealed to the darkest fears and prejudices of his audiences toward the Catholic (and eventually he would expand his condemnation to include 'Bolsheviks' and other 'disloyal' leftists) 'aliens' among them. Not infrequently, his rallies were accompanied by small-scale violence, sometimes directed toward Catholics or associated symbols, but just as often directed by Catholics toward members of the PPA, or even Elliot himself (he was once horsewhipped following a particularly inflammatory speech).

Without a doubt the conscription of clergy issue and the sectarian divisiveness it exacerbated fuelled the explosive growth of the PPA in 1917 and 1918. Each new branch when formed pledged to oppose the 'preferential treatment' of Catholic priests, teachers and theological students. Such a resolution elided the fact that the state's treatment of Catholic clergy was hardly preferential. The Cabinet in April 1917 did suspend the call-up of the drafted seminary students, and did manage to persuade all Military Service Boards to accept certificates that in effect exempted most Catholic priests, teachers and students. However, the Boards had already been inclined to accept most appeals for exemption from any mainstream clergy, Catholic or Protestant. The real difficulty lay in the fact that many Protestant clergy, when called up, felt duty-bound to refuse to appeal for an exemption. This was also true of teachers outside of Catholic schools, a fact which helped scuttle a Bill proposed in September 1917 that would have exempted all teachers, in religious and state schools, from conscription. In the end, the controversy over this particular aspect of conscription in New Zealand, the drafting of Catholic clergy, represented only the most virulent example in that Dominion of the larger tendency of compulsory service to act as an issue that defined and clarified conceptions of collective identity and their relationship to ideals of national or imperial community. As in Canada and Australia, the perceived willingness or unwillingness of various class, racial, ethnic or religious 'outliers' within New Zealand to serve and sacrifice in equitable numbers on behalf of a cause that was sacred for much of the predominant segment of society, on terms largely defined by that predominant segment, acted as a litmus test, or more precisely a loyalty test (or perhaps a test of faith?), to determine their worthiness or unworthiness for inclusion and acceptance within the national/imperial community. During the debate over conscripting clergy, one New Zealand newspaper asserted precisely this when it stated that if the country's Catholics saw themselves as subjects of the Pope before the King, then they were 'to all intents and purposes, Aliens.'[93]

The Wars Over the War: From Conscription to Commemoration

In many ways, the controversy within Canada, Australia and New Zealand over the nature and scale of the Dominions' participation in the war resulted in the extension to domestic politics of the imagery and rhetorical devices characteristic of the propaganda levelled against the countries' battlefield adversaries. As with the war overseas, opponents in the war on the home front in each nation did not hesitate to render the debate in crudely unambiguous terms that offered men and women stark choices between 'good' and 'evil', and that demonised those with contrary viewpoints as 'enemies' of the people. In this hysterical atmosphere born of a widespread sense of unprecedented crisis, attempts to shape public opinion were more often based on exploiting emotion and sentiment (high and low) than on appeals to reason.

While the hysteria of the war years would die down to a considerable extent in the inter-war period, the tendency to engage in what Paul Fussell has called 'gross dichotomizing,'[94] that is, to draw stark and uncompromising lines between one's own position and those of one's opponents, would linger on in the post-war cultural debates about the correct depiction or interpretation of the Great War's meaning. As we will see in the next chapter, this tendency would be less evident in post-war efforts to commemorate the dead through memorials and commemorative ceremonies, as there seemed to exist within the societies of Great Britain, Canada, Australia and New Zealand a general consensus about the appropriate forms and methods of performing this function. However, to a considerable extent, the dichotomising impulse would become more apparent as significant challenges to the interpretation of the war enshrined throughout the Empire on stone monuments or through civic commemoration rituals emerged over the course of the inter-war period. The form and consequences of the debates over the memory of the Great War that would result in all four nations between 1919 and 1939 is the subject of the final chapter.

5

'The Glory and the Sadness'

From the outbreak of the Great War until its end four years later, the men and women of Great Britain, Canada, Australia and New Zealand sought to justify to themselves and to the world the immense slaughter, the vast outlay of resources, and the social upheaval that seemed to be the price of victory. Destruction, loss and suffering endured and inflicted on the scale of 1914–18 had to have meaning beyond the acquisition of territory, the upholding of treaty obligations, or even the preservation of security. As the fighting dragged on and its human and material costs mounted, those who endeavoured in each country to sustain popular support for the war effort increasingly rationalized the conflict's terrible toll as a noble sacrifice in the name of various high-minded and transcendent goals. By the middle of the war, in imperial Dominions such as Canada, Australia and New Zealand, whose homelands remained distant from the principal battlefields and unthreatened by enemy troops, it became less and less satisfactory to justify continued involvement solely in terms of defending the Motherland or ensuring the Empire's survival. Thus, the conflict came to be represented ever more frequently in all three countries as a war to preserve freedom, or to protect 'civilization,' or to 'end all wars.' Furthermore, in the Dominions, these high-minded ideals were supplemented, and to a certain extent overshadowed, as justifications for fighting by narratives which validated the war as a means of achieving respect and status on the world stage, or of building a proud national identity within, or, less frequently, separate from, the British Empire.

For many citizens of Great Britain and the Dominions, the need to rationalize the conflict's terrible cost did not end when the guns fell silent in 1918. Consequently, much of the language and imagery employed with such near ubiquity during the war by those who strove to defend their nation's sacrifice did not by any means disappear from society. On the contrary, the rhetoric and imagery of justification and validation was immortalized in stone on countless war memorials, and rendered in text or on canvas in numerous war-related publications and art works aimed at mainstream audiences.

Recently, scholars have focused a great deal of attention on the development of a 'British' memory of the First World War. Between the late 1970s and early 1990s, scholarship concerning this subject generally followed the lead of Paul Fussell in concentrating on the emergence within the nation's culture of 'modern' forms of literary and artistic expression as a result of individual and collective war experiences. However, since the mid-1990s, a number of scholars, Jay Winter foremost among them, have shifted attention to the continued prevalence of 'traditional' literary and artistic approaches in inter-war British representations of the Great War. Those who, like Winter, see the development of inter-war British memory as being primarily defined by attempts to interpret the events of 1914–18 within traditional frames of reference, criticize their opponents for privileging a modernist perspective that characterized only a very narrow segment of inter-war British culture.

Supporting such criticism is the simple fact that the majority of inter-war British writers, artists and designers of monuments who tried to represent the experience of the Great War were not necessarily impelled to employ 'modernist' forms of expression in favour of more 'traditional' literary and artistic approaches. Indeed, representations of the war that relied upon romantic, religious or classical motifs characteristic of pre-war European culture, and which justified the appalling struggle in terms all-but identical to the more high-minded sentiments that during the war had validated the slaughter, dominated inter-war efforts to depict the conflict.[1]

Thus, during this period in Britain, in terms of the sheer volume of material produced, culturally conservative representations of the Great War far outnumbered avant-garde, or otherwise unconventional, interpretations of the conflict. However, as this and the next chapter will show, this does not necessarily mean that the country's public memory of the war can be accurately characterized as essentially traditional for the duration of the 1920s and 1930s. There is considerable evidence that the established modes of conceptualizing the Great War enjoyed less and less of a hold on the British public's imagination as the inter-war period progressed. The course of this development can, with somewhat broad accuracy, be charted chronologically. The period from 1919 to 1928 witnessed the high-water mark of local and national efforts to commemorate the war dead, which, as we will see, was for a number of reasons an inherently traditional project; at the same time, these years marked the appearance of the first scattered post-war challenges to the status-quo understanding of the war. Between 1928 and 1933, a well-documented wave of books, movies and other types of art, many of which were produced by war veterans, decisively contested the established representations and interpretations of the war. By the years between 1933 and 1939, it was evident that the introduction into the public discourse of the language, imagery and concepts which characterized these works had fundamentally altered the way the war's reality was imagined throughout all levels of British culture, and had generated new understandings of the war's meaning that were well on their way to becoming clichés in their own right by the eve of the Second World War. Of course, this is not to say that characteristically 'traditional' depictions and interpretations of the war did not continue to appear and to find a significant audience throughout the inter-war years. Furthermore, it is all-but impossible to determine conclusively whether this cultural development reflected a genuine change in the attitudes of a majority of Britons, since there were no public opinion surveys or large-scale interviews concerning the subject conducted at the time. However, the fact that the language and imagery employed by those who were imagining and interpreting the war for mainstream public consumption increasingly reflected influences originally identified with modernist or avant-garde perspectives offers compelling evidence that Britain's collective memory of the First World War continued to evolve over the course of the inter-war period.

By contrast, the same generalization cannot be made to the same extent about the collective memory of the Great War in Canada, Australia and New Zealand. The values, ideals and sentiments that during the war had been used to affirm the cause for which so many of the Dominions' young men were dying were duly enshrined on the innumerable monuments and memorials erected from Vancouver to Halifax, and from Perth to Auckland, in the years between 1919 and 1939. However, unlike Britain, Canada, Australia and New Zealand did not witness the appearance of any momentous home-grown cultural challenge to the dominance of the established understanding of the war experience, and of the meaning of that experience for the nation, local communities and individual soldiers. This despite the fact that, particularly in Canada and Australia, there was a publishing boom in war-related books – many of which were authored by veterans – that occurred at roughly the same time as the one which swept Britain. However, this outpouring produced almost no works that provided a counterpoint to the dominant representation and interpretation of the war experience. Rather, the overwhelming majority of Canadian, Australian and New Zealand war books re-inscribed conventional conceptualisations of the conflict's meaning. Those indigenous works that offered an alternative vision of the war and its meaning for Canada, Australia and New Zealand were quickly and forcefully marginalized, as were works from abroad which challenged the idealized understandings of the conflict that prevailed in the Dominions for the duration of the inter-war period. Why the collective memory of the war developed so differently in inter-war Canada, Australia and New Zealand than it did in inter-war Britain is the central question of this and the next chapter.

For Britain, Canada, Australia and New Zealand, the impulse to commemorate their fallen servicemen did not emerge only after the guns fell silent. In all three countries, the war years witnessed a variety of efforts to memorialise the ever-growing ranks of local boys who had been sacrificed to the cause. Such commemoration took many forms – the war not being over, much of it was not designed to be permanent, but there were exceptions. Mass open-air rallies, prayer vigils and church ceremonies, besides providing forums in which to reiterate support for the war effort, also served as sites where the bereaved might take comfort from the condolences and appreciation offered by their communities. Rolls of honour – lists of the community's dead that appeared weekly in local newspapers throughout the Empire, or which were enshrined in schools, churches, workplaces or other public spaces – served much the same purpose. In England, Anglican clergy, with the aid of publicity provided by the press and local businesses, encouraged the erection in many neighbourhoods of simple, inexpensive religious shrines listing the names of parishioners killed in the war. These transitory monuments, popular throughout the country after 1916 when a commercially manufactured version became widely available, served as sites where religious authorities could simultaneously express solace for the grief of their congregations and sanction the necessity of further sacrifices.[2]

Only in Australia were a large number of permanent stone memorials to the dead built before 1918. In all, 60 monuments (out of an eventual total of 1,455 Australian Great War memorials) were constructed throughout the country prior to the Armistice. Britain, Canada and New Zealand, by contrast, produced only a few such examples of precocious commemoration (for instance, only two out of a total of 366 First World War memorials in New Zealand were completed before 1918). In Australia the accelerated memorial impulse stemmed largely from the fact that there was a constant need to drum up recruits to fill the ranks of the nation's armed forces, which remained all volunteer for the duration of the war. The unveiling of monuments in towns and cities across the continent provided local authorities with opportunities to fan the flames of patriotism, and ideally to inspire a few more men to join the colours. Furthermore, by constructing war memorials, particularly in 1917 and 1918, communities overtly demonstrated where their loyalties (or at least the loyalties of the locality's elites) lay in the divisive debates that took place during this period over conscription and the Dominion's continued support for the war effort. Wartime home front battles over compulsory service and other aspects of the country's role in the conflict continued to inform the nature of commemoration in the Australia even after 1918. Australia was the only country in the Empire where it was possible to encounter many memorials to the Great War that not only listed the names of those who died in the conflict, but also those who served and returned (53.5 per cent of Australia's First World War memorials fit this category).[3]

Loyalist sentiments and attempts to generate support for the war largely underlay other forms of commemoration that emerged in Australia and elsewhere during the conflict. Anzac Day, for example, was first observed in many parts of Australia and New Zealand on the first anniversary of the 25 April 1915 landing at Gallipoli. In the case of Australia, Anzac Day celebrations from the beginning and for the duration of the conflict typically provided a platform for recruiting and fund-raising for the war. This was less true in New Zealand, which had instituted con-scription by August 1916. In both countries however, many of the same commu-nity leaders who headed area recruiting and morale-boosting campaigns comprised the local commemoration committees responsible for organizing the activities and ceremonies associated with the holiday. The forms of Anzac Day commemoration were remarkably similar wherever it was observed. The holiday usually began with church services, followed by speeches from local officials celebrating the soldiers of Anzac and the cause for which so many had died. Ceremonies typically con-cluded with a one-minute silence, and, in some cases, a march through city streets by returned servicemen.[4]

In Australia, there was no effort made at the federal level during the war to adopt Anzac Day as a national holiday, though politicians who supported the war, from Prime Minister Hughes on down, glorified 'The Day' and encouraged their countrymen to celebrate it at home and abroad. However, local Anzac Day com-memoration committees were often subordinated to the authority and regulation of State committees, which provided guidelines for the proper observance of the holiday. Many of the State committees also promoted the celebration of Anzac Day in State and Catholic schools, supplying institutions with pamphlets, paraphernalia and guest lecturers intended to inspire young minds to revere and emulate the country's heroes in khaki. Furthermore, members of various State commemoration committees corresponded with one another in efforts to promulgate the holiday as widely as possible, and to ensure some degree of nation-wide uniformity in the observances. [5] In New Zealand, the central government played a somewhat greater role in the movement towards Anzac Day becoming a national observance, declar-ing 25 April a nation-wide half-day holiday in 1916.[6]

Although the celebration of Anzac Day in Australia and New Zealand was by far the most well-organized and firmly established wartime commemorative cere-mony in any part of the Empire during the conflict, citizens in Britain and the Dominions also marked other war-related anniversaries, or invested pre-existing holidays with wartime connotations. For instance, 4 August, the date of Britain's entry into the conflict, was commemorated throughout England as 'Remembrance Day;' that is, until it was supplanted after the Armistice by 11 November as a more resonant symbol. In fact, almost any appropriately solemn religious holiday or suitably patriotic civic festival, from Easter to Empire Day to Trafalgar Day, could be, and very often was, utilized in Britain and the Dominions as an occasion for commemorating the nation's dead and/or validating their sacrifice.[7]

Regardless of the form taken by various examples of commemoration that ap-peared during the war, from temporary or permanent memorials to invented or co-opted traditions, one commonality that almost of them shared is the fact that they were neither conceived nor produced by national governments. Certainly Prime

Ministers, MPs and other national politicians often lent their rhetorical support to the ideal of commemoration, and even to specific commemorative projects such as Anzac Day or street shrines; in this respect they were no different from other influential elites – for instance, certain members of the clergy and the media – whose prominence gave them access to national audiences. However, in Britain and the Dominions most of the public commemoration observed in the course of the war emerged at the local level, and was not subject to centralized legislative or bureaucratic control. That is not to say that they were necessarily 'spontaneous' demonstrations of popular sentiment, though their general popularity and widespread support seems to indicate they were at least somewhat reflective of mainstream public ideals. For the most part, commemorative projects during the war were the brainchildren of community elites, and it was these same local leaders who promoted them to their constituents, congregations or clients, whatever the case may have been, and then oversaw their completion or observance.

After 1918, many of the same individuals responsible during the war for heading community efforts to honour local dead took the lead in campaigns to create permanent memorials in the parks and squares of the cities and towns where they had influence. More often than not, post-war commemoration committees in British and Dominion communities were led by and composed of men and women who had supported their nation's war effort, in many cases having run or participated in local recruiting or fund-raising drives. That does not mean, however, that dissenting elements of particular communities were left completely without a voice in the decisions that were made about commemoration. As Alex King has shown in his comprehensive examination of monument making in inter-war Britain, local memorial commission leaders often sought within their communities the input of individuals and groups representing different segments of society and a wide variety of opinions. Of course, the opinions of some individuals and groups – exservicemen and the bereaved, for instance – typically carried more weight than others. Community leaders generally wanted to avoid controversy in the choice of a war memorial, and used public meetings, representative bodies and local media to hammer out a consensus[8], though this process could in itself be extremely contentious (the chief proponent of a memorial project in New Zealand observed: 'I am satisfied that no subject on earth is more fruitful of controversy than that of war memorials.').[9] In this way, localities throughout the Empire built thousands of Great War memorials after 1918.

It is fair and accurate to say that most forms of wartime commemoration in Britain and the Dominions primarily served the needs of particular local communities. Shrines and ceremonies helped them to cope collectively with feelings of grief and loss, and also reaffirmed the loyalty and commitment of the majority to the cause of the wider community, whether defined as nation or Empire. Thus, such displays often served the purposes of national leaders, by encouraging at the local level support for the war in the form of tangible contributions of men and money, or less-tangible expressions of unity and high morale. However, these projects were neither envisioned nor implemented at the national level, and while much of their power and appeal might have depended on the depth of identification that many local citizens felt with some form of imagined national community – and on the degree to which as symbols these projects successfully expressed this sense of identification – they were generally not intended specifically to reach anything greater than a regional audience. Such would be the case as well for the overwhelming majority of Great War memorials produced during the inter-war period throughout Britain, Canada, Australia and New Zealand. However, one of the most significant developments of the years between 1919 and 1939 in terms of commemoration was the initiation in all four countries of a number of major 'national' projects aimed at memorialising the First World War.

The seeds of some of these projects were planted during the war itself. Almost from the beginning of hostilities, a number of individuals in Great Britain, Canada, Australia and New Zealand pondered the implications of the titanic struggle as a landmark event in the history of their countries, and set about envisioning methods by which some national memory of the struggle might be preserved to educate and inspire posterity. All four countries by the end of 1917 had established special organizations charged with the responsibility of gathering historically relevant records and artefacts related to their nation's role in the war. For Canada, this task was largely divided between the Canadian War Records Office and sections under the control of the Dominion Archivist. The New Zealand War Records section performed a similar function in that country. For Britain, the War Cabinet authorized in March 1917 the establishment of a National (later Imperial) War Museum whose staff was given the duty of collecting war records and battlefield relics to be eventually housed in a space wholly dedicated to the history of the Great War. Australia, for its part, formed the Australian War Records Section in May 1917 with much the same purpose in mind.[10] In Britain, Canada and Australia, these efforts would furnish the exhibits and collections housed in the national war museums created in the aftermath of the 1914–18 conflict. New Zealand would not build such an institution. The Auckland War Memorial Museum, completed in November 1929, emerged from pre-war plans for a city museum that were combined with post-war calls for a memorial to Auckland province's war dead.[11] The finished Museum, with an austere and imposing exterior evoking Classical Greek monuments, and an interior containing a second-floor hall of memories dominated by a wall inscribed with the names of the province's fallen, would serve as both a powerful local memorial (its grounds and the cenotaph unveiled there on the Museum's opening day became the site of the city's Anzac Day ceremonies) and a general history museum in which the

Great War (or any war, for that matter) comprised only a relatively small portion of the exhibits.[12]

Among the Dominions, Canada was first out of the gate in the effort to chronicle and preserve the history of its First World War experience when, in January 1916, Max Aitken (the future Lord Beaverbrook) set up at his own expense the Canadian War Records Office. The CWRO's mission was two-fold: To document and publicize the achievements of Canadian arms overseas, and to systematically maintain a record of Canadian involvement in the war. The initial purpose of the CWRO was primarily to act as a propaganda organ and an instrument of political pressure, but Aitken soon expanded the scope of the organization to include plans for the future commemoration of the Dominion's war effort. It was the CWRO that commissioned Richard Jack's canvas depicting the CEF's 1915 stand at Second Ypres, partly to remedy the dearth of available visual images of Canada's experience overseas, and partly to create a lasting record of what many at the time believed to be a seminal event in the development of the nation. The role that the CWRO played in making Jack's painting possible reflected Aitken's ambitions to sponsor artistic representations of the Great War that might one day comprise a significant collection documenting the Empire's experience in the conflict. It was this goal that underlay Aitken's creation in 1917 of the Canadian War Memorials Fund, an organization specifically devoted to supporting war art produced by Canadians and other members of the British Empire.[13] The record of the CWMF's patronage and its consequences for commemoration in Canada will be explored more fully in the next chapter.

Around the same time that Aitken was setting up the CWRO, the Dominion Archivist for Canada, Arthur Doughty (who would be assigned the honorary rank of Lieutenant Colonel during the war as a way of establishing the authority and credibility he would need in order to carry out his mission) was initiating a scheme to gather documents and artefacts related to Canada's war in the hopes that someday this material would form the collection of a museum solely dedicated to the massive conflict in which the nation was embroiled. After an initial expedition in April 1916, Doughty and two aides returned to Europe in June 1917 authorized by a Government Order-in-Council to carry out a Canadian War Archives Survey aimed at gathering as much documentary evidence and memorabilia related to Canada's role in the conflict as possible.[14] At the time, Doughty expressed the concern that without some attempt to compile and organize the records of Canada's involvement in the war while the Canadian armed forces formed a single 'living organism', future historians would be confronted by a sea of information diffused throughout various individual archives within the country and overseas. Therefore, according to Doughty, 'since the national history of a state is the unit from which a general history must be compiled, it would seem that we cannot too soon begin to prepare for the foundation of a history of our part in the war on an intelligent and scientific basis. This is necessary for our own satisfaction as well as for our own credit.'[15]

In the objective of gathering a large and diverse collection of material, Doughty and his team were remarkably successful. They obtained unit diaries and other documents that had been compiled by the CWRO, gathered information from members of the Canadian armed forces (as well as from members of other nations' armed forces who had evidence relevant to Canadian war activities), and added to their stockpile, initiated on their first mission in 1916, of weapons, armaments, photographs, signs, posters and other war-related relics and trophies. In December 1917 Doughty was appointed Controller of War Trophies, and a year later a Commission on War Records and Trophies was created to manage the staging of several exhibitions throughout North America that featured battlefield relics. The Commission was also charged with overseeing the allocation of derelict weapons and other military artefacts to Canadian localities.[16] The exhibitions, which took place between 1918 and 1919, proved extremely popular, attracting a total of 150,000 visitors in eight major Canadian cities and about 8 million attendees in 12 large cities across the U. S.[17] Furthermore, it seemed as if every metropolis and hamlet in Canada wanted one or more battle trophies to guard the local park or city hall. By December 1919 the captured stores on Canadian soil included 403 field guns, 108 howitzers, 349 trench mortars, 3,861 machine guns, 47 German airplanes and one tank.[18]

Doughty had always envisioned that the final repository of the massive amount of documents and artefacts gathered by the War Archives Survey would be a permanent museum devoted to the history of the Great War. As early as 1915 he had proposed that plans for a new Public Archive building in Ottawa include a wing to house such a museum. In addition, the 1918 final report of the War Archives Survey had concluded by reiterating this idea. However, while the Public (later National) Archives building that was completed in 1925 included a wing for storage of the documents collected by the War Archives Survey, as well as a separate facility built in 1924 to house war trophies, these structures did not represent the museum advocated by Doughty and others. The Commission which had been responsible for cataloguing and disposing of war trophies evolved during the 1930s into a Military Museum Board charged with planning the permanent facility, but the Canadian War Museum did not become a reality until 1942, six years after the death of Arthur Doughty.[19] This version of the museum was housed entirely in the trophies building of the National Archives, and almost immediately the amount of material on display in the relatively small space presented problems of congestion. In 1943 the Canadian War Museum Board wrote to the Canadian Secretary of State and the Minister of National Defense for the Army suggesting that the war museum be expanded. According to the Board, 'The existence of [an extensive public demand for the museum] is proved by the fact that since the Museum's opening – January

19, 1942 – more than 24,000 visitors have flocked to see its exhibits, though there has been no publicity except occasional news items in the local press.' The Board went on to articulate what it believed would be the function of a more ambitious version of the museum:

> A.) As a great national shrine and memorial, commemorating in a peculiarly fitting manner the united contribution of all Canadian citizens, – soldier, sailor, airman or civilian – to the all-out effort in defense of national liberty.
>
> B.) As a repository for the preservation and display of all forms of mechanical skill in construction and production methods, which will be invaluable in the technical education of future generations.
>
> C.) And finally, as a constant and powerful aid in fostering a Canadian spirit of unity, pride and loyalty.[20]

However, the Canadian War Museum would remain in its cramped quarters until it was ceded the entire National Archives building when the Archives were transferred to a new location in 1967.[21]

It is interesting to see that by 1943 the Canadian War Museum Board was promoting the commemorative function of an expanded museum. Doughty had consistently emphasized the usefulness of such a museum primarily as a centralized trove of archival resources and historical treasures that would record the story of Canada's experience in the Great War. There seems to be little evidence that Doughty's vision for the facility centred on the idea that it could also serve as a 'great shrine and national memorial.' Doughty's ideal echoed that of Britain's Imperial War Museum, which opened in London's Crystal Palace in 1920, before moving to an annex of the Imperial Institute in 1924, and to its final home in 1936 at the site of the former Bethlem Royal Hospital (the infamous 'Bedlam' insane asylum – a location whose irony was surely not lost on everyone). However, the fact that the Canadian War Museum Board by the 1940s highlighted the commemorative potential of the institution that they proposed may have reflected an appreciation of the innovative and impressive example of such a facility that had recently opened in Canberra, Australia.

The Australian War Memorial, which was dedicated on 11 November 1941, had no less prolonged a gestation, and perhaps an even more tortuous birth, than the Canadian War Museum. However, the finished product in Canberra represented the fulfilment of a much more ambitious and visionary concept than that proposed by the planners of the Canadian institution. The two individuals most responsible for conceiving and shepherding the Australian War Memorial to its completion were the redoubtable C. E. W. Bean, that figure who seems indispensable to the shaping of Australia's memory of the Great War, and John Treloar, who during the war oversaw the gathering of Australian records and battlefield relics in France, and would go on to serve as the AWM's director from 1920 until his death in 1952.[22]

At the time of its creation, the Australian War Memorial was unique among the war museums of Britain and the Dominions in that it functioned not only as a storehouse of archival records, and an exhibition displaying artefacts and memorabilia, but also as the country's principal national monument to its war dead. It was Bean who first came up with the idea of constructing a single grand edifice that combined the preservational function of a museum with the commemorative purpose of a memorial. He was first convinced of the necessity of a national monument to honour the achievements and sacrifices of Australian troops in the Great War when, in July 1916, he witnessed the men of the AIF withstand at Pozières their first major exposure to the horror and butchery of warfare on the Western Front.[23] In September 1917 Bean wrote an article that was published in several Australian journals in which he referred to the war diaries, photographs, maps, drawings and other materials documenting the Dominion's war as 'sacred records' which must be collected and preserved. This, the article went on to say, was the mission of the Australian War Records Section, which had been established four months earlier under the leadership of Lieutenant John Treloar.[24] The purpose of the AWRS bore much in common with that of Britain's Imperial War Museum and Canada's War Records Office and War Archives Survey, in that it was assigned the task of gathering and organizing documents and artefacts related to the country's war experience with the aim of eventually housing those items in a national museum devoted exclusively to the history of the conflict. The existence of British and Canadian organizations carrying on nearly identical work for their own nations did in fact serve both as a source of inspiration and as a source of rivalry for their Australian counterparts. Competition was particularly keen between the AWRS and the Imperial War Museum for battlefield relics.[25]

However, Bean and Treloar shared the goal of creating an Australian war museum that went significantly beyond in scope and purpose the objectives of similar institutions being planned in other parts of the Empire. In March 1918 Bean wrote to an Australian Senator, George Pearce, recommending that the massive amount of material then being collected by the AWRS be housed in a building located in the future Capital of the Commonwealth (at that time, plans to relocate Australia's federal capital from Melbourne to Canberra were still on the drawing board) that would serve not only as a Great War museum, but also as a memorial to the AIF. Bean outlined his vision of an edifice that would be regarded as 'the finest monument ever raised to any army,' and would include, along with an exhibition gallery and library, a central hall in which the photographs of Australia's war dead would be displayed.[26]

Convincing politicians and the public in Australia to support their ambitious project would be the greatest obstacle for Bean and Treloar as they struggled throughout the 1920s and 1930s to make the war memorial a reality. Although an Australian War Museum Committee had been established in 1917, and had busied itself since then with planning and promoting the proposed institution, it was not until 1923 that the Australian government publicly committed to the idea that the Australian War Museum would also be the national war memorial. This decision was reached not long after the Cabinet rejected suggestions from individuals and groups, including the RSL, to establish a tomb of the unknown warrior as Australia's primary Great War monument. The concept of a museum as national war memorial was not one which government ministers and the general public readily accepted, as it was an innovative idea, and one for which there were few, if any, models elsewhere in the world. Thus, the major work of Bean, Treloar and the War Museum Committee (which became the War Memorial Committee after 1923) involved building interest in the collection that would be housed at the site, and making their case that such a monument would be the most fitting way to honour the memory of the dead.[27]

Between April 1922 and January 1925, much of the Australian War Museum's collection was on display at the Melbourne Exhibition Hall. In its three-year span, a total of more than 780,000 visitors viewed the exhibition. According to Bean, in writing the guidebook for the display, he tried as much as possible to create an environment in which those viewing the collection would be compelled to appreciate the commemorative nature of the museum. Judging from the responses of reporters and others that reviewed the display, Bean was largely successful in his aim. An editorial in the Melbourne *Herald* promised that 'parents of fallen men will go [to the exhibition] in grief and come away in pride.'[28] In April 1925 the Australian War Museum's collection opened to the public in its new temporary home in the exhibition building of Sydney's Prince Alfred Park, where it would remain until 1935. The museum in Sydney proved to be even more popular than it had been in Melbourne. By 1932, over two million visitors had viewed the Prince Alfred Park exhibition.[29]

However, the initial effort of the museum's organizers to bring the collection to Sydney highlights the degree of hostility, which the idea of the institution could sometimes generate. Faced with the War Memorial Committee's request to open their exhibition in Australia's largest metropolis, a number of Labor Party members of the Sydney City Council declared themselves pacifists and recommended that the war museum's collection should be dumped into the Pacific. Such extremist rhetoric energized Labor's opponents in the local press and government, and guaranteed that these forces would unite to ensure that the museum secured a lease on the Prince Alfred Park building. Regardless of the animosity felt by some Sydney community leaders toward the museum, attendance at the exhibition was certainly not adversely affected by the heated debate surrounding its relocation. More than 10,000 people came to see the collection on its opening weekend (which coincided with the Easter holiday).[30]

The Sydney Labor Party council-members' hostility to the presence of the Prince Alfred Park exhibition is interesting because it highlights the fact that a certain degree of ambivalence and trepidation existed within Australian society regarding the message being sent by 'commemorative' projects such as the war museum. While the rhetoric of New South Wales Laborites on the matter may be seen as unrepresentatively radical in relation to mainstream opinion, given their traditional extremism, the Labor left in Australia during the 1920s was in general a powerful and vocal force, with a large and important constituency among the country's working class. The memories of the wartime conscription battles and the 1917 General Strike were still fresh, and the bitter feelings lingered over what many in this camp saw as the establishment's betrayal of democratic freedoms and working-class rights in order to prosecute an exploitative and murderous capitalist-imperialist war. Their understanding of what the war had meant for the Australian working man often induced them to contest what they saw as efforts to commemorate the conflict in a way that they believed re-inscribed the ideas of the hegemonic elites whom they accused of profiting from the subjugation and destruction of so many fellow citizens. One radical Sydney journal, for instance, argued that the war museum's Prince Alfred Park exhibit should show less of the romance and more of the ghastly side of warfare, including the attendant filth, disease and horrific casualties.31

Of course, this is exactly what most non-radical Australians dreaded seeing in a war museum. Their concerns over the message of such a facility sprang from an understanding, often as a result of personal experience, of the grief felt by so many citizens in the wake of the Dominion's tremendous losses. For many, the war was a dark chapter that they wanted to forget; they were leery of exacerbating their own pain and that of others, and they were apprehensive that a museum devoted to the conflict might encourage militarism that could lead to a repeat of the nightmare just ended. An Anzac Day editorial that appeared in a Melbourne newspaper only weeks after the museum's exhibition opened in Sydney summed up this perspective. The lesson of Anzac Day, according to the writer, is that 'there shall be no more war.' He continued: 'And if, because of the horror and suffering and heartbreak of the last great war, our minds are surely set in the direction of peace and loving kindness ... [the Anzacs'] sacrifices will have been justified.'32

Bean, Treloar and the war museum's other supporters were extremely sensitive to all such expressions of concern about the institution's message. They worked hard to ensure that the site's function as a monument commemorating Australia's war dead became paramount in the general public's understanding of the institution's purpose. For example, whenever possible Bean discouraged the use of the word 'trophies' to describe the captured stores and other battlefield mementos in the collection, preferring to employ terms such as 'relics' and 'records'. The museum's defenders often felt compelled to stress the absence of bellicosity in the way such items were displayed, having heard the accusation that their trove of martial tools and spoils of battle glorified war frequently enough to fear that it might turn opinion against them.

On the eve of a Bill being introduced in Parliament in 1925 that would officially establish the museum as Australia's national war memorial, Bean instructed the institution's Acting Director (Treloar was temporarily assigned to duties elsewhere) to keep all references to 'trophies' out of statements to the press about the museum, and to emphasize the fact that the structure would be first and foremost a memorial.[33] In presenting the Bill before Parliament, Senator Pearce called attention to the Hall of Memory, which would list the names of Australians killed on active duty in the war and was touted as the centrepiece of the proposed building. In the words of the Senator, 'standing in that silent hall, surrounded by the names of those who fell and a few of their most precious relics, visitors may, for all time, be impressed with the sense that they are standing in the actual presence of the dead, and realise their larger responsibilities to their memory.' He further declared that other nations had war museums, 'but none ... has been recognized as the National War Memorial of the country in which it exists.' The Australian War Memorial Act passed in both Houses of Parliament by 26 September 1925, without significant debate; one Representative objected to the lack of enlisted men on the War Museum Committee, but there was generally little political opposition toward the Bill from any quarter. In announcing his support for the Act, a Labor Representative declared: 'I do not advocate the establishment of this museum for the purpose of popularizing war; quite the reverse ... It is to be hoped that the exhibits will train the young minds of the future in the paths of peace.'[34]

For the war museum's backers, having it officially declared Australia's national memorial was a tremendous victory, as it assured that the structure would eventually be built. However, formidable obstacles remained for Bean, Treloar and their allies to overcome before the memorial was finally dedicated 16 years after the Parliament ratified its status. None of these barriers to the building's completion were political however, but stemmed from the frugality of the Federal government in the 1920s, and its absolute destitution during the Depression of the 1930s. The Cabinet in 1924 authorized a maximum of £250,000 to be spent on the construction of the memorial. Coming up with an aesthetically pleasing architectural design that could accommodate the ambitious scope and aims of the edifice for such a meagre sum proved exceedingly difficult. In the end, two architects were asked to work together to combine their separate designs for the building into a single structure. Their partnership proved to be an unhappy marriage that led to serious delays in the construction of the museum. A more serious problem was the fact that Parliament in 1928 voted the memorial £50,000 of the funds allotted to it, but only £10,000 could be spent before the Great Depression hit in 1929. Government sources of money immediately dried up, and the memorial was in danger being delayed indefinitely for lack of funds. Only through the ingenious money-raising schemes of Tre-loar to build up the War Memorial Fund was the institution able to continue to finance the planning and construction of the building taking shape in Canberra.35

The Australian War Memorial was finally completed in time to be opened to the public on Armistice Day, 1941, in a ceremony rich with symbolism that achieved heightened poignancy due to the fact that Australia was once again at war in sup-port of the Empire. The opening ceremony began in the morning with the mix of religious and secular observance characteristic of memorial dedications throughout the Britain and the Dominions during the inter-war period. Following a service complete with hymns, prayers and a benediction, and a brief interlude of band mu-sic (during which Catholic dignitaries invited to the ceremony could join the com-pany, having discretely avoided taking part in the religious service, with its objectionably Protestant character), participants observed the Two Minutes Silence at 11 a.m. (announced, as was traditional, with the bugling of the 'Last Post').[36] Two minutes after the conclusion of the Silence, Australia's Governor General, Lord Gowrie, who had won the Victoria Cross in imperial service in 1898 and been seriously wounded at Gallipoli as a major in the Welsh Guards, addressed the as-sembly. The keynote speech of this long-serving British soldier made no mention of the First World War as the crucible of Australian nationhood, nor of the spirit of the AIF as an inspiration to future generations, nor of any of the cherished cli-chés associated with the Anzac ideal. The Great War, according to Gowrie, 'caused universal destruction, desolation and distress without bringing any compensating advantage to any one of the belligerents. It was a war which settled nothing; it was a war in which all concerned came out losers.' Visitors to the Memorial would be led to reflect on the terrible cost of war, and all would 'declare with no uncertain voice, never again, never again.'[37] Such an unambiguous denunciation of the First World War as futile for all concerned was rarely expressed in connection with Aus-tralian commemoration of the war, and perhaps only a Briton could have said it in such a context; Gowrie in fact rejected a speech written for him by the Memorial staff that employed more traditional language and themes to validate Australia's sacrifices.[38]

After a few more speeches by various dignitaries, including the Prime Minister, John Curtin (who, despite being a member of the Labor Party, followed the tradi-tional line in characterizing the memorial as a monument to 'the deeds that helped to make the nation'), the participants were ushered into the building itself. To a certain extent, the intended emotional impact of the structure was muted by the fact that the Hall of Memory was incomplete and the Roll of Honour that would eventually line the walls of the commemorative courtyard was not yet installed. However, the courtyard itself, with its allusions to Classical and Islamic architec-tural styles, offered a dignified and attractive ingress to the part of the museum housing the collection. In these rooms and hallways, visitors could view the weapons, uniforms, vehicles, maps, photographs, paintings, dioramas and other items that were the heart and soul of the institution.[39] In the guidebook printed for the museum's opening, the Memorial staff, adhering to the preferred style of Bean and Treloar, used language that emphasized the sacred nature of the collection. For example, documentary records and material artefacts were typically referred to as 'relics' that were 'enshrined' in the building's galleries and archives.[40]

In its explicitly dual purpose as a national museum and a monument, the Australian War Memorial was unique among the commemorative structures raised to the dead of the Great War in Britain and the Dominions. However, in terms of the emotional responses that the planners hoped to inspire in those who viewed the edifice, in terms of the understandings about the war's meaning that they hoped to convey, and in terms of the themes and imagery that they employed to generate those responses and convey those meanings, Australia's war memorial was entirely consistent – albeit realized on a more ambitious scale than was common – with the social functions and ideological purposes of inter-war commemorative projects throughout the Empire.

In Britain, Canada, Australia and New Zealand, commemoration of the Great War began in earnest after the Armistice. Remembrance, whether at the national or local level, usually consisted of two often-interrelated activities: conducting ceremonies and building memorials. The monuments which became ubiquitous in the city parks and town squares – as well as in many schools, churches and businesses – throughout Britain and the Dominions, provided not only daily reminders of a community's sacrifice, but also symbolic focus points for that community's observances of commemorative rituals and ceremonies.

For Britain, by the end of the 1920s all of the most significant Great War memorials and ceremonies aimed at what were understood to be the national and imperial communities had been established. Armistice Day (also known as Remembrance Day), with its accompanying ritual of the Two Minutes' Silence, had first been observed in Britain and the Empire on 11 November 1919. The first Armistice Day also saw the unveiling of the permanent version of Edward Lutyens' national monument commemorating the First World War, the Cenotaph at Whitehall. The next year's observance of the holiday was marked by the burial of the Unknown Warrior in his Tomb at Westminster Abbey.[41] The most important British overseas monument to their war dead, the Menin Gate Memorial in Belgium, was inaugurated on 24 July 1927.[42]

For Canada, as for Britain, Remembrance Day served during the inter-war years as the premier occasion commemorating the Great War. In Australia, by contrast, Anzac Day on 25 April, after it appeared to be headed for extinction in most parts of the country during the early 1920s, had bounced back by the latter half of the decade to supersede 11 November as the nation's principal memorial observance (as it would in New Zealand as well). Interest in Anzac Day revived in the 1920s largely as a result of efforts by the Returned Soldiers' and Sailors' Imperial League of Australia (RSSILA) and their allies in politics and the media to promote some kind of nation-wide commemoration of the Great War that would uphold the heroic image of Australia's soldiers in order to validate their elevated status (by government policy ex-servicemen were given preference in employment) and perpetuate the loyalist establishment's representation of the war as a moment of national assertion. By 1927 every State in Australia had passed legislation mandating Anzac Day as an official holiday commemorating the Great War.43 The New Zealand government had already declared Anzac Day a national holiday in 1922, largely in response to the lobbying of the country's main veterans organization, the Returned Servicemen's Association.44

Compared to Britain, Canada, Australia and New Zealand were slow to complete their national First World War memorials. For Canada, the Peace Tower, which rises above the Centre Block of the Houses of Parliament (rebuilt after a 1916 fire) in Ottawa was finished in 1927, and the Memorial Chamber, which it houses, opened fittingly on 11 November 1928. It would be another 14 years before the Book of Remembrance containing the names of 66,665 Canadians who died in the country's armed forces between 1914 and 1922 assumed its place of honour upon an altar in the Memorial Chamber. Also in Ottawa, Canada's National War Memorial in Confederation Square was not unveiled until Remembrance Day, 1939. Three years earlier, the North American Dominion's most significant overseas memorial was dedicated on 26 July at Vimy Ridge, in a ceremony attended by thousands of Canadian 'pilgrims' who had made the long voyage across the Atlantic to witness the event.[45]

For Australia, besides the Australian War Memorial, which opened in Canberra in 1941, the Shrine of Remembrance in Melbourne is perhaps the only other memorial on the continent that can be genuinely regarded as a 'national' Great War monument. The massive structure, inspired by the pyramids of Ancient Egypt and Classical Greek mausoleums, was dedicated on Armistice Day 1934 in the presence of 300,000 spectators.[46] Four years later would see the inauguration of Australia's principal overseas monument, located at Villers-Bretonneux in France.[47]

As early as 1919, New Zealand's Parliament voted £100,000 for a national war memorial to be built in Wellington. However, government funding and planning for the project lapsed during the early 1920s. By the end of the decade, largely through the efforts of private citizens, the scheme was revived financially and reenvisioned aesthetically. A combination of government subsidies and private subscriptions would fund construction of the memorial, which was now conceptualised as an 'art deco' carillon tower rising before the new national art gallery and museum that were to be built on the same grounds. In this form, New Zealand's national war memorial was dedicated on Anzac Day 1932.[48]

For the Dominions, the relatively tardy completion of their national memorials by no means reflected any lack of political will power on the part of ruling administrations to carry out these projects. Rather, the explanations for the slow progress of these undertakings usually rested with the practical obstacles imposed by the difficulties of achieving consensus among various interested parties about the design and other characteristics of a 'national' memorial, and by the problems arising from the meagre financial resources available to Dominion governments to devote to such schemes during the 1920s, and particularly during the Depression years of the 1930s.

In Britain, Canada, Australia and New Zealand, it is possible to distinguish distinct commonalties in the language, imagery and motifs almost universally employed to convey the meanings of the national ceremonies and memorials commemorating the Great War. For the most part, these phenomena were consistent with the forms and themes associated with First World War memorials and ceremonies appearing at the local level as well. Examining how meaning was rendered in these commemorative acts, and how men and women articulated their interpretations of that meaning, is useful because it illuminates the interrelated utilitarian and ideological social functions of public remembrance for a given community.

The historian Jay Winter has rightly observed that scholars who focus their attention on forms of commemoration such as memorials or remembrance ceremonies will draw conclusions about the memory of the Great War as it developed in inter-war Britain that are quite different from those advanced by Fussell and others whose evidence comes largely from sources belonging to, or influenced by, the literary and artistic avant-garde. According to Winter's view, rather than responding to the ordeal of 1914–18 by rejecting 'traditional' pre-war ways of articulating and representing phenomena such as war, death, grief and loss, most of those during the inter-war years who tried to express, both literally and symbolically, the collective trauma resulting from the encounter with mass slaughter on an unprecedented scale strove to adapt established language and motifs to the experience, and to incorporate The Deluge into pre-existing narratives of national development and community consensus.[49]

Indeed, during the inter-war period in Great Britain, Canada, Australia and New Zealand the overwhelming majority of national and community war memorials and monuments relied, in their design and in the language used to dedicate them and to represent their meaning, on the forms and sentiments more typically associated with pre-existing cultural traditions than on modes of expression characteristic of inter-war 'modernist' movements. The same generalization can be made for the rituals and speech making related to commemorative ceremonies and holidays.

To a great extent, the conservatism of most projects commemorating the Great War can be explained largely by the fact that they were primarily designed to achieve two inter-connected aims: To provide consolation to the bereaved, and to legitimate the cause for which so many had died. It can be argued that the goal of consoling those grieving the loss of loved-ones in war demands an inherently conservative approach. In order to complete the process of healing and closure essential to overcoming loss, those left behind desire certainty that the one who died (in a death, given the youth of most combatants, that can only be regarded as untimely) did so for a good reason. Commemoration then, becomes first and foremost the act of reassuring the bereaved that this was the case. By paying homage to the dead, the community demonstrates its gratitude and appreciation for their sacrifice, and in this way offers at least some emotional compensation to the victims of loss.

However, as Alex King has pointed out, the critical stance, irreverent perspective and ironic tone characteristic of most modernist art was incompatible with commemoration because it offered no solace; it was, in fact explicitly antithetical to consolation and closure.[50] Samuel Hynes has described the version of the war's meaning presented by writers such as Sassoon, Graves and Owen, or painters such as Paul Nash, Wyndham Lewis and William Orpen, as Anti-Monuments.[51] It is a label that fits the spirit and agenda of these artists' anti-war project, which was fundamentally to *protest* the futile destruction of so many young men whose deaths the organizers of commemoration were seeking to validate. The next chapter will explore the modes of protest in the inter-war period more fully. The rest of this chapter will concentrate on the language and imagery by which commemoration served to validate the sacrifice and loss brought about by the First World War.

It does not require more than a cursory examination of the text, rituals and visual depictions produced in Britain, Canada, Australia and New Zealand during the inter-war period in connection with remembrance of the Great War to discern a fairly direct continuity between the forms and sentiments prevalent in much commemoration and the rhetoric and representation characteristic of post-1916 wartime efforts made by war supporters in all three countries to rationalize involvement in the conflict. For instance, commemorative ceremonies and memorial unveilings, particularly during the 1920s, were almost always marked by appeals from the press and the pulpit to follow the example provided by the nation's fallen soldiers and put aside class and sectarian differences to work to preserve in peacetime the order and stability of the societies that they fought for. A London newspaper in 1919 described the message of the Silence in this way: 'In quiet graves beyond the seas sleep a million British men who paid the price of victory ... It is our duty to see that they did not die in vain, and for the accomplishment of that duty all classes must combine as they did to win the war, unselfishly and harmoniously.'[52] Similarly, an Armistice Day editorial in a Montreal journal in 1927 characterized the cause of Canada's soldiers as 'a crusade ennobling our civilization as it breaks down the stronghold lusts of selfishness, and sets up a new standard of service, fellowship and covenantal [sic.] fealty whereby nations may better live.'[53] A 1922 Anzac Day editorial in the Melbourne *Age* provided a more strident example of this sentiment:

> Miserable strife from Europe has engendered strife among us here. We have been infected by foreign pestilences; always these pestilences have troubled us with vile sectarian wrangles affronting common sense and common decency, and with contemptible political and industrial strife, based on the common greed ... The question of Australians for this day may well be, shall we be tricked perpetually of the inheritance the Anzacs left us?[54]

The inter-war years in Britain, Canada, Australia and New Zealand shared similar domestic political contexts in which the establishments' use of the war dead to sanction their appeals for unity, loyalty and order must be understood. In the immediate aftermath of the war, three of these nations, Britain, Canada and Australia, experienced a high degree of class and sectarian conflict as their economies adjusted to the upheavals resulting from the First World War, and restive marginalized groups, many of whom had experienced a heightened sense of alienation from the ruling power structure as a consequence of wartime policies and attitudes toward them, increasingly challenged the dominance of established elites. Britain was embroiled in the uprising and subsequent civil war in Ireland during the first half of the 1920s, an event whose impact was also felt in the Dominions (especially Australia, with its large Irish-Catholic minority). Industrial strife was endemic in all three countries in the turbulent years immediately after the end of the war. The widespread strikes, riots and other manifestations of labour unrest that characterized Britain, Canada and Australia between 1919 and 1922 gradually waned in the Dominions with the advent of increasing domestic prosperity, but lingered on in Britain before culminating in the General Strike of 1926. Both Britain and Australia were home to a Communist Party by 1920, as were Canada and New Zealand not long after, thereby transforming the threat of Bolshevism from a hypothetical bogeyman into a tangible menace.[55]

The great bulk of inter-war commemoration on the national and local level in Britain, and on the local level in the Dominions, occurred during the 1920s, amidst an atmosphere of heightened anxiety among each nation's elites. While the planners and organizers of most Great War memorials and remembrance ceremonies typically characterized them as politically neutral, most, if not all, such phenomena actually conveyed at least implicit ideological meanings. Commemoration projects provided the men and women responsible for conceiving them and overseeing their completion with opportunities for re-inscribing and reaffirming established national or community values and ideals.[56] Such affirmations were made all the more compelling by the fact that they paid homage to individuals who could be represented as having willingly sacrificed themselves in order to uphold the very values and ideals being exalted. Furthermore, commemoration often served to help sustain or develop the celebratory and unifying conceptions of national identity that had played such an important role during the war in nourishing support for the conflict. These mythologies provided a counterpoint to alternative identities that seemed to many to threaten the cohesion, stability or traditional structure of society.

The conservative functions of memorials and commemorative ceremonies meant that those who were responsible for creating them and carrying them out generally relied on established concepts and modes of expression to convey their meaning. The dominant forms included religious, classical or chivalric motifs and language. However, within this conventional framework there existed considerable room for self-expression. Sir Edwin Lutyens' Cenotaph at Whitehall, for instance, was obviously influenced by classical precedents, but the austere, dramatic monument is difficult to classify. The same can be said of Sir Reginald Blomfield's Cross of Sacrifice, which combined classical, religious and chivalric elements into a single powerful image of a Latin cross rendered as a sleek, downward-pointing broadsword. This design would adorn the gravestones and monuments of the overseas war cemeteries established by the Imperial War Graves Commission. In many ways the Cenotaph and the Cross of Sacrifice were the archetypal examples of Great War commemoration in Britain; they were certainly the most imitated, owing perhaps as much to their notoriety as to their aesthetic merits. Traditional but austere, even stark, they encapsulated the sentiments of many Britons regarding the properly understated approach to commemorating this most terrible of all wars.[57] And not only in the Motherland were these designs popular. Montreal was just one of many cities in the Empire to centre its Remembrance Day ceremonies around a Cenotaph[58], and the Cross of Sacrifice adorns the entrance to the Memorial Chamber of the Peace Tower in Ottawa[59], among other sites.

It is significant to note that, besides avant-garde abstract designs (particularly designs that rely on irony as their dominant motif, deploying images that convey paradox, absurdity, bitterness or despair) certain other types of imagery are almost universally absent from memorials to the Great War in Britain and the Dominions. For instance, one is hard-pressed to find, even in figurative representations, anything evocative of the romantic glorification of war. There are no statues of generals on rearing steeds of the kind one might associate with war monuments of the nineteenth century. To a significant extent this reflects the democratisation of commemoration, underway in the Empire by the time of the Boer War, but established as a dominant trend in the wake of the First World War.[60] Figurative monuments throughout the Empire exalt the common soldier and his apotheosis in the years between 1914 and 1918, but generally not through the romantically heroic or sentimental motifs typical of Victorian depictions of war, and, actually, not atypical of artistic representations of the First World War. For every F. H. Varley who painted the grim reality of dead soldiers heaped unceremoniously in an oxcart, several artists such as John Byam Lister Shaw depicted immaculate corpses draped in flags, and a legion of Alfred Munnings' imagined stirring cavalry charges into the teeth of machine guns.[61] True, there is a horse represented among the figures straining through the arch of the National War Memorial in Ottawa, but it is pulling an artillery piece and conveys the same grim resolve resonating from the human sculptures.

The extreme realism of the figures depicted on the National War Memorial – reflecting an attention to historical accuracy which many who observed its creation demanded right down to the last buttonhole[62] – is not especially uncommon in the figurative statuary of Great War monuments in Britain and the Dominions. What are rare, however, are realistic representations of death. With a few exceptions (the Royal Artillery Memorial in Hyde Park, London, being one of the most noteworthy. This memorial includes the figure of a dead soldier lying on a stretcher, his face covered by a greatcoat. It is remarkably evocative of something one might actually encounter on a battlefield), death is rendered allegorically, and seldom serves as the central motif. Typically it is eclipsed by peace, victory, resurrection or some other hopeful, valedictory theme. Even the Cenotaph, with its ostensible neutrality of message – which Jay Winter sees as analogous to that of Maya Lin's 1982 Vietnam Veterans Memorial in Washington D.C.[63] – fits this pattern. The empty tomb that it represents, with its allusions to the empty tomb of Christ after Resurrection, signifies the hope of immortality as much as it does the centrality of death.

Of course, a memorial's message is not communicated solely through the images that it presents. The language associated with inscriptions, dedication ceremonies and media commentary also provides insight into the meanings that people attach to it. Rudyard Kipling, in his capacity as a member of the Imperial War Graves Commission, chose a passage from Ecclesiastes, 'Their Name Liveth For Evermore', as the inscription to adorn Lutyens' Stone of Remembrance that rested at the centre of each IWGC cemetery. Kipling also composed the inscription that would be carved into the headstones commemorating unidentified imperial soldiers: 'A Soldier of the Great War … Known unto God.' Kipling's role in choosing and creating the inscriptions that would mark the overseas graves of those who died in the service of the Empire was made all the more poignant by the fact that he too had lost a son in the Great War.[64] However, even if this had not been the case, the status of Kipling as the author whose work had most contributed to the mythology of Empire so fundamental to mainstream late-Victorian and Edwardian British identity would have made him a natural choice to express the sentiments of the Empire's citizens toward their war dead. Kipling was also chosen to write the poem read at the ceremony dedicating Melbourne's Shrine of Remembrance, in which he saluted the men of Anzac for 'Having revealed their Nation in earth's sight.'[65] However, it was Australia's premier Great War commander, John Monash, who had composed the monument's inscription, though he would not live to see it dedicated.[66] Its final version, slightly modified from Monash's original lines (which borrowed heavily from Pericles), read:

> Let all men know that this is holy ground. Neither decay nor time shall ruin this Shrine, for it is built, not only in stone, but also in the hearts of men. Therefore, instead of pity, praise. The sacrifice of a nation lies here.

What was written on or about a memorial offered those responsible for the lines a chance to express, perhaps more explicitly than was possible with imagery alone, the values and ideals that the structure was meant to affirm. This being the case, the language associated with First World War memorial inscriptions, and with the speeches and media commentary accompanying dedication ceremonies, was consistent with most monumental imagery produced in the 1920s and 1930s in terms of its conservatism and emphasis on conventional themes and forms of expression. For instance, Australia was not in the inter-war years known to be any more royalist or imperialist in sentiment than New Zealand, but about 16 per cent of the monuments in Australia, and 13 percent in New Zealand, validate the sacrifice of their young men in the name of the 'King', and about 11 per cent in Australia and eight per cent in New Zealand do so in the name of the 'Empire.'[67] Similarly, a 1933 draft of the dedication for Canada's Book of Remembrance read: 'These are the names of those Canadians who, serving in the Canadian and other forces of the British Empire, keeping the faith and remembering the traditions which they had been taught, gave up their lives in the Great War, 1914–1918.' A year later the writer modified the first part of the passage to read, 'Here are recorded the names of those Canadians who, loyal to the crown and to the traditions of their fathers…'[68]

Religion, chivalry, and classical allusions were the preferred motifs of most of the politicians who declaimed upon the meanings of the memorials, as well as of the reporters and pundits who articulated the messages of these structures for their readers. When the Canadian National Memorial on Vimy Ridge was unveiled in 1936, more than 6,000 Canadian veterans and their families journeyed across the Atlantic to witness the event. In the words of a Canadian commentator at the time, they did so 'not as excursionists prompted by curiosity to visit interesting scenes, but rather as worshippers venturing upon a service that inspired within them the noblest elements of their being.' The ceremony's planners referred to these spectators as 'Pilgrims,' and indeed the route of their trip through Belgium and France did resemble a trek through a Great War holy land, complete with CEF equivalents to the Stations of the Cross. The travellers disembarked at Boulogne and then proceeded to Paris, Cambrai, Mons, Brussels, LeHavre, Antwerp and Valenciennes before finally arriving in the vicinity of the front lines at Vimy.[69] There, the Pilgrims could view Walter Allward's massive fortress-like edifice, with its twin pylons towering over the Douai Plain, and perhaps those among them, particularly those returned men who, in the words of one author, 'felt the need … of seeking fresh courage for the battle of life by worshipping at the shrine of the glorious dead,'[70] would find sustenance.

In Britain, Canada, Australia and New Zealand the mainstream rhetoric and rituals articulated and performed at remembrance ceremonies, whether they were connected with the dedication of memorials or with holidays and other similar observances, seemed to comprise the gospel and the dogma of a civic religion. In all four countries, the central feature of this faith was a cult of the dead. The objects of veneration in this cult were the nation's servicemen killed in the war, who, despite their everyman status, had behaved individually and collectively as heroes by willingly sacrificing themselves for the greater good. For those who believed that these soldiers had been instrumental in accomplishing the stated goals of the war their sacrifice represented a triumphant epic. For those who saw the war as an absurd tragedy, however, the soldiers embodied its foremost victims. As we will see in the next chapter, by the 1930s, the ranks of those who held the latter perspective were growing in all four countries.

And while Britain, Canada, Australia and New Zealand all venerated their soldiers in the context of this cult, only the Dominions, particularly Australia and New Zealand, but Canada as well to a lesser extent, placed the returned man at the centre of the commemorative function. Leaders in Britain, by contrast, steadily marginalized veterans, whose politics could be unconventional and whose behaviour could be unruly, from decision making about how the war was to be commemorated. Remembrance in the Motherland became the province of civilians, and increasingly revolved around the bereaved.[71] In Australia especially, Anzac Day became, over the course of the inter-war period, more and more of a soldier's holiday, under the control of the country's major veterans' group (the RSSILA).[72]

The cult of the sacrificed Great War soldier was a powerful inter-war civic faith in Britain, Canada, Australia and New Zealand, but it was particularly prevalent in the Dominions, and its holy scripture took the form of an epic narrative that was unique to the experience of these three countries. As we have seen in previous chapters, many in Canada, Australia and New Zealand during the war perceived or represented the sacrifices and achievements of their soldiers as a 'right of passage' which earned their Dominions newfound status and respect as bona fide nations. One only has to examine the language and imagery surrounding holidays and other commemorative occasions to see that this interpretation of the war's meaning for Canada, Australia and New Zealand survived for the duration of the inter-war period, even if the idea of war itself was increasingly condemned. An Anzac Day editorial in 1919 declared that the Gallipoli campaign 'reminded Australia for the first time of its responsibilities as a young nation … the thousands of men who died in the campaign … did much to ennoble Australia … in the eyes of other nations. They were the envoys not of trade or commerce, but of Australia's manhood and spiritual force.'[73] A 1928 Anzac Day essay from a Brisbane newspaper proclaimed that at Gallipoli 'it was then that Australians were submitted to the greatest test of all – the fire test of courage in hard battle.'[74] On Armistice Day 1931 a Canadian general told a Montreal audience that 'out of the smoke and grime of battle … Canada emerged as a nation with national pride, a national consciousness and a national soul, and although her political birthday was July 1, 1867, her national birthday of full and acknowledged nationhood might well be November 11, 1918.'[75] An observer of the Vimy memorial dedication ceremony in 1936 reported that the keynote of the speakers was peace, but also 'pride in Canada and in the achievements of the Canadian Corps, sorrow for the sacrifice but joy in the spirit that had evoked the sacrifice.'[76] And finally, a Melbourne editorial writer on Anzac Day, 1939, had this to say about the country's mood on the holiday:

Australians are filled with pride, sorrow, gratitude, faith and wonder: the whole gamut of human emotions is awakened to expression as the mind contemplates the glory and the sadness and the misery of those four years of war.[77]

The idea of the war leading to the birth of the nation in Canada, Australia and New Zealand was a compelling narrative, and complemented the sense of national distinctiveness that was growing in each country. As we will see in the next chapter, this increasing sense of national identity and self-esteem in the Dominions could manifest itself in many different forms, and in many different realms, from art to foreign policy, but it had to be respected to some extent by the Motherland, be it through the Statute of Westminster or the small gesture of the King remaining bareheaded during the playing of the hymn (but not yet the national anthem) 'O Canada' at the Vimy memorial dedication.[78]

That said, while the conventional affirming and validating interpretations of the war, with their resonant and comforting traditional language and imagery, were powerful and nearly ubiquitous within the societies in question, there existed nevertheless significant challenges in Britain, Canada, Australia and New Zealand to the status quo understanding of the war's meaning. There were individuals, such as the Halifax editorial writer who wrote in 1919 of the lice, rats, decaying flesh and 'bodies gnawed bare and white' that were a feature of trench life, who had never accepted the euphemism and allegory by which the war's reality was hidden from civilians.[79] Or, to give another example, there were by the 1930s organizations like the Australian Congress Against War and Fascism, which chose to hold anti-war rallies and distribute leaflets in Melbourne the week that the Shrine of Remembrance was being dedicated. 'Give a smashing answer to the plans of humanity's common enemy, the Fascists and war-mongers!' they urged.[80] The nature of the challenges to the established version of the Great War's meaning, and the effect that these salvos against the commemorative project had on the development of the inter-war memory of the conflict in Britain, Canada, Australia and New Zealand, will be the primary subject of the next chapter.

6

'From Failing Hands We Throw ...'

Literary Disenchantment in Britain

In 1922, C. E. Montague, a veteran British journalist who in 1914 had enlisted in the British Army at the age of 47 and served on the Western Front before being invalided back into civilian war work in England, lamented the gulf between the ideals that the young men of Britain fought and died for in the Great War and the reality of the world that existed in the wake of the conflict. Montague listed several of the phrases employed by propagandists (of which he was one, following his return to the home front)[1] to represent the cause for which so much sacrifice had been demanded: ' "The freedom of Europe," "The war to end wars," "The overthrow of militarism," "The cause of civilization." ' He then declared:

> Most people believe so little now in anything or anyone that they would find it hard to understand the simplicity and intensity of faith with which these phrases were once taken among our troops, or the certitude felt by hundreds of thousands of men who are now dead that if they were killed their monument would be a new Europe not soured or soiled with the hates and greeds of old.[2]

The work from which this passage is drawn expresses the *Disenchantment* of its title in terms of a profound loss of faith. For Montague, the war had revealed just how illusory were his beliefs, which he felt he shared with so many others who had volunteered their lives for the country's cause, in the inherent excellence of British values and institutions, and in the capacity of war to generate spiritual renewal in individuals as well as in societies. The conflict had ripped the glamorous facade away from the ugly machinery powering the Edwardian 'bluff' to expose the corruption, malice, cynicism, prejudice, complacency and stupidity in high places that lay at its core. Or, in the words of Montague, 'At the heart of the magical rose was seated an earwig.'[3]

Montague was one of a small, but influential, number of British literati writing during the early post-war period who represented the conflict as primarily a narrative of disillusion and loss. The types of works through which these men and women expressed their interpretations of the war varied: Montague's manuscript was basically an extended essay, rather than a history per se, but it was more or less contemporary with works by H. G. Wells and C. F. G. Masterman, among others, that attempted to place the Great War within the larger context of British (and, in the case of Wells, human) history.[4] Two years before *Disenchantment* was published, the war correspondent Philip Gibbs penned a journalistic exposé of the horrors and futility of the Great War, and John Maynard Keynes wrote a scathing indictment of the peace imposed by the Allies at Versailles. That same year, Colonel Charles Repington published a memoir that chronicled the wartime behaviour of England's governing class at its decadent, cynical, incompetent, Machiavellian worst.[5] Prior to the mid-1920s, few soldiers who had served in the trenches produced accounts of their experiences, and fewer still challenged the then-prevailing mainstream notion of the war as a costly but righteous crusade. Nevertheless, two precursors of the more critical ex-combatant perspective on the war appeared in 1920 and 1919 respectively: a collection of poems by Wilfred Owen, and a novel by A. P. Herbert, *The Secret Battle*, which chronicled the tragic execution of a British serviceman for cowardice. In addition, the years in which many of these works were produced were marked by the publication of several examples of Modernist literature and poetry, destined to become classics, that, even if they did not specifically concern the war as a subject, were nevertheless pervaded by the presence of the war as the event or experience primarily responsible for the altered social, cultural and psychological landscapes that they documented.[6]

While the formats of these particular interpretations of Britain's war experience varied considerably, they typically shared essential similarities of message and purpose. They represented the meaning of the war in a fashion that was diametrically opposed to the consolatory, validating interpretation epitomized by the language and imagery associated with the monuments and commemorative ceremonies that were omnipresent in societies throughout the Empire in the immediate aftermath of the conflict. Where the commemorative project presented an understanding of the war's meaning that affirmed the transcendent ideals that ostensibly inspired so many to give their lives, the narrative of disenchantment offered no such reassuring rationale for the carnage of 1914–18. Writers like Montague represented the war as having achieved little except the physical destruction of men and material, and the spiritual destruction of peoples' faith in the values, assumptions and convictions that had underpinned their pre-war understandings of the societies in which they lived. In addition, where the commemorative project sought to integrate the Great War into the continuity of pre-existing national and local traditions and histories, the narrative of disenchantment emphasized the discontinuity of the world before the war and the one created in its wake.

C. F. G. Masterman declared that 'there is not one good cause which can be said to have been enriched by the murderous operation of this war.'[7] In a similar vein, Philip Gibbs surveyed the economic difficulties and social turmoil that wracked Britain in the immediate aftermath of the conflict and concluded gloomily that 'we won victory in the field and at the cost of our own ruin.' With prophetic foresight, the journalist predicted that, as a result of the war, 'some crash must come, tragic and shocking to our social structure.' He hoped only that the leaders and the people of Britain would respond to this future crisis with more wisdom, and less vitriol and self-interest, than they had to the crisis of the war. He declared:

It is only by that hope that one may look back upon the war with anything but despair. All the lives of those boys whom I saw go marching up the roads of France and Flanders to the fields of death, so splendid, so lovely in their youth, will have been laid down in vain if by their sacrifice the world is not uplifted to some plane a little higher than the barbarity which was let loose in Europe.[8]

For some of the writers expressing a disenchanted outlook, it was already clear that the sacrifices of the nation's soldiers had been in vain. Wrote the American expatriate Ezra Pound in 'Hugh Selwyn Mauberley':

There died a myriad,
And of the best, among them,
For an old bitch gone in the teeth,
For a botched civilization[9]

In all of the works cited above, Britain's soldiers embodied, literally and figuratively, all that the nation had lost as a result of the war. As they were represented in the narrative of disenchantment, it was the fighting men – particularly those who volunteered for service before conscription was instituted in 1916 – who not only symbolized the highest ideals of British society, but who also believed in those ideals most fervently and sincerely. Gibbs wrote that the imagination of the British people would be captivated 'for as long as history lasts' by the vision of the young men who went to the Western Front in 1915–16 'not as conscript soldiers, but as volunteers, for the old country's sake, to take their chances and "do their bit" in the world's bloodiest war.'[10] According to Montague, most of these volunteers were 'men of handsome and boundless illusions.'[11] And, as rendered by the narrative, a great number of these exemplary youth paid for their illusions with their lives, while many of those who survived found that their experiences in the trenches had shattered their faith and trust in British 'civilization' – in those who governed and shaped it, and in the institutions and values associated with it. In the words of Pound:

> Died some, pro patria,
> non "dulce" non "et decor" ...
> walked eye-deep in hell
> believing in old men's lies, then unbelieving
> came home, home to a lie,
> home to many deceits,
> home to old lies and new infamy;
> usury age-old and age-thick
> and liars in public places.[12]

The men who passed through the cauldron of war emerged, if not physically damaged, then spiritually or emotionally seared in some way. 'All was not right with the spirit of the men who came back,' declared Gibbs. Outwardly, and once again in civilian clothes, they looked like the same youth who had gone off to war, 'but they had not come back the same men. Something had altered in them. They were subject to queer moods, queer tempers, fits of profound depression, alternating with a restless desire for pleasure.'[13] Montague also discerned a change in the personalities of those who survived their military service, and attributed this phenomenon to the insights that they gained from the shattering experiences of 1914–18. At the very least, 'the adventure of finding our cooled and solid earth turning ... into a ball of fire under the foot would not have left the state of our minds quite as it had been,' he asserted. He further argued that the mentality of ex-soldiers was even more dramatically transformed due to the fact that 'most of us feel we have pulled through the scrape, scorched and battered, by our own sweat, and not by the leadership of those to whom we had too lazily given the places of mark in that rather childish old world before the smash came.'[14]

Within the narrative of disenchantment, the war played a different role as a historical force than it did within the project of commemoration. Those whose agenda was to affirm and rationalize the sacrifices of 1914–18 represented the war as having been fought either to preserve and uphold ideals and convictions (for example, vague but resonant concepts such as 'civilization' or 'duty') or to generally change the world for the better (for instance, by achieving 'peace' or 'freedom'). By contrast, for the disenchanted, the war had not accomplished any of the high-minded aims that ostensibly justified its horror and bloodshed, but rather had resulted in the pointless slaughter of thousands of youths who believed in the exemplary ideals and values that were hypocritically and insincerely invoked by the 'old men' who sent them to their deaths. The war was thus an agent not of preservation, but of transformation, and the form of that transformation was destruction and loss – spiritual destruction and loss at least as much as material. Faith in the continued march of Progress, certainty in the righteousness of social conventions and convictions, confidence in the superiority of British institutions, trust in the character and abilities of British decision-makers – all of these were shaken, if not obliterated, by the disillusioning experience of the war.

In many ways, the narrative of disenchantment articulated in these years was a critique aimed specifically at British society and culture. However, within this critique, the soldiers of Australia, Canada and other Dominions (as well as the United States) often played an important and consistent role. With striking frequency, writers such as Montague, Masterman and Gibbs represented the Dominion fighting men as embodiments of New World virtues that provided an exemplary contrast to the defects of the Motherland. Masterman described Australians, Canadians and Americans as possessing 'astonishing physical developments, an independence which the whole system of the British Army has discouraged,' and a sense of pride common to the 'great English-speaking races growing up beyond the oceans' in countries characterized by a degree of democracy and equality denied to most in the 'little overcrowded island of cities' that was England.[15] For Gibbs, the Australians and Canadians 'had all the British quality of courage and the benefit of a harder physique, gained by outdoor life and unweakened ancestry.'[16] Montague similarly idealized Dominion troops in a strikingly vivid passage of his own:

> You might survey from beginning to end a British attack up a bare ... slope, perhaps with home troops on the left and Canadian or Australasian troops on the right. You had already seen them meet on roads in the rear: battalions of colourless, stunted, half-toothless lads from hot, humid Lancashire mills; battalions of slow, staring faces, gargoyles out of the tragical-comical-historical pastoral edifice of modern English rural life; dominion battalions of men startlingly taller, stronger, handsomer, prouder, firmer in nerve, better schooled, more boldly interested in life, quicker to take means to an end and to parry and counter any new blow of circumstance, men who had learned already to look at our men with the half-curious, half-pitying look of a higher, happier caste at a lower.[17]

To a remarkable degree, the ideal of the Dominion soldier presented in the works of many disenchanted British literati duplicated several of the themes and images that had been central to the romanticized vision of colonial manhood prevalent in Australian, Canadian and New Zealand culture before and during the Great War. As previous chapters have demonstrated, the conception that the hardy outdoor lifestyle and greater egalitarianism and democracy that supposedly characterized the Dominions produced a breed of men in the colonies who were, on average, superior physically and intellectually to their British counterparts in the masses, was a notion commonly expressed by many in Australia, Canada and New Zealand who sought to articulate distinct Dominion identities and to encourage the development of national pride among their fellow citizens. Such ideas were readily adaptable to the martial context – it required only a short leap of imagination to argue that the same factors that created generally superior men also specifically produced superior soldiers – and during the Great War, the pervasive exaltation of Dominion troops, and the glorification of their exploits, introduced them to wider audiences in Canada, Australia and New Zealand than ever before.

As we will see, the idealized image of the colonial soldier, and the pride engendered by the widespread belief that his outstanding record on the battlefield had won for Australia, Canada and New Zealand new-found status and respect among the nations of the world, served as the primary components of a narrative of the Dominion war experience that during the inter-war period would dominate, in all three countries, mainstream representations of their role in the conflict. Furthermore, this narrative, unlike the affirming interpretation of the British war experience prevalent in that nation's culture during the years immediately following the war, would prove largely impervious to the contagion of disenchantment.

Significantly, the writings of individuals such as Montague, Masterman and Gibbs offer some indication of why this might have been the case. Each of these authors shared a perspective coloured to a greater or lesser extent by Victorian and Edwardian romantic and/or social Darwinist concepts that linked the rise and decline of national status with the condition of a nation's character, or of its 'racial' stock. The narrative of disenchantment presented a vision of Britain in decline – a decline that was either brought about, or exposed and exacerbated, by the war. The Dominion soldiers, who were perceived as fitter and smarter than the average British fighting man, both highlighted the flaws of the society that produced the sub-par Tommy, and symbolized the qualities that would one day allow the 'coming men' from the New World to ascend to supremacy over the Old World's degenerated civilization.

Cultural Nationalism in the Dominions

The contrast that the narrative of disenchantment drew between the social and cultural decay that the war had supposedly revealed or accelerated in Britain (and by extension, Europe), and the health and vigour of colonial societies that these countries' athletic, independent fighting men embodied, accorded in many ways with prevailing intellectual and artistic currents within Australia, Canada and New Zealand during the 1920s. As far as can be discerned, no writers in either Dominion produced works in this decade that shared the sense of post-war disenchantment expressed by Montague, Gibbs, Masterman and other British authors. On the contrary, the cultural scenes in Australia, Canada and New Zealand (to the extent that such a scene existed there in the 1920s), were dominated by a surge in nationalist sentiment. The forms which this nationalism took varied considerably in each country, depending on the specific agendas of those who promulgated it, but as a prevailing outlook, it characterized a cross-section of Dominion culture ranging from mass entertainment to the avant-garde.[18]

The 1920s in Canada and Australia, and the 1930s in New Zealand, witnessed concerted and systematic efforts by writers, artists and other members of each country's cultural establishment to generate interest in, and improve the quality of, the literary and artistic output of the nation. In the Dominions, those who shared these goals sought to define and represent in prose, verse or on canvas the distinctive features of Canadian, Australian or New Zealand society and identity, and to promote appreciation and respect for the literature and art of the Dominions at least somewhat comparable to that enjoyed by the British (and in Canada, American as well) works that still dominated markets and imaginations from Toronto to Melbourne and Wellington. There was nothing particularly new about this agenda, as previous chapters have shown. What was different about the 'cultural nationalism' of the interwar period in the Dominions from its antecedents in the late-nineteenth century was the extent to which a growing 'high cultural' scene in each country exercised a disproportionate influence on the nature and direction of this project.

In the case of Canada and Australia, the Great War seldom specifically served as a subject of those literary and artistic works associated with the nationalist outlook that were produced in these countries during the 1920s. Nevertheless the conflict did function as a significant catalyst for the emergence of these movements, primarily as a result of the pride and confidence engendered in the Dominions by their performance in the conflict, and the disaffection with the British and European 'civilization' responsible for the horrors and carnage of 1914–18. In New Zealand, by contrast, there appear in the first decade after the war only isolated examples of what might be regarded as self-conscious 'cultural nationalism', largely due to the general lack of an audience for home grown writing and art, and to the dearth in the country before the 1930s of supportive cultural institutions and infrastructure. Thus the direct impact of the First World War (as opposed to the Great Depression) on the formation and exploration of New Zealand identity as expressed within the inter-war culture is somewhat more difficult to discern for that Dominion than for Canada and Australia. However, the experience of the Great War visibly informs, or hovers meaningfully in the background of many of the seminal works associated with the emergence of a New Zealand 'national' culture. While painting and other forms of representational art reflected these trends in all three Dominions no less, and perhaps even more, than any other artistic field, for now the discussion will focus primarily on developments in literature and poetry, first in Canada and then in Australia and New Zealand.

Canada merits foremost consideration because cultural nationalism, as a comprehensive project within the arts establishment, seems to have been pursued there during the 1920s relatively more energetically than it was in Australia (or, obviously, in New Zealand) at that time. Three of Canada's premier twentieth-century literary magazines were founded in the first decade after the war. In the material that they printed and reviewed, the *Canadian Bookman* (1919–39), *Canadian Forum* (1920–) and the *Dalhousie Review* (1921–) focused on the developing arts scene in Canada, exercising toward their subjects a degree of discrimination and judgement that varied from the *Bookman*'s unabashed boosterism to the more balanced, critical perspective of the *Forum* and the *Review*. The post-war nationalist impulse in Canadian arts and letters also led in 1921 to the founding of the Canadian Authors Association. Through a variety of means, including literary prizes and lecture tours, the CAA – together with its official organ, the *Bookman* – strove to promote Canadian literature, sometimes without regard for the quality of the works being touted, so long as they were produced by Canadians.[19]

Compared to the years before 1914, the inter-war period did in fact witness a significant surge in the number of novels, short stories, poems and non-fiction published and read by Canadians. The majority of these made no attempt to treat specifically 'Canadian' subjects. For instance, most fiction of the 1920s and 1930s could be classified as generic romantic escapism. However, even escapism during this time increasingly reflected the cultural preoccupation with Canada's identity, as a growing number of authors chose to set their adventure stories in the Far North or West, and their historical romances in old Quebec or the Canadian prairies. 'Regional idylls,' that is, novels or short stories that celebrated the customs, values and landscape of a particular Canadian locality, also continued to experience the popularity they had enjoyed since the turn of the century.[20] Before the war, the Canadian humorist Stephen Leacock had thoroughly summed up the spirit of this genre in his preface to *Sunshine Sketches of a Little Town*, which was published in 1912. According to Leacock, the book was inspired by 'a land of hope and sunshine where little towns spread their trim maple leaves beside placid lakes almost within echo of the primeval forest.'[21]

The spirit of optimism, romance, and above all, hope, symbolized by Leacock's passage largely characterized the Canadian literature and art of the 1920s that was, more systematically than ever before, imagining and celebrating the landscape and character of the nation. For the most part, in this project there was room neither for the pessimistic, critical perspective, nor the innovative methods, associated with avant-garde movements in Europe and the United States. In fact, the critics and other members of the Canadian cultural establishment who promoted nationalism within the arts often explicitly emphasized the degree to which works produced by Dominion writers and artists avoided the offensive subject matter and 'decadent' styles that they correlated with European and American modernism. One critic asserted in 1926 that the Canadian poet was 'instinctively a romantic,' and that for some time to come Canadian literature 'will provide a refreshing haven of genuine romanticism to which the reader may retreat when he seeks an antidote to the intellectual tension imposed by the future progeny of [T. S. Eliot's] "The Waste Land" and [Edgar Lee Master's] "Spoon River".'[22] This same critic praised John McCrae's 'In Flanders Fields' as the 'single poem of highest importance' in Canadian literature.[23] The authors of a 1924 survey of English-Canadian literature declared that it was axiomatic that 'verse and prose rise to the dignity of literature when they express and promote existence ideally – by delighting the aesthetic senses, by consoling the heart, by inspiring the moral imagination, by exalting or transporting the spirit.' On the basis of this conservative premise they also lauded 'In Flanders Fields' as 'the supreme lyric of the world war.'[24]

Of course, not every Canadian writer was hide-bound by the traditional romantic conventions that dominated the cultural scene in the 1920s. For example, a number of Canadian poets embraced the influences of innovative European and American works, and produced exemplary verse that marked the appearance of characteristically 'modern' poetry in the North American Dominion. Particularly important in this regard were the poets A. J. M. Smith, F. R. Scott, Leo Kennedy and A. M. Klein, who edited and contributed to two short-lived but highly influential Montreal literary journals, the *McGill Fortnightly Review* (1925–27) and the *Canadian Mercury* (1928–29). Beyond the Montreal group, E. J. Pratt began in the 1920s his long and distinguished career as one of Canada's most original and accomplished poets, and by the end of the decade, Robert Finch and Dorothy Livesay were publishing innovative verse as well. Among Canadian novelists, the 1920s saw the publication of several works of realistic fiction and social criticism. Jessie Sime's *Our Little Life* (1921) was the first novel ever to realistically represent contemporary working-class life in a Canadian city (in this case, Montreal). In addition, writers such as Frederick Philip Grove, Martha Ostenso and Robert J. C. Stead presented unromantic depictions of life on the Canadian prairies. Stead's novel *Grain* (1926) offers one of the earliest examples in Canadian fiction of a protagonist whose response to the call of duty in the First World War is less than heroic.[25]

The arts in French Canada during the inter-war period in many ways provided a mirror image to their English-Canadian counterparts. The literature and poetry produced by French-Canadians in these years was by-and-large just as traditional and nationalist as that of English-Canada, but the form of nationalism represented in French-language works differed considerably from that espoused by English-Canadian writers. Just as the First World War had heightened many English Canadians' sense of having a distinct national identity, and encouraged them to see a role for Canada as a global power-player commensurate with its elevated national status, the conflict between English and French Canadians after 1916 over conscription led a number of the country's French-speaking intelligentsia to embrace a nationalism centred on maintaining Quebec as a French-Catholic nation in North America.[26]

This variety of nationalism was exemplified in French Canadian novels from the 1920s, such as Abbé Lionel Groulx's *l'Appel de la Race* and Jean-Charles Harvey's *Marcel Faure*, that demonized English Canadians. The conservatism that prevailed within French-Canadian arts and letters was reflected in works like Adélard Dugré's *La Campagne canadienne* (1925) and Harry Bernard's *La Terre vivant* (1925), which idealized the simplicity and piety of rural Quebec's inhabitants as exemplary contrasts to the decadence of modernity. However, like the English-Canadian poets and novelists who rejected the stultifying conventions that they believed kept the country's arts mired in mediocrity, a number of French-Canadian writers produced works that demonstrated their openness to influences emanating from the avant-garde in Europe and the United States. For instance, poets such as Robert Choquette, Simone Routier and Alfred Desrochers, whose verse was published in the progressive Montreal literary journal *Le Nignog*, employed styles, tones and themes similar to those found in works by some of the English-speaking Canadian modernists with whom they shared a city, but not a dialogue.[27]

However, Canadian authors and poets whose works reflected cutting-edge sensibilities, regardless of whether they wrote in English or French, definitely found themselves during the 1920s on the margins of the cultural scene in the North American Dominion. The dominant movement in these years was a celebratory, uncritical nationalism, and its primary – and most popular – purveyors were those individuals who expressed its ideals through traditional styles and subject matter. Given this fact, it is perhaps not surprising that the most successful Canadian writers during the first decade after the Great War continued to be the handful of men and women who were already established prior to 1914 as the Dominion's most popular and critically lauded literary figures. Best-selling novelists such as the adventure writer Ralph Connor (C. W. Gordon), Lucy Maude Montgomery (author of the Anne of Green Gables series) and Nellie McClung, along with poets such as Robert Service, Charles G. D. Roberts and Bliss Carman, had before the war set the standards for romanticized representations of Canada's land and people, and their status as the nation's pre-eminent literary luminaries remained unchallenged well into the post-war period.[28]

Turning attention now to the largest Pacific Dominion, it is easy to discern within Australia during the 1920s a number of literary and artistic currents very similar to the ones that were shaping Canadian culture in this decade. In Australia, as in Canada, the battlefield achievements of the AIF between 1914 and 1918 engendered among many citizens a sense of pride in the distinguished reputation won by their fighting men, and encouraged an optimistic outlook regarding the Dominion's future as a nation. At the same time, the perception that Britain's performance in the war had been comparatively lacklustre, and that the pathologies of modern European society had brought about and prolonged the conflict, spurred many Australians to express profound disillusion with British and European civilization and to turn inward to explore their own identity, with the goal of developing their own potential in isolation from the contagions emanating from the Old World. Vance Palmer, who enjoyed a long and distinguished career as one of Australia's most celebrated and influential poets of the twentieth century, articulated this sentiment shortly after returning from military service overseas. He wrote:

Europe is very old,
It has known wars and death,
The live past stirs within its mould,
Yet chill cometh its breath.
Pensive, subtle, profound,
It broods in secret prayer,
While dreams of dead men underground
Trouble the heavy air.

Palmer contrasted the gloomy, sepulchral atmosphere of Europe with the vibrant, radiant land of hope and promise awakening in the Antipodes. He declared:

I will go south and south,
There Life has scarce begun,
And lightfoot, with a laugh on its mouth,
Plays butterfly in the sun.[29]

Along the same lines, Zora Cross, an Australian poet who lost a brother in the war, lamented in 1921 the fact that so many idealistic young men of the Dominion had died for their love of the Motherland and received in return only 'England's cold, brown kiss.'[30]

Disenchantment, as far as it existed in Australia during the 1920s, was directed almost exclusively at Britain and Europe. The most important Australian literary movement of the decade involved the founding of the journal Vision by the writer Jack Lindsay, his artist/novelist father Norman, the bookseller Frank Johnson and the poet Kenneth Slessor. These individuals, who saw themselves as members of the creative vanguard in Australia, explicitly rejected art characterized by the jaded alienation and dense, pretentious imagery that they labelled the 'stigmata of Modernism.' They argued that, with the avant-garde in Europe enchanted by the decadent sensibility of Eliot, James Joyce and their disciples, the duty of the avant-garde in Australia was to initiate a new movement that relied on classical European forms, animated by the youthful vigour of the Australian environment, to create aesthetically beautiful, cultured art. The members of the Vision school were not nationalists in the conventional sense, given that they also rejected what they called 'Australianism' – that is, the romanticization of even the most banal qualities associated with Australian life, and the gratuitous glorification of the Australian vernacular and idiom. However, they did believe that Australian society and culture, which had not yet been debased by the degenerate intellectual movements and social forces operating in Europe, could serve as an incubator for a new artistic movement that might inspire and elevate the human spirit to transcend the miasma of modernity. As Lindsay put it:

> It is short-sighted Nationalism that can be proud only of verse about shearers and horses, and measures the reality of a work by its local references. If we wish to express an Australian spirit, let us make that spirit worth expressing by adding to it all the stimulus of sensuous and lyric imagery we can, by creating beauty so that the general consciousness may be further vitalised ... If a Cleopatra can be created in London, she can be created in Sydney ...[31]

In rejecting both the influence of the European (and American) avant-garde, and the traditional Australian nationalist project, the artists associated with Vision were attempting to paddle simultaneously against the prevailing cultural currents overseas and at home. Not that they had any need to be overly concerned about the inroads made by modernism on the Australian cultural landscape. As in Canada, Australia's war experience energized and advanced trends existing prior to 1914 that celebrated and romanticized the Dominion's land and people in the interest of solidifying among its citizens a unifying sense of national identity and an inspiring sense of national pride. Also similar to what occurred in Canada, the war, particularly the domestic turmoil associated with the issue of conscription, revealed for Australia the gravity of the class and ethnic cleavages threatening the cohesion of its society. The primary components of the nationalist project, as it existed in post-war Australia, emphasized ideals and aspects of life in the Dominion that suggested the unity, rather than the divergence, of experience. The Australian cultural scene in the 1920s, like that of Canada in the same decade, was dominated by idealizations of the Dominion's landscape and environment – facets of daily existence which were shared by all citizens – and by celebrations of essential 'national' traits, habits and qualities.[32]

The development of the visual arts in Australia and Canada during the 1920s epitomized these trends in the Dominions. In Australia, Melbourne's premier art museum, the Victorian Gallery, purchased in 1920 its first painting by a member of the Heidelberg School, a group of artists who had been active in the Dominion since the 1880s. The ranks of the Heidelberg School (named for a suburb of Melbourne where many of the artists were based) included Tom Roberts, Arthur Streeton, Frederick McCubbin and Charles Conder. In their work they strove to capture the distinctive qualities of the Australian landscape, and to represent the everyday pursuits and typical character of ordinary Australians. They eschewed the tendency of earlier artists to depict Australia's soil, trees and shrubs in the green and pleasant hues of England, and instead tried to render the distinctive blues, yellows and reds of the Antipodean environment in a way that would seem familiar to most of its residents. Similarly, Roberts, McCubbin and other members of the Heidelberg School contributed to the emerging mythologies of the 'Australian type' with their idealized compositions of sheep-shearers, cattle-drovers, bushmen and other quotidian figures. In the first decades after their appearance, the artists belonging to the Heidelberg movement encountered some hostility toward their work from within the Australian artistic establishment, many of whom remained convinced of the inherent superiority of European styles and subject matter over work that aimed to capture distinctly Australian images. However, by the 1920s, not only was the Heidelberg School institutionalised within the pantheon of high-culture in the Dominion, as the Victorian Gallery's aforementioned 1920 purchase of a canvas by Tom Roberts indicates, but European émigrés painting in Australia during this decade, including Elioth Gruner and Hans Heysen, captivated the general public and wealthy patrons alike with works that reflected themes and styles consistent with those often associated with the Heidelberg School.[33]

In Canada, an artistic movement similar to Australia's Heidelberg School cohered during the inter-war period around several artists known as the Group of Seven. Most of the members of this circle, which included James E. H. MacDonald, Lawren Harris, A. Y. Jackson, Fred Varley, Frank Carmichael, Arthur Lismer and Frank Johnston (who left the Group in 1924, to be replaced by A. J. Casson. Edwin Holgate and Lemoine Fitzgerald joined in the early 1930s), began their collaboration before the First World War. Four of the original seven – Lismer, Johnston, Varley and Jackson – served between 1914 and 1918 as official war artists commissioned by Max Aitken's Canadian War Memorials Fund, the entrepreneur's ambitious scheme to provide a record of the Great War on canvas and in sculpture. The individuals from the Group of Seven were some of the few Canadian artists commissioned by the CWMF (most of those working under its auspices were British), a situation that led to criticism of the organization in the Canadian press and from groups such as the Royal Canadian Academy of Art and the Ontario Society of Artists.[34] Nevertheless, the experience provided through the CWMF profoundly influenced the development of the Group of Seven's aesthetic. For those who served as war artists in France and Flanders, the bleak, battle-scarred landscapes of the Western Front increased their appreciation of the barren wilderness areas of northern Ontario, and provided them with a new palette of muddy brown, yellow ochre and cool grey hues that they would employ to great effect in their renderings of Canadian panoramas. Furthermore, exposure to the modernist styles of British artists working for the CWMF, including the painters William Orpen, C. R. W. Nevinson and Paul Nash, influenced the visual approach, if not the subject-matter, of several of the Group's members. For instance, two paintings that would become iconic of the Group's aesthetic, Lawren Harris' Above Lake Superior and A. Y. Jackson's First Snow, clearly show the impact of Nash in their form and composition, with their barren moonscapes rendered in sombre-hued, starkly vertical and horizontal lines.[35]

The Group of Seven's inaugural exhibition opened at the Art Museum of Toronto in May 1920. There, they outlined their vision for creating a distinctly Canadian art, one whose meaning was accessible beyond the salons of the cognoscenti, and that reflected the vitality and rugged beauty of the young nation. Their project had the stated aim of facilitating the development of national feeling among the Dominion's populace, and its appearance on the cultural scene coincided with, and contributed to, the post-war surge in Canadian national self-confidence and self-awareness. No artistic movement of the inter-war period more effectively channelled the era's prevailing cultural currents, and Canadian critics, along with the general public, largely responded to the Group of Seven with unabashed enthusiasm. Those few critics who panned the Group played into their hands by allowing the artists to portray themselves as embattled progressives confronting the enmity of the conservative cultural establishment. In truth, Canada's cultural establishment, along with many wealthy patrons, and much of the populace as a whole, supported the vision of the Group as an embodiment of what many hoped was an awakening national consciousness.[36] It is no coincidence that the paintings selected by Canada and Australia as their contributions to the 1924 British Empire Exhibition held at Wembley in London, the first major showcase in the metropole to display art from Britain and all the Dominions alongside one another, were dominated by the Group of Seven and the Heidelberg School respectively.[37]

The generalizations that can be made about Australian and Canadian cultural output during the 1920s can also be applied to New Zealand, though it is more difficult to describe a New Zealand 'cultural scene' in this decade. Without a doubt, however, the overwhelming majority of fiction, poetry and art produced in New Zealand at the time conformed in its subjects, themes and styles to the prevailing works in other Dominions that infused their otherwise conventional examples of storytelling, verse or visual representation with language and imagery distinct to their colonial setting. However, compared to the other Dominions, the amount of even such 'middlebrow' material created by and for New Zealanders was relatively sparse. To a much greater degree than was true in Canada and Australia, New Zealand before the 1930s lacked the supporting infrastructure of literary journals, publishing houses, art galleries and art patrons so essential to the development and promotion of an indigenous cultural scene. Therefore much of what issued from New Zealand writers and artists, whether it was the typical middlebrow fare or the more rare examples of modernist or cutting-edge literature and art – for example, the short stories of Katherine Mansfield, or the paintings of Frances Mary Hodgkins – was produced and published or exhibited outside of the country, and in many cases aimed for exposure beyond the limited audience of the small island Dominion. Though fewer in number, the most common art forms in New Zealand during the 1920s generally conformed to the decade's dominant forms in Canada and Australia: generic escapist fiction and conventional poetry or representational art embodying a descriptive, consensus, unifying understanding of 'national' identity. While a number of writers and artists in these years turned a critical lens on New Zealand society, or sought to render the Dominion's landscape, environment and people in original ways, they remained relatively isolated examples of innovation. What was almost entirely absent in New Zealand in the 1920s, as opposed to Canada and Australia in that decade, were the kind of self-conscious cultural movements to create a 'national' literature or artistic style in a way that reflected or confronted the experimental, modernist trends emerging in Europe and the United States. New Zealand's cultural scene would be transformed in the 1930s by the appearance of such movements.

In literature, this development was facilitated enormously by the creation in the early 1930s of two seminal New Zealand literary journals, *Phoenix*, short-lived at just four issues that were published in 1932–33, and the longer-running *Tomorrow* (1934–40). In its first issue, *Phoenix* declared: 'We are hungry for the words that shall show us these islands and ourselves; that shall give us a home in thought.' In an article in one of *Tomorrow*'s first issues, one of its founding editors, Frederick Sinclaire characterized New Zealand as 'a land of dreadful silence' in which 'no one says anything, in which no one is expected to say anything,' and challenged the magazine's readers to help invigorate the country's dormant cultural life. Like the *McGill Fortnightly Review* and the *Canadian Mercury* in Canada, or *Vision* in Australia, *Phoenix* and *Tomorrow* (along with the Caxton Press, established in Christchurch in 1932–33) provided a New Zealand forum for that Dominion's vanguard of writers and poets.[38] What appeared in the pages of these magazines, whether it was poetry by R. A. K. Mason, Allen Curnow, A. R. D. Fairburn and Charles Brasch, or fiction by Robin Hyde (whose 'Starkie' novels, *Passport to Hell* [1936] and *Nor the Years Condemn* [1938] contain episodes set during the First World War that, in their tone, style and imagery echo many of the characteristics associated with the anti-war canon emerging in Europe and America at the time) and Frank Sargeson, reflected the influence of innovative currents from overseas, but consciously applied its artistry to the project of defining 'New Zealandness' and scrutinizing and criticizing the society and 'national character.' Though such criticism from these writers could be excoriating, and their exploration of some of the more negative aspects of New Zealand society often engendered disapproval from the mainstream public, they nevertheless contributed to the prevailing cultural atmosphere in New Zealand in the 1930s of national self-assertion and self-discovery.

Developments in the visual arts in New Zealand reflected this general environment of self-conscious cultural awakening as well. Though no discernible national 'school' equivalent to the Group of Seven emerged in New Zealand during the inter-war period, a number of individual painters there produced works that revealed goals similar to those of their counterparts in Canada. New Zealand-based artists such as Christopher Perkins, John Weeks (like some members of the Group of Seven, both were First World War veterans) and Toss Woolaston endeavoured to represent the distinct features of New Zealand light and landscape through the application of 'modern' styles and techniques. During the inter-war years, this generally constituted an oeuvre reflecting the influence of European impressionism and expressionism, rather than the more avant-garde abstract experimentation and socialist realism that, by the 1930s, was already establishing a significant presence in the art scenes of Canada and Australia.[39]

By the 1930s in all three Dominions, as these countries like most of the rest of the world endured the social and political upheavals stemming from the Great Depression, the prevailing middlebrow, consensus version of cultural nationalism experienced unprecedented challenges from vanguard writers and artists inspired to render a more critical and complex understanding of Canadian, Australian or New Zealand society and identity. Many of the complacent, orthodox idealizations of these colonies as 'lands of hope and sunshine' were assailed as never before, and a harsh light shined for the first time on the flaws and dysfunctional elements of each society. However, though such critiques encompassed a myriad of topics, from economic inequalities to racial and gender discrimination, none of the Dominions witnessed in this period any widespread and influential effort within their culture to contravene the conventional interpretation or representations of the country's First World War experience comparable to that which emerged in Britain in the 1920s and, as will be discussed, gathered steam there at the end of that decade and the beginning of the next. In Britain the war experience was no less fair game for critical re-examination or innovative depiction than any other aspect of society in that period, but this was generally less true of the Dominions. There, the social criticism and artistic experimentation that characterized the 1930s took place in the context of a continuing cultural project of national self-exploration and self-expression, albeit one that now was often less unambiguously celebratory and more penetrating and sophisticated. Within this landscape, works that posited disenchantment or disillusion as the overarching sentiment emerging from the war experience often seemed alien and false to men and women who encountered them, even those who were relatively sympathetic to more 'realistic' depictions of the warfare and conditions that typified the setting. This partially explains why not only the disillusioned compositions produced in Britain, Europe and North America, but also the comparably few such works similar in style and tone coming from Dominion authors and artists, generally received receptions in Australia, Canada and New Zealand that ranged from icy to virulently hostile. Typically, critics and commentators who dismissed disenchanted representations of the war did so primarily on the grounds that they insulted or distorted the image of the nation's fighting men. Claude H. Weston, in the Forward to New Zealand veteran C. A. L. Treadwell's 1936 memoir *Recollections of an Amateur Soldier* praised the book for offering an 'antidote' to accounts that 'describe the effect of war upon the abnormal soldier.' In the words of Weston:

> From the reception of a certain type of war book one would imagine that the reaction to the circumstance of war by the few square pegs in round holes among the troops engaged finds a responsive harmony in its readers. But that kind of book misses the high spirit of the majority of our soldiers... whose mind and heart and soul saw the braver side... in the end the good soldiers found a serenity and gaiety that were as pure gold... No wonder that most ex-servicemen find it hard to be impressed by the Pacifists' wholesale condemnation of war; they cannot forget the steel in which their mates were forged even at the price of going through the flame. They can think of no process by which men are so purified...[40]

In Canada, Australia and New Zealand, the idealization of their fighting men from the Great War as almost sacred symbols of the nation's most sterling qualities, laudatory achievements and enormous collective sacrifice provided perhaps the most formidable obstacle to any widespread acceptance of the interpretation and representation of the war experience that characterized the 'disenchanted' perspective.

Mobilizing the Symbol of the Soldier in the Dominions

For Canada and Australia in the 1920s, cultural nationalism, together with the project of commemorating the war dead, provided a unifying ideal at a time when the societies in both Dominions found little else around which to build consensus. New Zealand saw comparably greater domestic tranquillity during this period,[41] but for Canada and Australia the first three years after the war especially were marked by a continuation – or even, in some cases, intensification of the social and political unrest that had characterized the Canadian and Australian home fronts from 1916 to 1918. In Canada, labour union membership had grown from 143,000 in 1915 to 378,000 in 1919. The swelling ranks of organized labour were increasingly militant as well, as they fought to keep industrial wages in line with the country's soaring cost of living, and agitated against restrictive government policies aimed at curbing the power of unions. Industrial strife, particularly acute in the western section of the country, culminated in 1919 with the Winnipeg General Strike, which shut down the city for over a month, and resulted in clashes between protestors and police that left one worker dead. Labour discontent was not the only source of division in these years. The war left various segments of society feeling alienated from the prevailing power structure: most obviously, French Canadians, but also, many Canadian farmers expressed growing dissatisfaction in the latter years of the war with the policies of the 'old-line' political parties that did not satisfactorily address their primary concerns. The grievances of the agricultural sector led by 1920 to the formation of a third political party, the National Progressives, that specifically represented the interests of the country's farmers, and that would offer a significant challenge – until the middle of the decade, at any rate – to the traditional dominance of the Liberal and Conservative parties. Many observers of Canadian society in the early 1920s might have agreed with the historian O. D. Skelton's bleak assessment at the time that Canada could no longer expect to remain immune from the ills being suffered by 'older civilizations.'[42]

Many of the same forces that were inspiring political turmoil and social unrest in Canada between 1919 and 1921 acted in Australia to make these years turbulent ones in that Pacific Dominion as well. Industrial strife had been endemic there in the last two years of the war, and 1919 saw more working days lost to strikes than any previous year in Australia's history. Several cities witnessed violent clashes that year between workers, police and strike-breakers (many of whom were returned soldiers), and Brisbane and Fremantle both briefly experienced something resembling open warfare between the forces of labour and their opponents. The divisions between rural and urban Australia were deepened as well by the war, much as they had been in Canada. The response of Australian agricultural interests was very similar to that of their counterparts in North America: In January 1920, members of the House of Representatives who represented rural electorates formed the Australian Country Party, which would remain a powerful political force for a much longer time than the Progressives did in Canada. During the inter-war period and beyond, the Country Party consistently aligned with the conservative parties opposed to the Australian Labor Party, which resulted in anti-Labor majorities at the federal level of government in all years but two during the 24 years between 1917 and 1941 (which contrasted with governments below the federal level, where Labor was at least competitive in most states). Finally, tensions between Irish Catholic Australians and the Protestant majority escalated between 1919 and 1921, largely due to Irish-Catholic anger at the brutal response of the British government to the violent unrest convulsing Ireland in these years. St. Patrick's day in Australia became an opportunity for both sides to hurl slurs at one another in the press, and on the street. Irish Catholics held massive demonstrations against 'British tyranny', and one Irish politician was expelled from Australia's Parliament for making remarks harshly critical of British policy.[43]

In both Canada and Australia, the turbulence of the early 1920s would give way by the middle of the decade to a state of tense, but relatively calm, political and social stability. Economic prosperity had more or less returned to both Dominions, and the class, sectarian, ethnic and regional divisions highlighted by the war years and their immediate aftermath, while not gone, and certainly not forgotten, were largely contained, as Canadians and Australians turned inward to focus on exploiting their potential for material growth, and on creating through their culture an identity worthy of their national aspirations. The groups that enjoyed political and cultural hegemony within the societies of the Dominions – English-Canadians in Canada, white Protestants of British heritage in Australia – promoted conceptions of national identity that constructed universalised ideals of the 'true Canadian' or the 'dinkum (real) Australian.' And more often than not, these were ideals that did not challenge the ruling establishment's claims to hegemony. There existed no more compelling Canadian or Australian ideal type of this sort than the Great War soldier.

The image of the Canadian or Australian First World War soldier represented in the art, literature and media of the Dominions during the 1920s typically restated the stereotypes of this figure that had emerged during the war out of even older idealized conceptions of colonial manhood. For example, Archibald Cameron MacDonell, a former CEF commander, wrote in a 1921 issue of the Canadian magazine Queen's Quarterly an article describing the average Canadian enlisted man whom he encountered on the Western Front to be 'splendidly cheerful, brave to a fault; ready to risk themselves for a friend; chivalrous, resourceful and full of initiative ... like knights of old.' MacDonell suggested that these traits were not common to all soldiers in every army, at least not to all enlisted men. Rather, they reflected the qualities that characterized men who, like those that served in the CEF, hailed from democratic societies, and came of age in a healthy, invigorating environment such as Canada's. According to MacDonell, the lesson for Canada and all democracies of the CEF's outstanding performance in battle was that 'a country of free men, engaged and proficient in the countless occupations of civil life, is always potentially formidable in war.' Furthermore:

> The Canadian soldier comes from a country of magnificent distances, large rivers, vast forests, broad lakes and lofty mountains. He is a man with fine traditions behind him ... He comes from people who for over 150 years have striven to preserve their individuality ... All this helps to build up a strong virile manhood such as our people proved they possessed on the Western Front.[44]

In Australia, no single representation of the First World War 'digger' did more to enshrine that figure as an icon within the nation's culture than C. E. W. Bean's official history of Australia's participation in the conflict, the first three volumes of which were published between 1921 and 1929. As has been discussed in the previous chapter, Bean's work reached an extraordinarily large audience for an official history, thanks to the ingenious subscription scheme conducted by John Treloar in order to raise money for the Australian War Memorial. Thus, many Australians might have been impressed as they read these lines assessing the performance of the nation's soldiers at Gallipoli:

> Long before the end of this great battle the Australian soldier had revealed ... what manner of fighter he was. He had not yet the astonishing mastery of the soldier's craft which marked him in 1918. But he had scattered to the winds ... the notion often reiterated, that an Australian force would be ineffective through lack of discipline.

However, in Bean's view, it was not discipline that explained the Australian fighting man's success. Rather, the secret of the 'diggers'' prowess lay in 'the mettle of the men themselves.' Bean continued:

> To be the sort of man who would give way when his mates were trusting to his firmness; to be the sort of man who would fail when the line, the whole force, and the allied cause required his endurance; to have made it necessary for another unit to do his own unit's work; to live the rest of his life haunted by the knowledge that he had set his hand to a soldier's task and had lacked the grit to carry it through – that was the prospect which these men could not face. Life was very dear, but life was not worth living unless they could be true to their idea of Australian manhood.[45]

For McDonell and Bean, the sterling qualities which made ordinary Canadians and Australians excellent fighting men might be innate within most colonial males by sheer virtue of the environment in which they were reared, but there was no question that it was the test of war that had brought them to the surface, and indeed revealed them to the world. In this sense, according to the message implicit in this logic, the war had served a positive function – perhaps its only positive function – by triggering the kinds of sublime virtues and exalted standards of heroism and self-sacrifice that largely lay dormant in civilian life. In the words of one Australian newspaper, the lesson of Gallipoli lay in the fact that 'there is a high courage in mankind that needs but great occasion to make it manifest, so that overnight, common men are transfigured, and life itself ... becomes as nothing in the hour of people's need.'[46] This was a theme that would appear time and again in mainstream

Canadian, Australian and New Zealand interpretations of the war's meaning for their countries. As an ideal, it stressed the ordinariness of the nation's fighting men, who only became paragons by virtue of their choice (a particularly compelling aspect of the theme in Australia, which maintained its all-volunteer army for the duration of the conflict) to lay their lives on the line for some cause greater than themselves, whether it was their civilization, their nation, or their fellow man. The individuals who died in this act served as objects of veneration, and as lessons in civic virtue, for those left behind. The soldiers who survived their ordeal earned an exalted status (at least in theory) as exemplary citizens within the democracy.

For the purposes of forming in Canada, Australia and New Zealand the central component of unifying myths of national achievement and self-assertion, the Dominions' dead soldiers were amenable to their appropriation. The living proved more problematic. Rhetorically, it was easy to celebrate the returned servicemen as not only embodiments of all that was best about Canadian, Australian and New Zealand manhood, but also as symbols of the glorious future that awaited the young Dominions if their citizens followed the example set by the unity and self-sacrifice of the countries' fighting men.[47] In reality, many politicians and commentators in the Dominions viewed returned soldiers with great trepidation as potential sources of future unrest, or as ticking time bombs of pent-up aggression. Upon the end of hostilities, governments in Australia, Canada and New Zealand initiated repatriation schemes that provided disability pensions to wounded veterans, settled many soldiers as farmers on tracts of land provided by the state (or also, in the case of Australia, granted them funds to start their own small businesses), and, in some instances, awarded limited gratuities for war service. In Australia, the Commonwealth and most state governments legislated that military veterans were to be granted preference in public service employment, and many local councils and some private employers also adhered to this policy of special consideration in the hiring of returned men. With the various efforts to compensate and provide for the welfare of ex-servicemen, not only were Dominion governments acknowledging the debt that society owed to the soldiers who had made such sacrifices for the common good, they were also attempting to pre-empt possible domestic turmoil growing out of veterans' discontent. Officials in all three countries contemplated with dread the prospect of legions of angry, unemployed and potentially lethal ex-soldiers suddenly demobilized and unleashed on the home front.[48]

During the turbulent first three years immediately after the war, many veterans in Canada and Australia did seem to be bearing out the worst fears of authorities over the potential of ex-soldiers as a destabilizing influence within society. Returned men played prominent roles on both sides of the barricades during the labour and sectarian clashes that characterized this period in the Dominions. In Canada, veterans led anti-labour and anti-immigrant riots in Vancouver and Toronto in 1918, and in Winnipeg and Halifax, among other cities, in 1919. During the Winnipeg General Strike, ex-soldiers demonstrated in the ranks of labour protesters and served in the ranks of the Royal-Northwest Mounted Police who rode them down.[49] In Australia during these years, the role of ex-servicemen was equally as prominent, and equally as ambivalent, as in Canada. Veterans among the striking workers in Fremantle used combat tactics learned in the war (along with revolvers and home-made bombs) to fend off police.[50] Two months earlier in Brisbane, a mob of several thousand citizens that included many returned men, spurred on by red baiting in the local press, had attacked radicals and members of the city's Russian community. In the week of violence that followed this initial clash, some veterans briefly banded together in a paramilitary 'Army to Fight Bolshevism.' This Australian version of a German Freikorps petered out along with the violence in Brisbane, but some saw its existence, however brief, as an ominous sign nevertheless.[51]

Opponents on either side of the ideological fence in Canada, Australia and New Zealand during the inter-war period strove to sanction their causes by linking them to the potent symbol of the soldier. As one of the few figures within the societies of the Dominions for whom genuine veneration was all-but universal across class, sectarian, ethnic and other dividing lines, the symbol of the soldier could prove a particularly poignant and compelling rhetorical device for those who sought to mobilize support for a particular ideological position. For instance, a radical left-wing Australian journal in 1930 used the image of the downtrodden 'digger' to highlight the gravity of social injustice in the country during the Great Depression. The editorial writer lamented that the men who 'went 12,000 miles to make Australia a place to live in, are down to bedrock, and have to loaf about the streets in order to obtain shelter from the rain. It is a sorry spectacle of civilisation, Christianity, and the glory of war...' The consistent image of the Great War soldier as represented by the Left in Canada, Australia and New Zealand during the inter-war period, particularly during the 1930s as the deprivations resulting from the Depression led to renewed class conflict and social unrest in all three nations, was as a victim of capitalist exploitation who had paid the price for his naive idealism in blood and suffering while profiteers and the ruling class reaped the rewards of his sacrifice. In the words of the aforementioned editorial, in the 'dreadful aftermath of the war ... The bugle no longer sounds, and the swashbuckler has no use for the slaves of jingoism ... the profiteer has filled his coffers, and now is hatching fresh schemes of exploitation by which he can accumulate more wealth at the expense of [the workers].'[52]

However, in inter-war Canada, Australia and New Zealand, the First World War soldier, both as a symbolic figure and as a flesh-and-blood constituent, was typically associated with political conservatism. Of course, cohorts as large and diverse as those comprised by Australian, Canadian and New Zealand veterans of the Great War cannot be accurately characterized as monolithic in their political ideologies. There were many examples of ex-soldiers in all three countries who embraced radical leftist ideologies, and a great number, particularly in Australia, who were active in trade unions before and after the war. However, the efforts of conservative forces in Canada, Australia and New Zealand, led in many cases by individuals associated with the loyalist establishments in these countries, to recruit veterans to their cause, and to harness the ideal of the soldier to their message, were much more systematic and energetic, and in the end proved more successful. It stands to reason that many ex-servicemen were inclined toward conservative perspectives in the first place, given the fact that most of them (all of them in Australia) had volunteered to fight, which was often a supreme act of loyalty in and of itself, and that the Left in all three Dominions had, to a greater or lesser extent, opposed the loyalist factions in power during the war. However, conservatives in inter-war Canada, Australia and New Zealand employed various tactics to ensure that the returned serviceman, and the ideal of national identity that he represented, was definitively associated with loyalist interpretations of the war's meaning for the nation, and with the preservation of the social status quo. In Australia, during the worst years of the Depression crisis, this agenda briefly led to the formation of a few extremist right-wing paramilitary organizations composed largely of ex-soldiers that resembled, on a much smaller and more localized scale, the Fascist black-shirts and brown-shirts active in Italy and Germany at the time. The New Guard, formed in July 1931 in New South Wales, and estimated two months later to have a membership of 36,000 in Sydney alone, was one such movement. During its brief existence (it had largely disbanded by 1935), members of the group harassed communists and other 'radicals' throughout New South Wales and Victoria, violently breaking up Communist Party meetings and in some cases forcing communists to flee various communities en masse. In December 1931 a contingent of New Guardsmen attacked a communist meeting in Ballarat; after physically assaulting several Party members they consigned communist literature to the flames while singing, 'Keep the Home Fires Burning.'[53] However, as dramatic as such extremist movements were in enlisting ex-soldiers to the cause of embodying and preserving the loyalist status quo in Dominion societies, they were relatively rare and their political impact was limited at best. The same could not be said of each country's dominant veterans' organizations, the most powerful and effective tools that loyalist establishments had at their disposal for mobilizing ex-soldiers to their banner.[54]

By the end of the Great War, Canada had seen the establishment of several different veterans' organizations of various ideological hues, ranging from the imperialist Army and Navy Veterans (ANV), to the conservative Great War Veterans Association (GWVA), to the more progressive Grand Army of United Veterans (GAUV), to the ultra-radical Soldiers' and Sailors' Labour Party. Of these, the largest and most prominent organization was the GWVA. In 1920 the association boasted 857 branches with an estimated 200,000 members. Its magazine,

The Veteran, reached 70,000 paying subscribers. Although its membership would decline over the course of the decade, the GWVA remained powerful enough to engineer, by 1927, its amalgamation with most rival veterans' groups into a single organization known as the Canadian Legion (the name of the magazine changed to *The Legionary*). In its constitution the Legion banned membership by Anarchists, Communists and 'any other person who advocates the destruction of ordered government in Canada.' Over the course of the inter-war period the Legion would achieve the goal of its leaders in becoming the recognized national movement of Canadian ex-servicemen, with influence in the circles of power largely denied to whatever veterans' organizations remained outside of its umbrella. As a result, the Legion would serve as a powerful advocate for government policies benefiting ex-servicemen. In addition, the Legion would play an important role in promulgating the establishment narrative of the war by becoming the driving force behind national commemoration projects such as the Canadian Memorial at Vimy Ridge, and by lending its influential voice to the chorus of opinion that shaped public reception to interpretations of the Dominion war experience that challenged the mainstream version.[55]

New Zealand's Returned Services Association (RSA), established by 1916 as the primary national organization representing the Dominion's veterans, and with a membership by 1920 of 57,000 out of a total of 80,000 returned soldiers, also proved a formidable advocate for its constituents and served as the driving force behind efforts to commemorate the war's dead and to honour and reward its survivors. Though the RSA never exercised the kind of stark political power prophesied by one commentator in 1918 who assured readers of the organization's journal Quick March that 'some day not far distant, [the RSA] will control a hundred thousand votes at least,' its influence as a pressure group was considerable on the national and local level.[56] As we have seen, the RSA was central in establishing and promoting the rituals associated with Anzac Day in New Zealand. They, more than any other single group, also ensured that the landing would be commemorated on April 25 as a national holiday and moreover, observed as a 'holy day', with hotels, racetracks, theatres, shops and other businesses closed along with schools and government offices. Even during the mid-1920s, when the membership of the RSA dropped below 7,000, its lowest point during the inter-war period, the organization remained vital in shaping national and local commemoration. The Auckland War Memorial Museum, completed in 1929, was just one such project in which the input of the RSA decisively determined how a given community would symbolically represent and interpret the meaning of its collective sacrifice. In that example, as in most others, the RSA presented itself as the advocate not just of ex-soldiers, but also of their loved ones and dependents, including those left behind by the fallen.[57] Such advocacy was greatly appreciated during the Depression, which saw the organization's membership surge above 30,000 once again. An additional factor in the revival of the RSA in the 1930s may have been its spirited defence of the conventional understanding of the First World War's meaning for New Zealand, and of the revered image of the country's fighting men. Responding in 1935 to isolated condemnations of Anzac Day and calls for its abolition from members of New Zealand's nascent and relatively miniscule Pacifist movement, the RSA vowed to combat 'to the utmost' any attempts to do away with the holiday.[58]

In Australia, the country's dominant veterans' organization, the Returned Soldiers' and Sailors' Imperial League of Australia (RSSILA) – which had absorbed all of the Dominion's other veterans' groups by 1918 – achieved an even more total monopoly of access to Commonwealth policy-makers than that enjoyed by the Canadian Legion or New Zealand's RSA. The Australian government after 1918 officially recognized the RSSILA as the sole representative of returned soldiers. It was awarded a seat on all Federal repatriation committees, and was one of the few organizations granted the right to lobby the Cabinet.[59] In return the RSSILA was given a mandate to contain radical elements among returned soldiers. The RSSILA embarked on this mission first within its own ranks: By 1919 most of the organization's most vocal left-wing members were muzzled or expelled. The RSSILA, like the Canadian Legion, cast itself as a non-partisan organization, and avoided direct participation in electoral politics. However, the loyalist worthies of a given community established most RSSILA branches, and prominent ex-officers who had become businessmen or professionals generally filled State and national leadership posts. And while the organization might have officially renounced direct participation in party politics, it was steeped to the gills in support of the loyalist power structure. During the turbulent years in Australia immediately after the war, even as conservative politicians and members of the establishment media demonised radical 'diggers' by associating them with the menace of Bolshevism, RSSILA branches were not above supplying the 'muscle' to physically enforce the power structure's efforts to maintain 'law and order.' By 1919, the RSSILA listed 167,000 members on its rolls – a higher proportion of returned servicemen than belonged to comparable veterans' groups elsewhere in the Empire and in the United States – and essentially had no rivals in the power that it wielded to influence Australian government policy regarding the country's ex-soldiers. Consequently, perhaps, Australia's veterans enjoyed an officially sanctioned privileged status unsurpassed anywhere else in the British Empire. The preference given to servicemen in hiring was the cornerstone of this privilege. The fact that it had been obtained – and that it continued to be safeguarded[60] – by the RSSILA, ensured that during the dark days of the Great Depression the rolls of the veterans' organization remained full of grateful ex-servicemen.[61] Therefore, to cite one example, when the Federal Executive of the RSSILA recommended in 1930 that Erich Remarque's anti-war novel *All Quiet on the Western Front* should be banned in Australia, it proved to be far more than a symbolic gesture.[62]

The War Books Boom in Britain and the Dominions

Of course, those who most determined the principal themes, images and language by which the Great War was represented, and its meaning interpreted, within the inter-war cultures of Great Britain, Canada, Australia and New Zealand would naturally be the soldiers themselves. Personal narratives of the war that were produced by former combatants could be expected to attain a level of authenticity, legitimacy and poignancy unavailable to civilians, but there was a dearth of such accounts in all three countries for most of the 1920s. With a few exceptions, ex-soldiers during these years remained silent about their experiences in the conflict. That silence would be shattered suddenly, first in Britain and then in the Dominions, by a cacophonous barrage of novels and memoirs penned by ex-servicemen that broke upon the cultural scenes of all four countries at the end of the 1920s and the beginning of the 1930s. Most of the personal narratives written by Dominion veterans share certain superficial similarities with most of the accounts produced by ex-soldiers from Britain. Besides the similar timing of their publication, many British and Dominion narratives recount a similar war experience (almost all of them were written by men who served as infantrymen on the Western Front), and the authors all hail from countries that share broad similarities of culture and heritage. However, there are significant differences between the styles, tones and motifs that characterize the overwhelming majority of personal narratives written by ex-soldiers from the Dominions, and the modes of expression and themes that distinguish a sizeable, and disproportionately influential, number of the works produced by British veterans.

Though an absolutely precise periodisation is somewhat artificial, one can chart with reasonable accuracy the beginning of the British war books 'boom' at around 1926–27, about three or four years before it began in the Dominions. In Britain, the wave crested in 1929, whereas it peaked in the Dominions around 1933. Given this chronology, it seems appropriate to discuss the British war books first. Some of the best-known and best-reviewed works produced during Britain's 'boom' included Herbert Read's *In Retreat* (1926), Edmund Blunden's *Undertones of War*, Siegfried Sassoon's *Memoir of a Fox-Hunting Man* (both 1927), Ford Madox Ford's *Parade's End* (1928), R. C. Sherriff's play *Journey's End*, the English translation of Erich Maria Remarque's *All Quiet on the Western Front*, Robert Graves' *Good-bye to All That*, and Richard Aldington's *Death of a Hero* (all 1929). These works, many of them by authors whose literary ambitions pre-dated 1914, rendered the experience of war into narrative with a skilful artistry that captured the imagination of critics and the public. According to scholars such as Paul Fussell and Samuel Hynes, these manuscripts did more than any others to help fix the prevailing conception of the British war generation's martial experience in the nation's imagination.[63]

When one surveys this literary outpouring after the nearly decade-long draught that preceded it, an obvious question is, why did it occur when it did? On the surface, it might seem that for any articulate former soldier, the experience of fighting on the Western Front in the First World War would lend itself to immediate and unproblematic conversion into narrative. Nothing could be further from the truth. So extraordinary was the drama played out on those muddy killing fields that it seems to have long-boggled the creative faculties of many of these writers. In the 'Preliminary' to Undertones of War, Edmund Blunden described his own difficulties in depicting, objectively and accurately, the reality of what he lived through in the trenches:

> I tried [to write the novel] once before ... But what I then wrote, and little enough I completed, although in its details not much affected by the perplexities of distancing memory, was noisy with a depressing forced gaiety then very much the rage ... And I have been attempting the "image and the horror of it" ... Even so, when the main sheaves appeared fine enough to my flattering eye, it was impossible not to look again, and to descry the ground, how thickly and innumerably yet it was strewn with the facts and notions of war experience.[64]

Along the same lines, Richard Aldington described the war as an 'incommunicable' experience.[65] Perhaps it is also the case that events in Britain and the world, combined with the fact that 1928 marked the ten-year anniversary of the Armistice, inspired a retrospective mood among these ex-combatants. After all, the peak of the war books wave in Britain coincided with the collapse of the world economy, the enfranchisement of women on equal terms with men, and the election of a second Labour government. If nothing else, these developments might have decisively convinced some observers that the war had fundamentally changed their world, and that England's old ruling order was dead forever.[66]

The dark common thread that winds its way through all of the classic British war novels and memoirs is the theme of loss: Loss of men, loss of innocence, loss of illusions, loss of order, loss of values and loss of hope. Even the war's successful conclusion for the Allies does not mitigate this central motif. Victory is only another occasion for bitter irony. For example, in Good-bye to All That, Robert Graves declared that news of the Armistice sent him 'walking alone along the dyke above the marshes of Rhuddlan ... cursing and sobbing and thinking of the dead.'[67]

Besides the theme of loss, there are other common aspects of tone, style and content in the works of Graves, Sassoon, Blunden and the other British war authors. For instance, combat and death are never portrayed as glorious or heroic. More often, combat is represented as bewildering, absurd or anti-climactic. Death is depicted as, at best, banal, at worst, bestial and ghastly. Technology is ugly and unnatural, but it rules over men on the industrialized battlefield. The home front is alien and decadent, and soldiers who return there during the war soon long again for the front. Finally, the war is a crime being perpetrated by the 'Old Men' of the establishment who are willing to sacrifice England's young warriors on the altars of greed and hate.[68]

The motifs and sentiments that appeared in these British ex-soldiers' war novels and memoirs echoed in many ways the perspective articulated by the men and women who produced the British narratives of disenchantment in the early 1920s. Like Montague, Masterman and Gibbs, the war authors sought to express protest and lamentation, as opposed to consolation and validation. They made common cause with the narrative of disenchantment in their consciousness of all that had been lost, and in their anger and sadness over the waste of it all. Perhaps the major difference between the war authors (or more accurately, the anti-war authors) and the disenchanted literati of the early 1920s was that the ex-soldiers, writing at the end of a decade that had not shown the world to be a better place in the wake of the war, were even less hopeful about the future, whether it was theirs or Britain's. Referring to the post-war world, Ford Madox Ford's hero in Parade's End declares: 'There will be no more parades ... There won't, there damn well won't ... No more Hope, no more Glory, no more parades for you and me any more. Nor for the country ... nor for the world, I dare say ...'[69]

This passage conveys the idea that the world before the war, the one of parades and capitalized ideals like Hope and Glory, became little more than a memory after the guns fell silent. From Ford's novel, to Good-bye to All That, to Sassoon's Memoirs of a Fox-Hunting Man, there is a clear dichotomy drawn between the time and place in which the author existed before the conflict and the one that he inhabits afterwards. Between the two realities, the war experience lies like a great, gaping fissure.

Significantly, all of the authors listed above who published war books during the British 'boom', with the exception of Remarque who served in the German army, served as junior officers in the infantry of the British Army on the Western Front. All of them were volunteers as well.[70] Chapter One discussed the implications of this experience, in terms of the disproportionately high casualties that junior officers suffered as a result of taking a leading role on the battlefield, and in terms of how the feudal ethos that guided the behaviour in battle of the upper and upper-middle-class men who comprised their ranks commingled with the lethality of modern warfare (and, the anti-war authors would add, the incompetence, greed and callousness of the 'Old Men' who ran the war) to create a formula for their destruction. In many cases, the result, at least intellectually, for the members of this cohort who survived this ordeal was to be left bereft of the romantic notion that immutable traditions, noble virtues, breeding and conviction could inoculate them against the dark forces of modernity. They too could be brutalized and slaughtered, and their sterling qualities as individuals would not save them. In a review of All Quiet on the Western Front, the soldier-novelist Herbert Read wrote:

No idealism is left in this generation. We cannot believe in democracy, or socialism, or the League of Nations. To be told at the front that we were fighting to make the world safe for democracy was to be driven to the dumb verge of insanity. On a mutual respect for each other's sufferings we built up that sense of comradeship which was the war's only good gift. But death destroyed even this, and we were left with only the bare desire to live, although life itself was past our comprehension.[71]

The perspective of these British war authors provides a stark contrast to that found in the majority of novels and memoirs written by ex-soldiers from Canada, Australia and New Zealand. Most of the Dominion authors were veterans of the same experience of industrialized warfare on the Western Front that so disillusioned many of their counterparts in Britain. However, with a few notable exceptions[72], the sense of loss and futility that pervades the works of Graves, Sassoon, Blunden and other British ex-servicemen is entirely absent from the typical Canadian, Australian or New Zealand war book. Not that Dominion authors were at all squeamish about representing the horrors of war. H. R. Williams, in the memoir of his experience as an infantryman in the AIF, related the following incident:

The words were scarcely out of my mouth when there came the whistle and roar of an exploding shell ... My mouth was open and rigid, my hands clutched my stomach, and my limbs felt as if they had been petrified. My face was turned to the spot where only a few minutes before I had been relieved on post. Instead of a man there was a heap of tumbled earth that still smoked from the explosion of the shell, and intermingled with the smoking mass was blood, flesh and fragments of clothing. My face, arms and head were smothered with the poor wretch's minced flesh and warm blood.[73]

However, this same author articulates a meaning for the bloodshed and suffering of 1914–1918 that provides an explicit counterpoint to the interpretation offered by the narrative of disenchantment. 'It is the fashion to depict the war solely as ghastly, sordid, even unnecessary,' Williams wrote. He continued:

No one wishes to glorify war; but any man who saw it first hand for any length of time realized that through all the horror, filth, and suffering there shone something inspiring, stimulating, sacred. This was the heroism, the selflessness of the men who fought for the country, died for their country, taking only what consolation there is in the submerging of self in country.[74]

From all available evidence it seems that the 'fashion' of excoriating the Great War to which Williams referred was a mode far more characteristic of Britain and

Europe than Australia, Canada or New Zealand. The war books 'boom' in the Dominions was a least as prolific as the one in the Motherland. In Canada it included Wilfred Brenton Kerr's *Shrieks and Crashes* (1929), F. W. Bagnall's *Not Mentioned in Despatches* (1933), Will R. Bird's *And We Go On* (1930), and Peregrine Acland's *All Else Is Folly* (1929). Australia saw the publication of titles such as William's aforementioned memoir, Joseph Maxwell's *Hell's Bells and Mademoiselles* (1932), E. J. Rule's *Jacka's Mob* (1933), and G. D. Mitchell's *Backs to the Wall* (1934), to name just a few. In New Zealand the output was fewer, but included C. A. L. Treadwell's *Recollections of an Amateur Soldier* (1936), James Elliot's *Scalpel and Sword* (1936), John Robertson's *With the Cameliers in Palestine* (1938), and Clutha Mackenzie's *The Tale of a Trooper* (1938). Most of these works now languish in obscurity even in the countries where they were published (and some deservedly so), but many of them sold well[75] and garnered good reviews when they initially appeared in Canada, Australia and New Zealand. For instance, one Canadian critic declared that Acland's *All Else Is Folly* 'is great art, because it is life. It is enduring literature, because of its truth and the beautiful, blinding expression of a hideous thing, which grows glorious from the way that it is endured.'[76] An Australian newspaper critic in 1933 opined that, even though readers might be 'generally tiring of war books,' they should not for this reason ignore E. J. Rule's *Jacka's Mob*. The reviewer declared that the novel 'bears the impress of truth, and hence its power and effectiveness.'[77]

Whether or not critics and readers in the Dominions believed that a war novel bore the 'impress of truth' about its subject was a critical factor in the way that it was received in these countries. Furthermore, novels and memoirs that represented the war, or interpreted its meaning, in a way that contradicted the mainstream understanding of the conflict's nature and significance often met with harsh criticism, and sometimes even suppression, in Australia, Canada and New Zealand. In March 1930 the Federal Executive of the RSSILA recommended that the organization request that the Commonwealth government prohibit all war books that 'defamed the soldiers of the Empire.' The RSSILA leadership further recommended that 'all war books should be censored by the war historian [presumably they were referring to C. E. W. Bean] before being admitted to the Commonwealth.'[78] In fact, in 1930 *All Quiet on the Western Front* was banned in New South Wales[79], and a year earlier the Commonwealth Minister for Customs had prohibited Ernest Hemingway's *A Farewell to Arms* from being sold in Australia.[80]

As for Canada, Jonathan Vance has chronicled the firestorm of controversy that greeted the 1930 publication of Charles Yale Harrison's *Generals Die In Bed*. The book, which was written by an American who served in the CEF, was published in England, and in its tone, style and imagery, shared more in common with British and American anti-war novels than with most accounts that were produced by Canadian ex-soldiers. As Vance observes, the aspect of Harrison's book that critics and others in Canada who condemned it found most infuriating was in its depiction of the nation's soldiers as brutal, fornicating, prisoner-killing animals.[81] In a typical passage, Harrison described what happened to a group of unarmed German soldiers who attempt to surrender to Canadian troops:

[The Germans] throw themselves into the crater of a shell-hole. They cower there. Some of our men walk up to the lip of the hole and shoot into the huddled mass of Germans. Clasped hands are held up from out of the funnel-shaped grave. The hands shake eloquently asking for pity. There is none. Our men shoot into the crater. In a few seconds only a squirming mass is left.[82]

After arousing some extremely vitriolic denunciations from prominent critics, including *Saturday Night*'s Nathaniel Benson, respected military men, including Archibald Macdonnell and Arthur Currie, and popular war authors, including W. B. Kerr and Will R. Bird[83], Harrison's novel was banned in Canada. This move prompted the book's British publisher to defend his decision to put out the novel by stating that 'the fighting men know what a fake the traditional glamour is, but it is essential that the young should also know that war is a nasty business.'[84]

It was not always necessary to invoke the heavy hand of government censorship to erect barriers to interpretations of the Great War's nature and meaning that challenged prevailing representations in the Dominions of that conflict and of the soldiers who experienced it. Journalists, critics, ex-soldiers and members of the general public in Australia, Canada and New Zealand consistently condemned in numerous articles, reviews, editorials and letters to the editor, not only the way that many British, European and American war books of the late 1920s and early 1930s characterized the war as futile and pointless, but also the way that they depicted the degradation in mind and spirit experienced by many soldiers who endured its horrors. The Melbourne Legacy Club in 1930 defeated a motion deploring war books, such as *All Quiet of the Western Front*, that were 'counterfeit' because they did not 'give a true picture of the behaviour of a soldier of any army.' The group decided that their condemnation would be gratuitous, since books such as Remarque's would be 'quickly forgotten.'[85] A Canadian critic characterized Richard Aldington's writing style in *Death of A Hero* as sometimes resembling the behaviour of 'the small boy who, having just been punished for using a naughty word, goes out and scrawls it with chalk on all the fences.'[86] A 1930 editorial in the *Sydney Morning Herald* complained that the tendency of many war books recently published overseas was to 'belittle the character and achievements of the fighting man.' According to the writer, 'the dire circumstances over which [the serviceman] so often triumphed' brought forth 'some of the finest resources of human nature.'[87] A work that did not conform to the accepted Dominion narrative of the war could even be

sabotaged by its own foreword, as occurred with J. Talbot Hobbs' ambivalent introduction to the Australian war author Edgar Morrow's 1934 anti-war novel *Iron
in the Fire*. 'Mr. Morrow was apparently an extremely sensitive youngster…and
some things seared his soul which had little effect on older and more sophisticated
men,' Hobbs wrote. 'The sensitive type was fairly numerous, and formed an important, if not very articulate cross-section of an army that was made up of all types'[88]

In Britain, by the middle of the 1930s, the narrative of disenchantment, which
was a representation of the war's meaning that had been articulated as a challenge
to the consoling, validating interpretation established by the commemorative project (which was in many ways a re-inscription of the loyalist narrative that during
the conflict justified the nation's sacrifices), had become much more characteristic
of the mainstream British understanding of the war than had been the case when it
first appeared in the early 1920s. In February 1933, when the young students of the
Oxford Union debating society approved a resolution stating that they would 'in
no circumstances fight for King and Country' (a declaration that would have
seemed almost as unthinkable in 1924 as in 1914), their motion was much less a
blanket refusal to take up arms than an explicit rejection of the jingoism, imperialistic sentiment and patriotic high diction excoriated within the narrative of disenchantment as the 'Old Lies' with which the 'Old Men' lured the country's youth to
their destruction between 1914 and 1918.[89] Furthermore, as Adrian Gregory and
Alex King have shown, the language and rituals associated with commemorative
ceremonies did undergo a change over the course of the 1930s. By the end of the
decade, almost the only acceptable meaning that could be attached to the conflict
in the rhetoric of commemoration was as an abject lesson in the necessity of end-
ing war once and for all.[90]

In Australia, Canada and New Zealand by contrast, the dominant narrative that
mitigated the losses, horror and turmoil of the nations' war experiences by emphasizing the 'positive' outcomes of the war – the achievement of elevated national
status, and the revelation to the world of the exemplary qualities of Australian,
New Zealand and Canadian manhood – remained largely unruffled on its pre-
eminent perch within Dominion culture. An Australian school textbook published
in 1931 reflected the predominance of this understanding within Dominion society.
According to the author:

> It is impossible within the compass of this work to do justice to the history
> and the deeds of the Australian Imperial Force … all that has been attempted
> is to summarize some of the more outstanding performances battles and fig-
> ures of the great "baptism of fire" which has made Australia a nation, given
> her a voice in the council chambers of the world …[91]

A popular inter-war history of the New Zealand Division in the First World War expressed similar sentiments in its depiction of New Zealand's reaction to news of their troops' successful landing at Gallipoli:

Deeper than all other feelings... was a sense of profound exultation. They had been tried and not found wanting. Twenty-four hours before they had been untried troops; now they had done deeds of arms that would go down in history. There was a thrill of exalted feeling running through the hearts of all. They had faced fire and not flinched. For the New Zealanders it was the beginning of that sense of nationality which was to grow so deep and strong as they marched from one ordeal of terror to another.[92]

Along the same lines, a New Zealand ex-soldier writing in 1938 could describe without irony his introduction to combat at Gallipoli as 'the dawn of a mysterious new life, when men met men in mortal fight, when the false standards of civilization went to the devil, and man was man' and declare that 'it was good to be alive; to be one of that brigade of fine hefty fellows on the edge of the great adventure, when they would join in the greatest sport on earth.'[93]

Of course, however, as Rosa Maria Bracco has shown, even in Britain, the narrative of disenchantment did not achieve cultural near-ubiquity in the way that the dominant interpretation of the war did in Canada, Australia and New Zealand. The novels and memoirs of Graves, Blunden, Ford and Sassoon were daring, challenging, intellectually sophisticated and artistically accomplished literature, and as in any society, they were extraordinary. In any genre, the mediocre examples always outnumber the excellent, and war books were no exception. Bracco has thoroughly examined the flood of what she calls 'Middlebrow writing,' some of which was very popular at the time, that accompanied the wave of ex-soldier literature with which most people are familiar. Bracco proposes that middlebrow fiction, with its adherence to conventional styles and tones, its conventional emphasis on continuity with the past (accompanied by hope for the future), and its conventional attempts to present a life-affirming message even in the face of the darkest of subject matter, may more accurately reflect the prevailing sentiments regarding the war held by the majority of middle-class British men and women in the 1920s and 1930s than does the literature of disenchantment. Given that middlebrow fiction was usually written with the conscious goal in mind of appealing to the widest possible mainstream audience, she may be right. However, that does not change the fact that the perspective expressed by individuals such as Montague, Masterman, Owen and Read exercised a profound, and perhaps disproportionate, influence upon British inter-war culture in a way that had no parallels in the Dominions.

Leaving aside the political organizations, pressure groups and cultural institutions that help explain this, one of the primary reasons why disenchantment never seriously threatened in the inter-war period the prevailing Great War narrative in Canada, Australia and New Zealand was the relative absence of an intellectual tradition in the Dominions that would support a perspective premised on loss and decline. The white populations in the Dominions were steeped in a long-standing ideal of themselves as young healthy countries, isolated from the ills of the Old World and destined to produce strong men and women who would one day inevitably claim their birthright as the uncorrupted heirs of British supremacy. The Great War, for all of its carnage and discord, had confirmed the potential and the destiny of these – no longer colonies – nations. Ironically, as we have seen, it was a point of view sometimes shared within the ranks of the disenchanted in the Motherland, who occasionally saw at least a glimmer of hope in the brave New Worlds emerging beyond the seas, even as their own world, with its insulating cocoon of romance and immutable certainty, seemed to transforming before their eyes into a wasteland, alien in its gloom.

Conclusion

This book charts the process by which rhetoric, language and images were used to shape and preserve compelling, and in some cases dominant, interpretations of the experience of the First World War expressed within the societies of Great Britain, Canada, Australia and New Zealand between 1914 and 1939. For Britain, these years witnessed the development of a narrative version of the war experience that emphasized the human, material, social and spiritual cost of the conflict. According to this narrative, the achievement of victory was overshadowed by all that the country lost as a result of the war, and the satisfaction that should have resulted from the nation's triumph was denied by the disenchantment resulting from the way that the conflict revealed the flaws and hypocrisies resting at the heart of British and European civilization. Many of the central themes and motifs associated with this understanding of the war's meaning reflected the pre-war outlook and the wartime experience of a particular segment of British society, namely the members of the upper and upper-middle-class, many of whom volunteered for service during the early days of the war, and served as junior officers in the British Army on the Western Front.

For Canada, Australia and New Zealand, by contrast, the interpretation of the war's meaning that prevailed within the cultures of these countries focused on what was achieved during the conflict by the nation and its soldiers, rather than on what was lost in the process. This was the case despite the fact that the material cost of the war for each Dominion was proportionally comparable to that experienced by Britain. However, the understanding of the war's meaning that emphasized the exemplary qualities of the nation's soldiers, and the achievement of an elevated national status that their outstanding battlefield performance helped to bring about, survived in Canada, Australia and New Zealand during the inter-war years as the dominant narrative representation of these nations' war experience. Interpretations that emphasized loss or some other negative element of that experience were successfully relegated to the cultural margins in the Dominions to a degree not duplicated in the Motherland.

From the evidence provided in the preceding chapters, it seems beyond question that the narrative presented here as characteristic of Dominion representations of their war experience, once it emerged during the war years, came to dominate the political and cultural discourse in these countries related to efforts to define the meaning of the war in ways that served to validate particular ideological positions. In this sense, the prevailing Dominion narrative conforms to the definition of a dominant, or established, collective memory. As a representation of the country's war experience, the celebratory, affirming narrative of national ascendance achieved near-ubiquity within the realm of public culture in Canada, Australia and New Zealand, and thus can legitimately be characterized as the established or mainstream understanding within Dominion society of the 1914–18 conflict. To the extent that the dominant narrative was challenged, whatever alternative interpretations of the war experience emerged during these years were successfully marginalized and ultimately proved limited in their impact upon conventional understandings of the conflagration.

However, in the case of the British narrative explored here, while it remains the 'memory' of the war that enjoys authority within British culture today, it is more difficult to prove that its dominance was already established during the inter-war years to the same extent as that which characterized the mainstream Dominion narratives. The 'disenchanted' interpretation of the war experience was itself a challenge to the mainstream representation of the war and its meaning that had emerged in Britain between 1914 and 1918, and subsequently been enshrined on memorials throughout the country, and validated in numerous works produced by 'Middlebrow' authors during the 1920s and 1930s. Consequently, rather than a status as the 'established' inter-war interpretation of Britain's experience – that is, as the public memory that was culturally ubiquitous and that marginalized successful alternative understandings – the narrative articulated by members of the country's 'Lost Generation', through its role as a compelling counterpoint to the mainstream myth of the war, profoundly altered the forms and language associated with how the conflict was imagined at various levels of inter-war society, from commemoration to artistic representation.

The primary aim of the preceding chapters has been to explore the question of why the narrative of disenchantment, as a mode of representing and interpreting the costly but undeniably victorious war experience of Britain, Canada, Australia and New Zealand, only became a formidable cultural force within inter-war Britain. Or conversely, why only in the Dominions did a celebratory, largely validating understanding of the country's war experience continue to dominate the domain of inter-war public culture even in the face of challenges from alternative interpretations? The conclusion reached in this analysis is that the answer lies in how the narrative of disenchantment in the Motherland, and the narrative of national awakening in the Dominions, engaged with certain long-standing discourses associated with the definition of different kinds of identity in Britain, Canada, Australia and New Zealand. For instance, the disenchanted perspective was inextricably linked to the degree to which the British aristocracy and upper-middle-class were deeply invested in romantic notions that they believed embodied the enduring virtues of England. Such conceptions were symbolized by the neo-feudal code of the gentleman, which encouraged the kind of behaviour in battle that not only made the elite 'natural' exemplars of brave leadership, but also ensured that the encounter between these young men and the lethal technology of industrialized warfare would have particularly tragic implications for their class. In Canada, Australia and New Zealand, on the other hand, the narrative that represented the typical Dominion soldier as a 'natural' warrior superior in physique and intellect to his counterpart serving in the ranks of the British Army cohered neatly with ideas, prevalent in the Dominions since the late nineteenth century, that the rugged frontier environment and the democratic societies of the colonial fringe produced a specimen of manhood several cuts above that produced in the urban slums and class-ridden society of the Motherland.

Also, as detailed in the preceding chapters, the nature and operation of particular political and cultural institutions in Britain, Canada, Australia and New Zealand during and after the Great War played a key role in determining how the conflict was remembered within inter-war culture in all four countries. In the Dominions, the more conservative elements of the political and cultural establishment controlled the instruments and infrastructure most crucial for defining the identity, and the political identification, of the nation's soldiers to an extent not paralleled in Britain. Furthermore, culture produced in the Dominions between the World Wars reflected a consensus celebration of nationalism, and a consensus veneration of the soldier as a symbol of national ascendance, to a degree that did not characterize British culture.

However, the fundamental explanation for the development of certain nationally distinctive memories of the Great War in Britain, Canada, Australia and New Zealand lies in the compelling continuity between pre-war conceptions of identity prevalent in, and specific to, each country, and the interpretations of the war's meaning that drew upon, and refashioned, these ideas to make powerful and appealing new myths.

Notes

Introduction

1 Siegfried Sassoon, 'On Passing the New Menin Gate,' *The Norton Anthology of English Literature* (New York: W.W. Norton & Company, 1986), pp. 1900–1901.

2 Will R. Bird, *Thirteen Years After* (Toronto: The Maclean Publishing Company, 1932), p.79.

3 Paul Fussell, *The Great War and Modern Memory* (New York: Oxford University Press, 1975).

4 Samuel Hynes, *A War Imagined: The First World War and English Culture* (New York: Collier Books, 1990). John Onions, *English Fiction and the Drama of the Great War, 1918–1939* (New York: St. Martin's Press, 1990). See also, Hugh Cecil, *The Flower of Battle: British Fiction Writers of the First World War* (London: Secker and Warburg, 1995).

5 Jay Winter, *Sites of Memory, Sites of Mourning: The Great War in European Cultural History* (Cambridge: Cambridge University Press, 1995). Adrian Gregory, *The Silence of Memory: Armistice Day, 1919–1946* (Oxford: Berg Publishers, 1994). Rosa Maria Bracco, *Merchants of Hope: British Middlebrow Writers and the First World War, 1919–1939* (Oxford: Berg Publishers, Ltd. 1993), Alex King, *Memorials of the Great War in Britain: the Symbolism and Politics of Remembrance* (Oxford: Berg Publishers, Ltd., 1998).

6 K. S. Inglis remains the premier scholar of the Australian and New Zealand memory of the First World War, having published more than a dozen books and articles related to Great War commemoration and the development of the Anzac tradition. Other notable works dealing with commemoration in Australia include Michael McKernan, *Here is Their Spirit: A History of the Australian War Memorial, 1917–1990* (St. Lucia: University of Queensland Press, 1991), and Alan Seymour and Richard Nile (eds), *Anzac: Meaning, Memory and Myth* (London: Sir Robert Menzies Centre for Australian Studies, 1991). The much smaller body of scholarship on the Great War and Canadian memory includes two particularly significant studies, Denise Thomson's 'National Sorrow, National Pride: Commemoration of War in Canada, 1918–1945,' *Journal of Canadian Studies* 30:4 (March 1996), pp. 5–27; and Jonathan F. Vance's *Death So Noble: Memory, Meaning and the First World War* (Vancouver: UBC Press, 1997).

7 In Margaret Higgonet, et al (eds) *Behind the Lines: Gender and the Two World Wars* (New Haven, Yale University Press, 1987), p. 29.

8 Hynes, *War Imagined*, p. xi.

9 Higonnet, et al, *Behind the Lines*, p. 5.

10 Pierre Nora, *Realms of Memory: Rethinking the French Past* (New York: Columbia University Press, 1996); Peter Novick, *The Holocaust in American Life* (Boston: Houghton Mifflin,

1999); Daniel J. Sherman, *The Construction of Memory in Interwar France* (Chicago: University of Chicago Press, 1999).

11 Alistair Thomson, *Anzac Memories: Living With the Legend* (Oxford: Oxford University Press, 1994).

12 In the realm of visual art, to take one example, artistic movements, such as the Group of Seven in Canada, and the Heidelberg School in Australia, that emphasized the visual distinctiveness of these nations enjoyed increasing popularity and critical acclaim. Crucially, these movements rejected the tendency of earlier dominion artists to ape the techniques and motifs of European artists in rendering the Canadian or Australian landscape and people, and strove to create a uniquely 'national' visual style. The Heidelberg School predated World War I, but it was not embraced by the Australian artistic establishment until the inter-war years, within a larger context of predominant cultural nationalism. Four of the original seven Canadian artists who took part in the Group of Seven's inaugural exhibition in 1920 had served as official Canadian war artists during the 1914–18 conflict, and their experience of the Western Front, as well as their exposure to the images of 'modernist' British war artists such as William Orpen, C. R. W. Nevinson, and Paul Nash, heavily influenced their subsequent paintings.

13 Which had the effect of automatically muting or marginalizing in this narrative the war experiences of many citizens who had not served as soldiers and yet were direct participants in the conflict in some way – for instance women nurses, munitions workers, conscientious objectors, anti-war activists, etc. Even within the ranks of servicemen, not every experience was equal: non-combat personnel, POWs, and to a certain extent even those who were conscripts rather than volunteers, did not feature as prominently in the dominant post-war narrative. That this was also true for Britain is the conclusion of Janet S. K. Watson's *Fighting Different Wars: Experience, Memory and the First World War in Britain* (Cambridge: Cambridge University Press, 2004).

14 There are numerous examples of wartime and inter-war idealizations of the Australian and Canadian soldier: See, for example, C. E. W. Bean's influential and best-selling *Official History of Australia in the War of 1914–1918* (Sydney: Angus and Robertson, 1929), and A. Fortescue Duguid's *Official History of Canada in the Great War, 1914–1919* (Ottawa: J. O. Patenaude, 1938). Some contemporary scholars continue to make the case that the battlefield record of Dominion troops sets them a cut above most units in the British Army. See, Shane Schreiber, *Shock Army of the British Empire: The Canadian Corps in the Last 100 Days of the Great War* (London: Praeger, 1997), and Denis Winter, *Haig's Command, A Reassessment* (London: Viking, 1991). However, recent scholarship by Peter Simkins and Paddy Griffith, among others, has questioned whether the performance of Dominion troops was any more remarkable than that of British soldiers, particularly given the much larger proportion of British units to Dominion units on the Western Front. Paddy Griffith, *Battle Tactics of the Western Front: The British Army's Art of Attack, 1916–1918* (New Haven: Yale University Press, 1994); Peter Simkins, 'Co-Stars or Supporting Cast? British Divisions in the "Hundred Days," 1918' in Paddy Griffith (ed.), *British Fighting Methods in the Great War* (London: Frank Cass, 1996).

15 Jeffrey Grey, *A Military History of Australia* (Cambridge: Cambridge University Press, 1990). Desmond Morton and J. L. Granatstein, *Marching to Armageddon: Canadians and the Great War* (Toronto: Lester and Orpen Dennys, 1989).

16 J. L. Granatstein, *Canada and the Two World Wars* (Toronto: Key Porter Books, Ltd., 2003). Christopher Pugsley, *The ANZAC Experience: New Zealand, Australia and Empire in the First World War* (Auckland: Reed Publishing Ltd., 2004).

17 H. G. Wells, *Outline of History* (1920). John Maynard Keynes, *The Economic Consequences of the Peace* (1920). C. F. G. Masterman, *England After the War* (1923). Philip Gibbs, *Realities of War* (1920). C. E. Montague, *Disenchantment* (1922).

18 Montague, a veteran newspaper journalist, enlisted in the British Army at the age of 47 in 1914, and served on the Western Front before being invalided in 1916 back to England and civilian war work.

19 Robert Graves, *Good-bye to All That* (1929). Siegfried Sassoon, *Memoirs of a Fox-Hunting Man* (1927) and *Memoirs of an Infantry Officer* (1930). Edmund Blunden, *Undertones of War* (1927). Herbert Read, *In Retreat* (1926). R. C. Sherriff, *Journey's End* (1929). The English translation of former German soldier Erich Maria Remarque's *All Quiet on the Western Front* (1929) was also a best seller in Britain during these years.

20 Robert Wohl was one of the first scholars to propose a connection between the disproportionate casualties suffered by Britain's elite and the emergence there of a bitter interpretation of the war experience. See *The Generation of 1914* (Cambridge, Mass.: Harvard University Press, 1979).

21 For an examination of one aspect of this ethos, as represented by the revival of the mediaeval code of chivalry in nineteenth-century Britain, see Mark Girouard, *The Return to Camelot: Chivalry and the English Gentleman* (New Haven: Yale University Press, 1981). For a more general exploration of the connection between British and American conceptions of masculinity and the increasingly bellicose cultural mood in those countries on the eve of the Great War, see Michael C. C. Adams, *The Great Adventure: Male Desire and the Coming of World War I* (Bloomington: Indiana University Press, 1990).

22 One of these notable exceptions is CEF veteran Charles Yale Harrison's *Generals Die in Bed* (London: Douglas, 1929).

23 H. R. Williams, *The Gallant Company: An Australian Soldier's Story of 1915–18* (Sydney: Angus and Robertson, 1933), p. 127. Other works that reflect this perspective include, for Australia, J. Maxwell's *Hell's Bells and Mademoiselles* (1932), E. J. Rule's *Jacka's Mob* (1933), and R. E. Lording's *There and Back* (1935). Positive Canadian narratives include Wilfred Benton Kerr's *Shrieks and Crashes* (1929), F. W. Bagnall's *Not Mentioned in Dispatches* (1933), Will R. Bird's *And We Go On* (1930), and Peregrine Acland's *All Else Is Folly* (1929). Among such works for New Zealand are C. A. L. Treadwell, *Recollections of an Amateur Soldier* (1936), James Elliot, *Scalpel and Sword* (1936), John Robertson, *With the Cameliers in Palestine* (1938), and Clutha N. Mackenzie, *The Tale of a Trooper* (1938).

Chapter One

1 J. F. C. Fuller, *The Last of the Gentlemen's Wars* (London: Faber and Faber Ltd., 1937), pp. 5–6.

2 Ibid., p. 7.

3 See A. C. Martin, *The Concentration Camps: 1900–1902: Facts, Figures and Fables* (Cape Town: H. Timmins, 1957); Thomas Pakenham, *The Boer War* (New York: Random House, 1979); S. B. Spies, *Methods of Barbarism? Roberts and Kitchener and Civilians in the Boer Republics: January 1900-May 1902* (Cape Town: Human and Rousseau, 1977).

4 Fuller, *Gentlemen's Wars*, p. 6.

5   Philip Bateman, *Generals of the Anglo-Boer War* (Cape Town: Purnell and Sons, 1977), p. 67. See also, Roy Macnab, *The French Colonel: Villebois-Mareuil and the Boers, 1899–1900* (Cape Town: Oxford University Press, 1975).

6   Of the combatants in the Great War, only the airmen seem to have consistently engaged throughout the conflict in documented displays of chivalry and sportsmanship toward one another. Furthermore, so strong was the aura of romance associated with the 'knights of the air' that even members of the other services were sometimes inspired to pay homage to them, as when 'The Red Baron', German fighter ace Manfred von Richtofen, was buried in 1918 with military honors by the Australian infantrymen who shot him down. See Peter Kilduff, *Richtofen: Beyond the Legend of the Red Baron* (New York: John Wiley and Sons, Inc., 1994), pp. 200–204. However, sportsmanship was not necessarily uppermost in the mind of a fighter pilot during combat, as Cecil Lewis confirms in his memoirs of his career in the British air service during World War I : 'So, like dueling, air fighing required a set steely courage, drained of all emotion, fined down to a tense and deadly effort of will. The Angel of Death is less callous, aloof and implacable than a fighting pilot when he dives [for the kill].' *Sagittarius Rising*, (London: Giniger/Stackpole Books, 1936), p. 170.

7   See David Cannadine, ed., *Admiral Nelson: Context and Legacy* (New York: Palgrave Macmillan, 2005); Terry Coleman, *Nelson: the Man and the Legend* (London: Bloomsbury, 2001); Andrew Lambert, *Nelson: Britannia's God of War* (London: Faber and Faber, 2004); Brian Lavery, *Horatio Lord Nelson* (New York: New York University Press, 2003).

8   Robert Southey, *Life of Nelson* (London: J. M. Dent & Sons, Ltd., 1813), p. 268.

9   See Ann Uhry Abrams, *The Valiant Hero: Benjamin West and Grand-Style History Painting* (Washington, D.C.: the Smithsonian Institution Press, 1985).

10 Linda Colley, *Britons: Forging the Nation, 1707–1837* (New Haven: Yale University Press, 1992), pp. 177–193.

11 A war that produced one of the most influential and enduring models of British martial virtue and heroic self-sacrifice, the doomed cavalry unit celebrated in Tennyson's 1854 poem, 'Charge of the Light Brigade.'

12 Brian Bond (ed.), *Victorian Military Campaigns* (London: Hutchison, 1967), pp. 309–311.

13 See Richard Collier, *The Great Indian Mutiny* (New York: E. P. Dutton and Company, 1964); Edward Gilliat, *Heroes of Modern India* (London: Seeley and Co., 1910); Christopher Hibbert, *The Great Mutiny* (New York: Viking Press, 1978); John Kaye, *History of the Indian Mutiny* (London: W. H. Allen and Co., 1888).

14 quoted in John William Kaye, *Lives of Indian Officers* (London: A. Strahan and Co., 1867), pp. 490–491.

15 J. Cave-Browne, *The Punjab and Delhi in 1857* (London: William Blackwood and Sons, 1861), p. 194.

16 High-strung in temperament and Puritanical in his religious convictions, Havelock had a number of well-publicized conflicts with his fellow officers, most notably with General James Neill. Havelock is also alleged to have given the order for rebellious Sepoys to be blown from the mouths of cannons in revenge for the massacre of British women and children at Cawnpore, according to W. H. Fitchett, *The Tale of the Great Mutiny* (London: John Murray, 1912), p. 193. Nevertheless, Havelock's success on the battlefield and his devout Christianity helped make him in the public's eyes one of the most captivating figures to emerge from the conflict. See John M. MacKenzie, 'Heroic Myths of Empire,'

in John M. MacKenzie (ed.), *Popular Imperialism in the Military, 1850–1950* (Manchester: Manchester University Press, 1992), pp. 116–121.

17   Quoted in John Clark Marshman, *Memoirs of Major-General Sir Henry Havelock* (London: Longmans, Green and Co., 1885), pp. 451–452.

18   Fitchett, *Great Mutiny*, p. 170.

19   Bond, ed., *Victorian Military Campaigns*, pp. 201–240. See also, Michael Barthorp, *Slogging Over Africa: the Boer Wars, 1815–1902* (London: Cassell, 2002), pp. 32–43.

20   Robin Neillands, *The Dervish Wars: Gordon and Kitchener in the Sudan* (London: John Murray, 1996), pp. 95–141.

21   John Pollock, *Gordon: The Man Behind the Legend* (London: Constable, 1993), p. 311.

22   Anthony Nutting, *Gordon of Khartoum: Martyr and Misfit* (New York: Clarkson N. Potter, 1966), p. 315.

23   Demetrius C. Boulger, *The Life of Gordon* (London: T. Fisher Unwin, 1897), p. 337.

24   *Times* (London), 24 April 1912, p. 1.

25   Reginald Pound, *Scott of the Antarctic* (New York: Coward-McCann, Inc., 1966), p. 310.

26   Dominic Hibberd, *The First World War* (London: MacMillan Ltd., 1990), p. 16.

27   Leonard Huxley (ed), *Scott's Last Expedition: Being the Journals of Captain R. F. Scott* (Smith, Elder & Co., 1913), pp. 597–600.

28   Ibid., p. 592. Naturally this heroic act was depicted on canvas, this time by J. C. Dollman in 1913.

29   Girouard, *Camelot*, pp. 4–6.

30   See J. V. Beckett, *The Aristocracy in England, 1660–1914* (New York: Blackwell, 1986); Lawrence Stone and Jeanne C. Fawtier Stone, *An Open Elite?England 1540–1880* (Oxford: Oxford University Press, 1984); Martin J. Wiener, *English Culture and the Decline of the Industrial Spirit* (Cambridge: Cambridge University Press, 1981).

31   As Mark Girouard has shown, the idea of chivalry enjoyed an enthusiastic revival across a wide segment of nineteenth-century British society, with the language and imagery associated with the knights of the Middle Ages and their ideals infiltrating the cultural and political discourse of groups as ideologically disparate as Radical Reformers and reactionary Tories. Mediaeval chivalry had been a code of conduct for an elite warrior class, and had been designed to soften the potential barbarity of their martial livelihood. Chivalry in the nineteenth century emerged out of a rediscovery and reappraisal of the history, culture and values of the Middle Ages that had begun in the late-eighteenth century and intensified during the Romantic cultural movement of the early 1800s. Victorian and Edwardian chivalry was part and parcel of a wave of enthusism for things mediaeval, including such superficial trappings as castles, heraldry, suits of armor, and even tournaments. As a code of conduct, nineteenth-century chivalry was still highly colored by its martial origins, but no longer restricted to society's hereditary warrior elite. Adherence to its principles demonstrated the good breeding that many thought requisite for members of society's higher echelons.

32   Gilliat, *Modern India*, p. 294.

33   Lionel J. Trotter, *The Bayard of India: A Life of General Sir James Outram* (London: William Blackwood and Sons, 1903), p. 289.

34   W. S. R. Hodson, *Twelve Years of a Soldier's Life in India* (Boston: Ticknor and Fields, 1860), pp. 50–51.

35   Kenelm Digby, *The Broad Stone of Honour, or the true sense and practice of chivalry* (London: G. Quaritch, 1877).

36 Thomas Carlyle, *Past and Present* (New York: The Macmillan Company, 1927 [reprint]), pp. 186–187.

37 Ibid., pp. 198–199.

38 Ibid., p. 166.

39 Girouard, *Camelot*, pp. 130–145.

40 Thomas Hughes, *Tom Brown's Schooldays* (London: Macmillan, 1857), pp. 11–12.

41 Ibid., pp. 73–74.

42 See Rupert Wilkinson, *Gentlemanly Power: British Leadership and the Public School Tradition; A Comparative Study in the Making of Rulers* (London: Oxford University Press, 1964).

43 J. A. Mangan, *Athleticism in the Victorian and Edwardian Public School* (Cambridge: Cambridge University Press, 1981).

44 John Chandos, *Boys Together: English Public Schools, 1800–1864* (London: Hutchinson, 1984), p. 150.

45 T. L. Papillon, quoted in Mangan, *Athleticism*, p. 9.

46 Henry Newbolt, *The Island Race* (London: E. Mathews, 1898), p. 75.

47 For discussions of Social Darwinist theory, see Greta Jones, *Social Darwinism and English Thought: The Interaction Between Biological and Social Theory* (Brighton, Sussex: Harvester Press, 1980); Paul Crook, *Darwinism, War and History* (Cambridge: Cambridge University Press, 1994); Edward Caudill, *Darwinian Myths: The Legends and Misuses of a Theory* (Knoxville: University of Tennessee Press, 1997); E. J. Hobsbawm, *The Age of Empire, 1875–1914* (New York: Pantheon Books, 1987).

48 Charles Sorley, *The Collected Letters of Charles Hamilton Sorley* (London: Cecil Woolf, 1990), p. 35.

49 See Richard A. Preston, Alex Roland, Sydney F. Wise, *Men In Arms: A History of Warfare and its Interrelationships with Western Society* (Fort Worth: Holt, Rinehart and Winston, 1991).

50 Norman McCord, *British History 1815–1906* (Oxford: Oxford University Press, 1991), p. 464.

51 Rupert Brooke, *The Collected Poems of Rupert Brooke* (London: Sidgwick and Jackson, Ltd., 1924), pp. 5, 7.

52 J. B. Priestley, *Margin Released: A Writer's Reminiscences and Reflections* (New York: Harper and Row, 1962), p. 136.

53 David Cannadine, *The Decline and Fall of the British Aristocracy* (New Haven: Yale University Press, 1990), p. 82.

54 Ibid., p. 83.

55 J. M. Winter, *The Great War and the British People* (Cambridge, Mass.: Harvard University Press, 1986) p. 93. The experience of Harrow was fairly typical of British public schools in the First World War. Of the 2,917 Harrovians who served in the military during the conflict, 690 were wounded and 644 – 22 per cent – were killed. Christopher Tyerman, *A History of Harrow School* (Oxford: Oxford University Press, 2000), p. 442.

56 Ibid., p. 87.

57 *Times* (London), 26 April 1915, p. 1.

58 Denis Winter, *Death's Men* (London: Penguin Books, 1978), p. 255.

59 Winter, *Great War*, p. 68.

60 H. H. Asquith, *Memories and Reflections* (Boston: Little, Brown and Co., 1928), p. 189.

Chapter Two

1   C. E. W. Bean, *Gallipoli Correspondent: The Frontline Diary of C. E. W. Bean* (Sydney: Allen and Unwin, 1983 [reprint]), p. 83.

2   Ibid., pp. 153, 155.

3   Quoted in Stephen Alomes, *Australian Nationalism* (New South Wales: Angus and Robertson, 1991), p. 9.

4   Including Newfoundland, which prior to 1934, when it returned to direct rule by Britain before becoming a Canadian province in 1949, remained the British Empire's 'other' self-governing Dominion in North America. In 1907, Newfoundland's governor, Sir Cavendish Boyle, celebrated the Dominion with these lyrics: 'When blinding storm gusts fret thy shore and wild waves lash the strand; though spin drift and tempest roar we love the wind-swept land.' *Newfoundland, an Ode* (London, Novello and Co., Ltd., 1907).

5   Dorothea Mackellar, *My Country: A Poem by Dorothea Mackellar with decorations and illustrations by J. J. Hilder* (Sydney: Greenhouse Publications, 1915), p. 2.

6   Charles Mair, *Canadian Poems* (Toronto: William Briggs, 1901), p. 251.

7   Mackellar, *My Country*, p. 1. Similarly, for the protagonist of the New Zealand poet David McKee Wright's 1897 verse 'Our Cities Face the Sea', a growing affection for the flora and landscape of the Pacific Dominion signifies a growing sense of New Zealand identity:

> He had learned the charm of the mountains, the breath of the tussocks he knew;
> He had lived in the land of sunshine, under skies of cloudless blue;
> And the charm of the old had faded, as the charm of the new had grown,
> Till he hailed the windy islands with their flax and fern as his own.
> *Station Ballads and Other Verses* (Dunedin: J.G. Sawell, 1897), pp. 106–108.

8   Mair, *Canadian Poems*, p. 253.

9   Bill Wannan (ed.), *A Marcus Clarke Reader* (Melbourne: Landsdowne Press, 1963), pp. 55–57.

10 New Zealand at the turn of the century was particularly celebrated by observers inside and outside of the Dominion as a model of social and political progress. Universal male suffrage – including for the Maori – was established in New Zealand by 1867, and in 1893, New Zealand became the first nation to grant women the right to vote. Other measures enacted prior to the First World War, including old age pensions and progressive labor legislation, cemented New Zealand's reputation – particularly among reformers in Europe and North America – as a democratic, egalitarian social laboratory worthy of study and emulation. See James Belich, *Paradise Reforged: A History of New Zealanders from the 1880s to the Year 2000* (Honolulu: University of Hawaii Press, 2001); Michael King, *The Penguin History of New Zealand* (Auckland: Penguin Books, 2003).

11 R. G. Haliburton, *The Men of the North and Their Place in History. A Lecture delivered before the Montreal Literary Club, March 31st, 1869* (Montreal: Montreal Gazette, 1869), pp. 2–16.

12 Wannan, *Marcus Clarke*, pp. 26–30.

13 Alomes, *Australian Nationalism*, p. 104.

14 Henry Lawson, *In the Days When the World Was Wide and Other Verses* (Sydney: Angus and Robertson, 1903), pp. 116–117.

15   Francis Adams, *The Australians: A Social Sketch* (London: T. Fisher Unwin, 1893), pp. 170–171.

16   W. Sanford Evans, *The Canadian Contingents and Canadian Imperialism* (London: T. Fisher Unwin, 1901), pp. 6–7.

17   The Maori descended from Polynesians who settled in New Zealand during the thirteenth century A.D.

18   A. H. Adams, *Tussock Land: A Romance of New Zealand and the Commonwealth* (London: Fisher and Unwin, 1904), p. 34.

19   E. C. Buley, *Glorious Deeds of Australasians in the Great War* (London: Andrew Melrose, Ltd., 1916), pp. 183–186.

20   T. G. Marquis, *Canada's Sons on Kopje and Veldt* (Toronto: The Canada's Sons Publishing Co., 1900), p. 189.

21   Alomes, *Australian Nationalism*, p. 94.

22   Carman Miller, *Painting the Map Red: Canada and the South African War, 1899–1902* (Montreal and Kingston: McGill-Queen's University Press, 1993), pp. 3, 429.

23   Gavin Souter, *Lion and Kangaroo: The Initiation of Australia, 1901–1919* (Sydney: Collins, 1976), p. 65.

24   Pugsley, *ANZAC Experience*, p. 49.

25   For a more comprehensive discussion of 'imperial nationalism' in Canada and Australia, see Carl Berger, *The Sense of Power: Studies in the Ideas of Canadian Imperialism, 1867–1914* (Toronto: University of Toronto Press, 1970); Peter Russell (ed.), *Nationalism in Canada* (Toronto: McGraw-Hill, 1966); W. G. McMinn, *Nationalism and Federalism in Australia* (Oxford: Oxford University Press, 1994); Thomas W. Tanner, *Compulsory Citizen Soldiers* (New South Wales: Alternative Publishing Cooperative, Etd., 1980). This last work deals with the Australian side of a policy instituted in Australia and New Zealand prior to the First World War that is particularly revealing of the complex motives combining self-interest and loyalty underlying 'imperial nationalism' in the Dominions. Australia by 1911, and New Zealand by 1912, enacted compulsory military training for boys and young men between the ages of 12 and 26 in Australia, and 18 and 25 in New Zealand. In both countries, this program was motivated by increasing security concerns (particularly in light of Japan's victory in their 1905 war with Russia, and Britain's repositioning of an increasing preponderance of their naval strength to the Atlantic in order to counter Germany's naval buildup), and a consequent desire to create a corps of trained citizenry who could comprise a self-defense force that could hold off an invading enemy (at least until reinforcements from Britain arrived), and who might also potentially provide the nucleus of an expeditionary force to be sent overseas in support of Britain. For more on compulsory military training in New Zealand, see Pugsley, *ANZAC Experience*, pp. 51–70.

26   Belich, *Paradise*, p. 111.

27   *Bulletin* (Sydney), 28 September 1901, p. 6.

28   The marginality of this opposition is demonstrated by the fact that only five out of 45 members of Australia's House of Representatives voted against sending a Commonwealth contingent (previous contingents raised prior to Federation had been contributed by individual states) to South Africa. Alomes, *Australian Nationalism*, pp. 145–147.

29   See Casey Murrow, *Henri Bourassa and French-Canadian Nationalism* (Montreal: Harvest House, 1968).

30   *Argus* (Melbourne), 3 August 1914, p. 1.

31   Ibid., 1 August 1914, p. 1.

32   *The Globe* (Toronto), 4 August 1914, p. 1.

33   Grace Morris Craig, *But This Is Our War* (Toronto: University of Toronto Press, 1981),
     p. 26.

34   *Mercury* (Hobart) 4 August 1914, p. 1.

35   Pugsley, *ANZAC Experience,* p. 63.

36   Granatstein and Morton, *Canada*, p. 335; Pugsley, *ANZAC Experience,* pp. 276, 307–308.
     Perhaps the most poignant losses were those of Newfoundland. The overwhelming ma-
     jority of its war dead belonged to the Newfoundland Regiment, the Dominion's primary
     contribution to the Empire's war effort on land. Of the approximately 6,000 men who
     served in the Regiment, 1,305 did not survive the war. Newfoundland's population be-
     tween 1914 and 1918 stood at about 250,000. G. W. L. Nicholson, *The Fighting New-
     foundlander: A History of the Royal Newfoundland Regiment* (St. John's: Government of
     Newfoundland, 1964), pp. 508–509.

37   Quoted in Robert Craig Brown and Ramsay Cook, *Canada, 1896–1921* (Toronto:
     McClelland & Stewart Ltd., 1974) p. 263.

38   *Worker* (Brisbane) 6 August 1914, p. 9.

39   *Direct Action* 22 August 1914, p. 3.

40   Brown and Cook, *Canada*, p. 251.

41   *Le Devoir*, 8 September 1914, p. 1. The relatively benign nature of Bourassa's comments
     did not prevent Canadian authorities from prohibiting him on at least two occasions
     from uttering them in public. See Henri Bourassa, *The Duty of Canada at the Present Hour*
     (Montreal: Le Devoir, 1914).

42   *Bathurst National Advocate*, 6 August 1914, p. 2.

43   Souter, *Lion and Kangaroo*, p. 214.

44   *Bulletin* (Sydney), 6 May 1915, p. 9.

45   *Courier* (Brisbane), 10 August 1914, p. 4.

46   Harry Gullet, 'Australia', *United Empire: The Royal Colonial Institute Journal* (October,
     1914), p. 22.

47   Fuller quoted in Morton and Granatstein, *Armageddon,* p. 48.

48   Only a few months after this article was published, Australian and New Zealand troops
     were living up to the worst stereotypes of colonial hooliganism with their riotous indis-
     cipline while stationed in Egypt.

49   Gullet, 'Australia,' p. 23.

50   Jeffrey Grey, *Military History*, p. 91. Paul Baker, *King and Country Call: New Zealanders,
     Conscription and the Great War* (Auckland: Auckland University Press, 1988), p.17.

51   King, *New Zealand*, p. 280.

52   Buley, *Glorious Deeds*, p. 304.

53   A. M. DeBeck, 'How Canada Answered the Call,' *Canada in Khaki* (London: The Cana-
     dian War Records Office, 1916), p. 36.

54   Morton, *Armageddon*, p.10.

55   Duguid, *Official History*, pp. 226–421. Duguid's 'Official History' of Canada in the Great
     War actually only covers the years 1914–15. Other sources for Second Ypres include
     Morton, *Armageddon*, pp. 58–62; G. W. L. Nicholson, *Canadian Expeditionary Force, 1914–
     1919* (Ottawa: R. Duhamel, 1962); Bill Freeman and Richard Nielson, *Far From Home:
     Canadians in the First World War* (Toronto: McGraw-Hill Ryerson, 1999).

56   Gilbert Parker, 'The Spirit of Heroism,' *Khaki*, pp. 11–16.

57 Morris-Craig, *Our War*, p. 28.

58 *With the First Canadian Contingent* (Toronto: Hodder and Stoughton, 1915), p. 85.

59 *Khaki*, p. vii.

60 Reproduced in Sandra Gwyn, *Tapestry of War* (Toronto: Harper Collins, 1992), p. 163.

61 Quoted in Gwyn, *Tapestry*, p. 149.

62 John McCrae, *In Flanders Fields, and Other Poems* (London: G. P. Putnam's Sons, 1919), p. 3.

63 Gallipoli was also, technically, the baptism of fire for the Newfoundland Regiment, though they saw little combat on the Peninsula, losing 43 men during the four months that they were stationed in the theater. Nicholson, *Newfoundlanders*, p. 172.

64 For an in-depth discussion of the strategy behind the Dardanelles campaign, see Jeffrey D. Wallin, *By Ships Alone: Churchill and the Dardanelles* (Durham, N.C.: Carolina Academic Press, 1981); Geoffrey Miller, *Straits: British Policy Towards the Ottoman Empire and the Origins of the Dardanelles Campaign* (Hull: University of Hull Press, 1997).

65 E. M. Andrews, *The Anzac Illusion: Anglo-Australian Relations During World War I* (Cambridge: Cambridge University Press, 1993), p. 51.

66 A. St. John Adcock, *Australasia Triumphant* (London: Simpkin, Marshall, Hamilton, Kent and Co., 1916) pp. 61–62.

67 See Alan Moorehead, *Gallipoli* (London: H. Hamilton, 1956); Cecil Malthus, *Anzac: A Retrospect* (Christchurch: Whitcombe and Tombs, 1965); Robert Rhodes James, *Gallipoli* (London: Batsford, 1965); Nigel Steel and Peter Hart, *Defeat at Gallipoli* (London: Macmillan, 1994); Michael Hickey, *Gallipoli* (London: John Murray, 1995); John Lee, *A Soldier's Life: General Sir Ian Hamilton* (London: Macmillan, 2000); Edward J. Erickson, *Ordered to Die: A History of the Ottoman Army in the First World War* (Westport, Conn.: Greenwood Press, 2001); Bill Gammage, *The Broken Years: Australian Soldiers in the Great War* (Victoria, Australia: Penguin Books, 1975), p. 110.

68 *Argus* (Melbourne), 8 May 1915, p. 1.

69 Buley, *Glorious Deeds*, p. 379. The stereotype of the Anzacs as 'natural warriors' inspired Buley and other commentators to label them 'white Ghurkas', after the British Army's elite South Asian units (largely recruited from Nepal) long celebrated for their prowess and ferocity in battle. However, even Buley acknowledges that this nickname had little appeal among the Anzacs, and it does not seem to have survived the first years of the war. Buley, *Glorious Deeds*, pp. 279–287. Also, Frank T. Lind, 'The White Ghurkas', *Daily News* (St. John's, Newfoundland), 1915. In a similar vein, boosters of Canada's fighting men sometimes compared them to North America's Native American warriors, as in these lines of verse appearing in a Newfoundland newspaper: 'The Germans call them Indians white,/For they know how to fight,/For the right and the light'. Arthur Wheeler, 'The White Indians', *Evening Telegram* (St. John's), 4 July 1916, p. 3.

70 Dorothea Mackellar, 'Australia's Men' (1915), in J. T. Laird (ed.), *Other Banners: An Anthology of Australian Literature of the First World War* (Canberra: The Australian War Memorial, 1971), pp. 45–46.

71 Nancy Croad (ed.), *My Dear Home: The Letters of Three Knight Brothers Who Gave Their Lives During World War I* (Auckland: Nancy Croad, 1995), p. 61.

72 Ronald East (ed.), *The Gallipoli Diary of Sergeant Lawrence of the Australian Engineers, 1st AIF, 1915* (Melbourne: Melbourne University Press, 1981), pp. 59, 75.

73 Geoffrey Serle, *John Monash: A Biography* (Melbourne: Melbourne University Press, 1982), p. 243.

74 Andrews, *Anzac Illusion*, pp. 57–58.

75 See Lewis, *Our War: Australia During World War I* (Melbourne: Melbourne University Press, 1980); Major Fred Waite, *The New Zealanders at Gallipoli* (Auckland: Whitcombe and Tombs, Ltd., 1921), pp. 294–295.

76 *West Australian*, 22 December 1915, p. 3.

77 Andrews, *Anzac Illusion*, p. 53.

78 Grey, *Military History*, pp. 98–99.

79 Andrews, *Anzac Illusion*, p. 3.

80 Serle, *Monash*, p. 223.

81 Anzac Diary of Percival Clennell Fenwick, Auckland War Memorial Museum, MS 1497, p. 8.

82 By 1917 Australian and New Zealand soldiers were widely known as 'diggers,' a nickname that Bean helped popularize in regard to the Australians, and that was possibly appropriated from Australian and New Zealand working-class traditions. The true origins of the term, and whether it originated with Australian or New Zealand troops, was and is hotly disputed. Some scholars assert, as Bean did, that the term pre-dated the First World War, originating as a nickname that New Zealand and Australian miners and/or gum diggers gave themselves. See K. S. Inglis, 'The Anzac Tradition', *Meanjin Quarterly* (March, 1965), p.28. Other scholars argue that the term emerged only during the war, and was used first by New Zealanders (who took pride in the British high command's acknowledgement of their prowess in that essential soldierly skill, digging), before spreading to the Australians who eventually, according to Christopher Pugsley, 'colonized' the nickname so that in current parlance, it specifically and exclusively refers to Australian soldiers. Pugsley, *Anzac Experience*, p. 30.

83 Andrews, *Anzac Illusion*, pp. 60–61.

84 Quoted in Inglis, 'Anzac Tradition,' p.28.

85 Bean, *Gallipoli Correspondent*, p. 83. A New Zealand soldier serving on the Peninsula also expressed admiration for what he perceived as a characteristically colonial streak of independence evident among both Australians and New Zealanders, but described, at the same time, what he perceived as subtle distinctions between how Australians and New Zealanders expressed that independence. The Australians, he wrote, were 'as independent as the devil and with the same recklessness [as the New Zealanders], yet one finds their independence of a stiff, unyielding kind, without any of the ranting vaunting of New Zealanders.' E. P. Williams, *A New Zealander's Diary: Gallipoli and France, 1915–1917* (Christchurch: Cadsonbury Publications, 1998), p. 57. Williams' assessment provides an interesting reversal of the conventional stereotype of the Australian soldier as more prone to 'ranting vaunting' than his New Zealand counterpart.

86 Inglis, 'Anzac Tradition', p. 29.

87 Bean, *Gallipoli Correspondent*, p. 155.

88 Inglis, 'Anzac Tradition', p. 29.

89 *Ibid.*, p. 35.

90 Another influential Australian writer whose work in 1915–16 employed stereotypes, language and settings evocative of the Australian working class in order to promote support for the war effort was the poet C. J. Dennis. In 1915 Dennis had published *The Songs of a Sentimental Bloke*, a book-length narrative poem about a love-sick Melbourne larrikin that sold over 50,000 copies in its first nine months on the market [Alec H. Chisolm, *The Making of a Sentimental Bloke* (Melbourne: Georgian House, 1946), pp. 46–47].

The poem, which was written in the vernacular of the Melbourne working class, was the *Canterbury Tales* of Australian slang and idiom. Brian Lewis recalls how in 1915, 'no social evening could avoid a recitation from it and it was quoted more than any other book, apart from the Bible.' (Lewis, *Our War*, pp. 2–3) In 1916 Dennis followed up the *Sentimental Bloke* with another narrative poem, *The Moods of Ginger Mick*. In this work, Dennis had the larrikin protagonist of the story join the AIF, become a hero on Gallipoli, learn to think of himself as a member of a nation and race rather than as a member of a class, and finally, demonstrate the value of self-sacrifice by dying in battle. *Ginger Mick* was also a huge success, selling more than 40,000 copies in its first six months in print.

91 Thomson, *Anzac Memories*, pp. 66–68.

92 All New World soldiers enjoyed a reputation for indiscipline out of the line, irreverence toward authority and indifference to spit and polish. It was an image (and sometimes a reality) that may have perturbed British (and many colonial) commanders, but that appealed to rank and file colonial soldiers, and to commentators and the general public in the Dominions. Significantly, this image conformed to expectations of behavior by soldiers hailing from lands idealized as havens of democracy, egalitarianism and individualism, especially when compared to the Old World. Newfoundland recruits were certainly not unique in being represented as men 'who until their enlistment had said "sir" to no man, and who gloried in the reputation given to them by one inspecting officer as "the most indisciplined lot he'd ever seen."' John Gallishaw, 'Gallipoli: The Adventures of a Survivor', *Century*, vol. 9, July 1916, pp. 371–382.

93 C. E. W. Bean, ed. *The Anzac Book* (London: Cassell and Co., 1916).

94 Thomson, *Anzac Memories*, p. 70.

95 Lewis, *Our War*, p. 172.

96 Christopher Brennan, 'Lions of War' (1916), in *Other Banners*, p. 46.

97 *Anzac Memorial* (Sydney: Returned Soldiers Association of New South Wales, 1916), pp. 51–97.

98 Though this conclusion was still disputed by some in the Dominions, as indicated by these lines penned by a New Zealand poet in 1916:

> Nay, 'tis not failure! Away with the name of it! Sons
> Of the South Land triumphant we see:
> Grand their achievement and deathless the fame of it –
> Fighting a tyrant that men may be free.

Jay Liddell Kelly, 'The Failure – Gallipoli, 1916' in *Anzac Memorial*, p. 85.

99 *Ibid*, p. 89, 63.

100 J. D. Burns, 'For England!', in *Other Banners*, p. 10.

101 *Argus*, 25 April 1916.

Chapter Three

1 The Newfoundland Regiment was not so fortunate. The First Battalion of that unit participated in an attack near the village of Beaumont Hamel on 1 July. Out of a total of slightly more than 1000 men, the Battalion suffered casualties of 14 officers and 219 other ranks killed, 12 officers and 374 other ranks wounded, and 91 other ranks missing. The casualty rate for officers who took part in the attack was 100 percent. The

slaughter at Beaumont Hamel was the single worst disaster in Newfoundland's history to that time. See Nicholson, *Fighting Newfoundlander*, pp. 274–275.

2   Grey, *Military History*, p. 103.

3   C. E. W. Bean, *The Official History of Australia in the War of 1914–1918 vol III: The A.I.F. in France: 1916* (Sydney, Angus and Robertson, 1929), p. 444.

4   Ibid., pp. 444–446.

5   C. E. W. Bean, *Anzac to Amiens: A Shorter History of the Australian Fighting Services in the Great War* (Canberra: Australian War Memorial, 1952), p. 236.

6   Astonishingly, each division was cycled through a *second* tour of the Pozières sector between mid-August and the end of the operation in early September.

7   Bean, *Official History*, p. 862.

8   Gammage, *Broken Years*, pp. 165–166.

9   Bean, *Official History*, pp. 871–872.

10   Generals J. W. McCay and H. V. Cox were sacked after Fromelles, General J. G. Legge was relieved after Pozières.

11   Bean, *Official History*, p. 872.

12   Gammage, *Broken Years*, pp. 165–169.

13   Andrews, *Anzac Illusion*, pp. 108–114.

14   Lewis, *Our War*, p. 213.

15   Ibid., p. 216.

16   Reginald H. Roy (ed.), *The Journal of Private Fraser* (Victoria, B. C.: Sono Nis Press, 1985), p. 195.

17   This battle was also notable for the first use in combat of tanks. The British employed several 'armored caterpillars' in support of their attack on Courcelette, but their effectiveness in this engagement was limited by the fact that there were too few of them and commanders at the time did not know how best to use them tactically. Nicholson, *Canadian Expeditionary Force*, pp. 169–170.

18   Morton, *Armageddon*, p. 116; Matthew Wright, *Western Front: The New Zealand Division in the First World War, 1916–1918* (Auckland: Reed Publishing, 2005), p. 82.

19   *Globe* (Toronto), 21 September 1916, p. 1; 20 September 1916, p. 7.

20   Gwyn, *Tapestry*, p. 295.

21   Desmond Morton, *A Peculiar Kind of Politics: Canada's Overseas Ministry in the First World War* (Toronto: University of Toronto Press, 1982), pp. 72–73.

22   Ibid., pp. 78–89.

23   Ibid, p. 89. Perley would be succeeded in December 1917 by A. E. Kemp.

24   George Perley, 'The Dominion at War,' *Khaki* (London: Canadian War Records Office, 1917), p. 9.

25   Andrews, *Anzac Illusion*, pp. 110–111.

26   Morton, *Politics*, pp. 110–111.

27   Robert Laird Borden, *Memoirs*, vol. 2 (New York: The Macmillan Company, 1938), pp. 621–625.

28   Nicholson, *Canadian Expeditionary Force*, pp. 261–266.

29   *Globe* (Toronto), 11 April 1917, p. 6.

30   *Free Press* (Manitoba), 12 April 1917, p. 7.

31   Schreiber, *Shock Army* (London: Praeger, 1997).

32   The Australians were actually pulled from the line in October 1918, their under-strength divisions having been in action since the German Spring offensives. The Canadians,

who were not in the line for those battles, remained in action until the Armistice was declared in November, as did the New Zealand Division, despite having been heavily employed on defense during the Spring offensives, and on offense during the Hundred Days. See Bean, *Official History, vol. VI*; Nicholson, *Canadian Expeditionary Force*, pp. 461–483.

33   Andrews, *Anzac Illusion*, pp. 140–141.

34   Ibid., p. 99.

35   Bean, *Official History*, pp. 354, 544.

36   Gammage, *Broken Years*, pp. 208, 240.

37   Conrad, *Knight Brothers*, p. 163.

38   F. M. Cutlack, *The Australians: Their Final Campaign, 1918* (London: Sampson Low, Marston & Co., Ltd., 1918), p. 235.

39   C. E. W. Bean attributed the origin of the nickname 'digger' to describe Australian or New Zealand troops to New Zealanders who inherited the term from the gum-diggers of their country (Bean acknowledged that it might also have originated with Australian miners in the AIF). By 1917, 'digger' was the most popular nickname used by Australian and New Zealand soldiers on the Western Front to describe themselves. *Official History, vol. IV*, pp. 732–733.

40   Gammage, *Broken Years*, p. 248.

41   Bean, *Official History, vol. IV*, p. 354.

42   Bean, *Official History*, pp. 441–1044.

43   Cutlack, *Australians*, p. 13.

44   Bean, *Official History, vol. VI.*, pp. 407, 753.

45   Col. H. Stewart, *The New Zealand Division: A Popular History Based on Official Records* (Auckland: Whitcombe and Tombs, 1921), p. 616.

46   J. F. B. Livesay, *Canada's Hundred Days* (Toronto: Thomas Allen, 1919), p. 397.

47   Bean, *Official History*, p. 464.

48   Livesay, *Hundred Days*, p. 399.

49   See Denis Winter, *Haig's Command*.

50   Peter Simkins, 'Co-Stars or Supporting Cast? British Divisions in the "Hundred Days", 1918' in Griffith (ed.), *British Fighting Methods*, pp. 50–57; Robin Prior, Trevor Wilson, *Command on the Western Front: The Military Career of Sir Henry Rawlinson, 1914–1918* (Cambridge, Mass.: Blackwell, 1992).

51   Pugsley, *Anzac Experience*, pp. 165–244.

52   See Griffith, *Battle Tactics; British Fighting Methods*.

53   Cutlack, *Australians*, p. 14.

54   C. E. W. Bean, *Letters from France* (Melbourne: Cassell and Company, 1917), p. 133.

55   Bean, *Official History vol. III*, p. 137.

56   Ibid., p. 858.

57   F. A. McKenzie, *Canada's Day of Glory* (Toronto: William Briggs, 1918), p. 23.

Chapter Four

1   G. W. L. Nicholson, *The Canadian Expeditionary Force, 1914–1919* (Ottawa: Government Printing Office, 1962), pp. 546–547.

2   J. L. Granatstein and J. M. Hitsman, *Broken Promises: A History of Conscription in Canada* (Toronto: Oxford University Press, 1977), pp. 23–24.

3 Ibid., pp. 36–37.

4 Granatstein and Hitsman, *Broken Promises*, pp. 36–37.

5 Brown and Cook, *Canada*, p. 212.

6 Granatstein and Hitsman, *Broken Promises*, p. 36.

7 Daphne Read, *The Great War and Canadian Society: An Oral History* (Toronto: New Hogtown Press, 1978), p. 93.

8 According to the 1911 census, the total number of Canadian-born males between 18 and 45 had been 1,112,000, of whom 667,000 were English-speaking and 445,000 were French-speaking. Elizabeth Armstrong, *The Crisis of Quebec* (McClelland and Stewart, Ltd., 1937), p. 122.

9 By comparison, there were 9,635 English-Canadian members of this contingent. The overwhelming majority of these recruits, 21,035 men, had been born in the British Isles (including Scotland and Wales). Ibid., p. 122.

10 Granatstein and Hitsman, *Broken Promises*, pp. 23–28. As the authors acknowledge, precise figures for the number of French-Canadians in the CEF are hard to come by. Recruits were not required on enlistment to state whether they were English or French speaking, but only whether they were Canadian born. Government figures for the French-Canadian composition of the CEF were estimates compiled by adding together the number of men serving in French-Canadian battalions and the number of men with 'French' names serving in other battalions.

11 *Globe* (Toronto) 18 September 1916, p. 6.; 17 July 1916, p. 5.

12 In 1912, the government in Ontario dealt a severe blow to bilingual education in the province by issuing 'Regulation 17,' which effectively proscribed the use of French as a language of instruction in Ontario schools receiving public funds. In 1916, the government of Manitoba followed suit by abolishing all bilingual schools in the province. These policies met with bitter and vocal opposition from many members of the French-speaking community throughout Canada. Brown and Cook, *Canada,* p. 256.

13 Granatstein and Hitsman, *Broken Promises*, p. 26.

14 Armstrong, *Crisis of Quebec*, p. 104. In fairness to Hughes and other military decision-makers, at least two of the French-Canadian commanders denied important appointments were passed over for possibly legitimate reasons: Fifty-five-year-old Major-General Lessard, the highest ranking officer of the pre-war militia, was judged too young for a significant command, while Colonel Pelletier, a South African War veteran, was stone deaf. Morton, *Armageddon*, p. 33.

15 Desmond Morton, 'French Canada and War, 1868–1917: The Military Background to the Conscription Crisis of 1917,' J. L. Granatstein and R. D. Cuff, eds., *War and Society in North America* (Toronto: Thomas Nelson and Sons, 1971) pp. 84–103.

16 O. D. Skelton, *Life and Letters of Sir Wilfrid Laurier* (McClelland and Stewart, Ltd., 1965), pp. 167–168.

17 Granatstein and Hitsman, *Broken Promises*, pp. 29–30.

18 Skelton, *Wilfrid Laurier*, p. 167.

19 Reprinted in Henri Bourassa, *The Duty of Canada at the Present Hour* (Montreal: Devoir, 1914), p. 4.

20 Bourassa, *Duty of Canada*, pp. 7, 24.

21 See Henri Bourassa, *Que Devons-Nous à L'Angleterre?* (Montreal: Le Devoir, 1915).

22 Henri Bourassa, *Canadian Nationalism and the War* (Montreal: Le Devoir, 1916), p. 14.

23 Armstrong, *Crisis of Quebec*, p. 234.

24 From an anti-Bourassa pamphlet reprinted in Bourassa, *Duty of Canada*, p. 3.

25 Armstrong, *Crisis of Quebec*, p. 148. Local priests in the province tended to support Bourassa, however, presumably because they were more in touch with the true sentiment of their parishioners toward serving overseas.

26 Gwyn, *Tapestry of War*, pp. 316–318. Bourassa was not the only French-Canadian commentator to make such a comparison. *Le Droit* of Ottawa published in 1916 an open letter to French Canadians serving overseas which drew an analogy between the 'Prussianism and barbarity' assailing Europe and the persecution of French speakers in Canada. Brown and Cook, *Canada*, p. 258.

27 Quoted in Gwyn, *Tapestry of War*, pp. 321–322.

28 Bourassa, *Canadian Nationalism*, pp. 16, 30.

29 Robert Craig Brown, *Robert Laird Borden: A Biography* (Toronto: Macmillan, 1980), pp. 111–125.

30 *Globe* (Toronto) 19 September 1916, p. 6.

31 Craig, *Our War*, p. 148.

32 Skelton, *Laurier*, p. 183.

33 Granatstein and Hitsman, *Broken Promises*, pp. 45, 189.

34 Ibid., pp. 60–63.

35 Borden, *Memoirs*, p. 698.

36 Canada, Parliament, *Parliamentary Debates* (Commons), vol. 127 (1917), pp. 1540–1542.

37 *Globe* (Toronto) 19 May 1917, p. 6.

38 *Free Press* (Manitoba) 1 May 1917, p. 9.

39 *Devoir*, 3 January 1918, p. 1.

40 Brown and Cook, *Canada*, p. 272.

41 Skelton, *Laurier*, p. 184.

42 Armstrong, *Crisis of Quebec*, p. 203.

43 *Globe* (Toronto) 11 December 1917, p. 11.

44 *Free Press* (Manitoba) 11 December 1917, p. 5.

45 Granatstein and Hitsman, *Broken Promises*, p. 77.

46 Armstrong, *Crisis of Quebec*, p. 204.

47 Henri Bourassa, *Win the War and Lose Canada* (Montreal: Le Devoir, 1917), p. 14.

48 Brown and Cook, p. 273

49 Ibid., p. 271.

50 Skelton, *Laurier*, p. 183.

51 Granatstein and Hitsman, *Broken Promises*, p. 89.

52 L. L. Robson, *The First A.I.F.: A Study of its Recruitment, 1914–1918* (Melbourne: Melbourne University Press, 1982), p. 85.

53 Andrews, *Anzac Illusion*, p. 44.

54 Canadian census figures from 1911 show that the British-born constituted about 16 per cent of the total male population aged between 18 and 45. Armstrong, *Crisis of Quebec*, p. 104.

55 Lewis, *Our War*, pp. 216–217.

56 *Daily Telegraph* (Sydney), 11 September 1915, p. 13.

57 L. F. Fitzhardinge, *The Little Digger: William Morris Hughes, A Political Biography, vol. II* (Sydney: Angus and Robertson, 1979), p. 171.

58 At the time of the 1911 Census, about 21 per cent of Australians were Catholics. I have no precise numbers on Australian membership in trade unions during World War I, but

according to the historian Russell Ward, by the last decade of the nineteenth century, 'trade unionism in Australia was stronger than in any other country at the time.' Russell Ward, *Australia* (New Jersey: Prentice Hall, 1965), p. 85.

59 From a leaflet reprinted in J. M. Main, ed. *Conscription: The Australian Debate, 1901–1970* (Melbourne: Cassell Ltd., 1970), p. 37.

60 *Morning Herald* (Sydney) 2 August 1916, p. 2.

61 Fitzhardinge, *Little Digger,* pp. 179–183.

62 Ibid., p. 183.

63 L. C. Jauncey, *The Story of Conscription in Australia* (Melbourne: Macmillan, 1968), p. 215.

64 Fitzhardinge, *Little Digger*, p. 265.

65 *Daily Telegraph* (Sydney), 27 October 1916, p. 1.

66 Reprinted in Main, *Conscription*, p. 70.

67 *Australian Worker* (Sydney), 15 November 1917, p. 3.

68 *Labor Call* (Sydney), 26 October 1916, p. 3.

69 *Australian Worker* (Sydney) 26 October 1916, p. 1 See Ward, *Australia*.

70 See Ward, *Australia*.

71 Reprinted in Main, *Conscription*, p. 65.

72 *Australian Christian World* (Sydney) 27 October 1916, p. 2.

73 *Argus* (Melbourne) 18 September 1916, p. 1.

74 *Argus* (Melbourne) 24 October 1916, p. 1.

75 *Advocate*, 8 December 1917, pp. 13–14.

76 Souter, *Lion and Kangaroo*, p. 262.

77 Ibid., p. 258.

78 A comparable situation did not prevail in Australia. Even though the most potent forces of dissent were associated with the industrial working class and the Irish-Catholic minority, it would have been impossible for their opponents to portray these groups as contributing less than their share of men to the cause. About 41 percent of the AIF had been employed in industry, transport and commerce (the most heavily unionized occupations in Australia) as civilians, while Catholics comprised 21 percent of the AIF, a number roughly proportional to their percentage in the population as a whole. Grey, *Military History of Australia*, pp. 91–92.

79 Fitzhardinge, *Little Digger*, pp. 236, 280.

80 *Australian Worker* (Sydney) 15 November 1917, p. 3.

81 Reprinted in Main, *Conscription*, p. 89.

82 Main, *Conscription*, p. 91.

83 The 'Warwick Egg' incident led indirectly to the establishment of the Commonwealth Police. In the aftermath of the episode, the Hughes government created a small commonwealth police force, which was disbanded in 1921. Four years later, another federal police body, the Peace Officers, was established. This force would merge with the Commonwealth Investigation Service in 1960 to become the current Commonwealth Police. Souter, *Lion and Kangaroo*, pp. 260–261.

84 Jauncey, *Story of Conscription*, p. 312.

85 Robson, *First A.I.F.*, p. 196. See also Pugsley, *Anzac Experience,* pp. 272–277.

86 Baker, *King and Country*, p. 155.

87 Ibid., p. 163.

88 See Archibald Baxter, *We Will Not Cease* (Eddie Tern Press, 1980) and H. E. Holland, *Armageddon or Calvary: The conscientious objectors of New Zealand and 'the process of their conversion'* (Brooklyn: H. E. Holland, 1919).

89 Baker, *King and Country.*, p. 99.

90 Ibid., pp. 210–222.

91 Keith Sinclair, ed., *The Oxford Illustrated History of New Zealand* (Oxford: Oxford University Press, 1997), p. 331.

92 King, *New Zealand*, p. 316; Baker, *King and Country*, p. 127.

93 *Daily Times* (Otago), 23 February 1917.

94 See Fussell, *Great War.*

Chapter Five

1   King, *Memorials*, pp. 44–61.

2   Ibid. pp. 44–61.

3   K. S. Inglis and Jock Phillips, 'War Memorials in Australia and New Zealand: A Comparative Survey' in J. Richard and P. Spearritt (eds), *Packaging the Past? Public Histories* (Melbourne: 1991), pp. 185–186.

4   *Age* (Melbourne), 25 April 1932, p. 7.

5   Thomson, *Anzac Memories*, pp. 129–130.

6   Keith Sinclair, *A Destiny Apart: New Zealand's Search for National Identity* (Sydney: Allen & Unwin, 1986), p. 182.

7   King, *Memorials*, p. 45.

8   Ibid. pp. 86–103.

9   George Gould, quoted in Chris Maclean and Jock Phillips, *The Sorrow and the Pride: New Zealand War Memorials* (Wellington: Historical Branch, Department of Internal Affairs, 1990), p. 94.

10 Paul Gough, 'Canada, Conflict and Commemoration: An Appraisal of the New Canadian War Memorial in Green Park, London and Reflection on the Official Patronage of Canadian War Art,' in *Canadian Military History* 5 (Spring 1996), 1: 29–30; Mckernan, *Spirit.*

11 Scott Worthy, 'Communities of Remembrance: Making Auckland's War Memorial Museum', *Journal of Contemporary History*, 39/4 (2004), p. 601.

12 Maclean and Phillips, *Sorrow*, p. 124.

13 Gough, 'Canada', 29–30.

14 Edward Atkinson, 'Colonel Doughty and the War Museum,' in *The Archivist* 16, (July–August, 1989), 4:7–8.

15 Letter from Arthur Doughty to Sir George Foster (Acting Prime Minister), 22 March, 1917, Record Group (RG) 37, Vol. 352, National Archives of Canada (NAC).

16 Atkinson, 'Doughty,', *Archivist*, p. 9.

17 Letter from Arthur Doughty to Canadian Secretary of State, 29 March, 1919, RG 37, Vol. 366, NAC.

18 Report, December 1919, RG 37, Vol. 366, NAC.

19 Atkinson, 'Doughty,' *Archivist*, pp. 8–9.

20 Letter from Canadian War Museum Board to the Minister of National Defense (Army) and the Secretary of State for Canada, 6 January, 1943, RG 37, Vol. 302, NAC.

21 Atkinson, 'Doughty,' *Archivist*, p. 9.

22 McKernan, *Spirit,* p. 67.

23 Ibid. p. 30.

24 *Commonwealth Gazette,* 15 January 1918, pp. 45–47.

25 McKernan, *Spirit,* pp. 39–41.

26 Letter from C. E. W. Bean to George Pearce, March 1918, Australian War Memorial 93.

27 McKernan, *Spirit,* pp. 66–78.

28 *Herald* (Melbourne), 27 April 1922, p. 1.

29 Ibid. pp. 74–76.

30 Ibid. p. 84.

31 Ibid. p. 86.

32 *Age* (Melbourne), 25 April 1925, p. 15.

33 Letter from Bean to Treloar, 19 April 1925, Bean papers, AWM 38, 3 Donated Records List 6673, item 667.

34 Commonwealth of Australia, *Parliamentary Debates* (Senate and House of Representatives) Vol. 111 (1925): pp. 1642–1643, 2480–2481.

35 Treloar's War Memorial Fund initiatives consisted of a number of different schemes, including efforts to raise money through the sale of 'scrap' souvenir items such as helmets and ammunition boxes as vases and ornaments, and the exhibition of war art such as Will Longstaff's popular 1929 painting 'Menin Gate at Midnight' (which depicts the ghosts of dead soldiers marching on the newly constructed Menin Gate Memorial in Belgium). However, by far Treloar's most successful fund-raising drive involved the sale in the 1930s of Bean's *Official History of Australia in the Great War* to ex-soldiers working for the Public Service of the Commonwealth and State governments (of whom there were many during the Depression – veterans were given preference in the relief work that Public Service offered) who could gradually purchase sets of the series by having the Treasury Department make an automatic deduction from their salary of a few shillings per paycheck. At deductions of £3/3/ per year, it generally took about four years for a subscriber to complete payment for a set. Largely as a result of this scheme, which was initiated in 1933, the income of the Memorial Fund jumped from £8,532 in 1931–32 to £38,903 by 1936–37. It must be noted that despite all their funding difficulties, the museum's organizers consistently rejected suggestions that the institution charge for admission, on the grounds that to do so might alienate the public and would violate the memorial character of the collection. McKernan, *Spirit,* pp. 132–137, 79–80.

36 Ibid. p. 4.

37 Official opening of the Australian War Memorial, address by the Governor General, 11 November 1941, AWM 93, pt. 4.

38 McKernan, *Spirit,* p.4.

39 Ibid. p. 19.

40 *Guide to the Australian War Memorial* (Canberra: Australian War Memorial, 1941), p. ix.

41 Gregory, *Silence of Memory,* pp. 8, 25.

42 The gate commemorated those of Britain and the Empire who fell in the Ypres salient and whose bodies were never recovered. Philip Longworth, *Unending Vigil: A History of the Commonwealth War Graves Commission* (London: Constable, 1967), p. 105.

43 Thomson, *Anzac Memories,* p. 131.

44 Sinclair, *Destiny,* p. 183.

45 Herbert Fairlie Wood and John Swettenham, *Silent Witnesses* (Toronto: Canadian War Museum Historical Publications, 1974), pp. 64, 132.

46 John Rickard, *Australia: A Cultural History* (United Kingdom: Addison Wesley Longman, 1996), p. 123.

47 Longworth, *Unending Vigil*, p. 126.

48 Maclean and Phillips, *Sorrow*, pp. 119–122.

49 Winter, *Sites of Memory*, pp. 1–11.

50 King, *Memorials*, p. 4.

51 Hynes, *War Imagined*, p. 283.

52 *Daily Express* (London), 11 November 1919, p. 6.

53 *Gazette* (Montreal), 11 November 1927, p. 12.

54 *Age*, (Melbourne), 25 April 1922, p. 7.

55 For a discussion of Britain in the 1920s, see Kenneth O. Morgan (ed) *The Oxford History of Britain* (Oxford: Oxford University Press, 1991), pp. 582–662. For Canada, see John Herd Thompson and Allen Seager, *Canada, 1922–1939: Decades of Discord* (Toronto: McClelland and Stewart, 1985), pp. 14–192. For Australia, see Russell Ward, *Australia* (Englewood Cliffs, New Jersey: Prentice Hall, 1965), pp. 107–115. For New Zealand, see King, *New Zealand*, pp. 305–344.

56 King, *Memorials*, pp. 1–16.

57 Ibid. pp. 141–155.

58 *Gazette* (Montreal), 12 November 1928, p. 2.

59 Wood and Swettenham, *Silent Witnesses*, p. 130.

60 King, *Memorials*, pp. 40–43.

61 On the painters, see Maria Tippett, *Art at the Service of War: Canada, Art and the Great War* (Toronto: University of Toronto Press, 1984), pp. 19, 21, 34.

62 Jonathan E. Vance, 'The Great Response: Canada's Long Struggle to Honour the Dead of the Great War,' *The Beaver* (October-November, 1996), p. 31.

63 Winter, *Sites of Memory*, p. 104.

64 Longworth, *Unending Vigil*, pp. 37, 43.

65 *Age*, (Melbourne) 12 November 1934, p. 6.

66 Serle, *Monash*, p. 473.

67 Inglis and Phillips, *War Memorials*, p. 190. Australia and New Zealand are the only countries within the scope of this study where comprehensive inventories of First World War memorials have been conducted that provide figures tabulating the total number of such monuments throughout the nation, and the prevalence of certain imagery and inscriptions.

68 Draft dedications for the Canadian Book of Remembrance, 1933, 1934, RG 35/5, Vol. 1, NAC.

69 W. W. Murray, 'The Vimy Pilgrimage,' *Canadian Geographical Journal* (December 1936), pp. 407–426. By the 1930s, the tradition of 'pilgrimages' to Great War battlefields was pretty well established throughout the Empire. See David W. Lloyd, *Battlefield Tourism: Pilgrimage and the Commemoration of the Great War in Britain, Australia and Canada, 1919–1939* (Oxford: Berg, 1998).

70 John Hundevad, *The Epic of Vimy* (Ottawa: The Legionary, 1936), p. 6.

71 Gregory, *Silence of Memory*, pp. 51–92.

72 Thomson, *Anzac Memories*, p. 133.

73 *Herald* (Sydney), 25 April 1919, p. 9.

74 *Courier*, (Brisbane), 25 April 1928, p. 11.

75 *Chronicle* (Halifax), 11 November 1931, p. 1.

76 Murray, 'Vimy Pilgrimage,' p. 425.

77 *Argus*, Melbourne, 25 April 1939, p. 6.

78 Murray, 'Vimy Pilgrimage,' p. 421.

79 *Chronicle* (Halifax), 11 November 1919, p. 3.

80 *Workers' Weekly* (Melbourne), 7 September 1934, p. 5.

Chapter Six

1   Hynes, *War Imagined*, p. 308.

2   C. E. Montague, *Disenchantment* (London: Chatto and Windus, 1922), p. 180.

3   Ibid., p. 219.

4   C. F. G. Masterman, *England After the War* (New York: Harcourt, Brace and Co. , 1923); H. G. Wells, *Outline of History* (New York: The Macmillan Company, 1920).

5   Philip Gibbs, *Realities of War* (London: W. Heinemann, 1920); John Maynard Keynes, *The Economic Consequences of the Peace* (London, 1920); Charles Repington, *The First World War* (London: Constable and Company, 1920).

6   Examples include T. S. Eliot's poem 'The Waste Land' (1922), Virginia Woolf's novel *Mrs. Dalloway* (1925), and Ezra Pound's poem 'Hugh Selwyn Mauberley' (1920).

7   Masterman, *England*, p. 15.

8   Gibbs, *Realities of War*, pp. 556–557.

9   Ezra Pound, 'Hugh Selwyn Mauberley', in *The Norton Anthology of American Literature*, (New York: W. W. Norton & Company, 1989), pp. 1790–1791.

10 Gibbs, *Realities of War*, p. 70.

11 Montague, *Disenchantment*, p. 2.

12 Pound, 'Mauberley,' *American Literature*, pp. 1790–1791.

13 Gibbs, *Realities of War*, pp. 547–548.

14 Montague, *Disenchantment*, p. 87.

15 Masterman, *England*, p. 35.

16 Gibbs, *Realities of War*, p. 529.

17 Montague, *Disenchantment*, pp. 152–153.

18 See H. M. Green, *A History of Australian Literature, vol. II* (Sydney: Angus and Robertson, 1961); Carl F. Klinck, *Literary History of Canada: Canadian Literature in English, vol. II* (Toronto: University of Toronto Press, 1965); John McLaren, *Australian Literature: An Historical Introduction* (Melbourne: Longman Cheshire, 1989); John Rickard, *Australia: A Cultural History* (United Kingdom: Addison Wesley Longman, 1988).

19 Klinck, *Literary History*, pp. 5–10.

20 Ibid., pp. 168–180.

21 Stephen Leacock, *Sunshine Sketches of a Little Town* (London: John Lane, 1912), p. xii.

22 Lionel Stevenson, *Appraisals of Canadian Literature* (Toronto: The Macmillan Company, 1926), pp. 61–62.

23 Ibid., p. 65.

24 J. D. Logan, Donald G. French, *Highways of Canadian Literature* (Toronto: McClelland & Stewart, 1924), pp. 16, 345.

25 Klinck, *Literary History*, pp. 186–193, 240–258.

26 Thompson and Seager, *Canada*, p. 172.

27 Ibid., pp. 173–175.

28 Klinck, *Literary History,* p. 5.

29   Printed in Laird, *Other Banners*, pp. 127–128.

30   Ibid., p. 124.

31   Jack Lindsay, 'Forward,' *Vision* 1 (May 1923), pp. 30–35.

32   See Rickard, *Australia*, pp. 124–133.

33   See Alomes, *Australian Nationalism*, p. 90; Rickard, *Australia*, p. 127; Ward, *Australia*, p. 83.

34   Gough, 'Canada', *CMH*, pp. 29–32.

35   Maria Tippett, *Art at the Service of War: Canada, Art, and the Great War* (Toronto: University of Toronto Press, 1984), pp. 108–109.

36   Thompson and Seager, *Canada*, pp. 162–164.

37   Christine Boyanoski, 'Selective Memory: The British Empire Exhibition and national histories of art', in Annie E. Coombes, ed. *Rethinking Settler Colonialism: History and Memory in Australia, Canada, Aotearoa New Zealand and South Africa* (Manchester: Manchester University Press, 2006), pp. 156–170.

38   *Tomorrow* also served as a forum for (generally left-leaning) political opinion.
     See Rachel Barrowman, *A Popular Vision: The Arts and the Left in New Zealand, 1930–1950* (Wellington: Victoria University Press, 1991), pp. 27–60.

39   Gil Docking, *Two Hundred Years of New Zealand Painting* (Auckland: David Bateman, 1990), pp. 124–160.

40   Claude H. Weston in C. A. L. Treadwell, *Recollections of an Amateur Soldier* (New Plymouth, New Zealand: Thomas Avery and Sons, 1936), pp. vii–ix.

41   The relative quiescence, compared to Australia and Canada, of organized labour that had characterized wartime New Zealand continued in the 1920s as well. Union membership in New Zealand remained relatively low and the labour movement (generally united under the leadership of the Labour Party) continued to favour working within the political system over militant industrial action. The Great Depression would alter this situation significantly, if temporarily, and the early 1930s would see the nation's worst class conflict since the years immediately preceding the First World War, with major rioting in 1932 by unemployed workers in Auckland, Wellington and Dunedin. In 1935, New Zealand elected its first Labour Party government, which proceeded to enact reforms that transformed the Dominion by 1938 into a model Welfare State. The greatest source of domestic division in 1920s New Zealand continued to be the anti-Catholic activism of the Protestant Political Association, whose national membership peaked at 200,000 in 1919. However, with the end by 1921 of the Rebellion in Ireland, the power and popularity of the PPA in New Zealand declined precipitously, as did sectarian conflict throughout the country.

42   Brown and Cook, *Canada*, pp. 309–320.

43   Crowley, *Modern Australia*, pp. 316–341; Ward, *Australia*, pp. 107–111.

44   Archibald Cameron MacDonell, 'The Canadian Soldier As I Knew Him on the Western Front,' *Queen's Quarterly* 28, (April-June, 1921), pp. 339–350.

45   Bean, *Official History, vol. I*, pp. 605, 607.

46   *Argus* (Melbourne), 25 April 1932, p. 6.

47   Vance, *Death*, pp. 136–162.

48   See Desmond Morton and Glenn Wright, *Winning the Second Battle: Canadian Veterans and the Return to Civilian Life, 1915–1930* (Toronto: University of Toronto Press, 1987); Thomson, *Anzac Memories*, pp. 105–117.

49   Morton and Wright, *Second Battle*, pp. 80, 120–122.

50 Thomson, *Anzac Memories*, p. 115.

51 *Courier* (Brisbane), 26 March 1919, p. 1; *Worker* (Brisbane), 27 March 1919, p. 3.

52 *Labor Call* (Melbourne), 11 December 1930, p. 1.

53 Alomes, *Modern Australia*, pp. 509–510.

54 See Humphrey McQueen, 'Shoot the Bolshevik! Hang the Profiteer! Reconstructing Australian Capitalism, 1918–21' in E. L. Wheelwright and K. Buckley, eds., *Essays in the Political Economy of Australian Capitalism, vol. 2* (Sydney: Australian and New Zealand Book Company, 1978), pp. 185–206; Thomson, *Anzac Memories*, pp. 120–128; Morton and Wright, *Second Battle*, pp. 62–83.

55 Morton and Wright, *Second Battle*, pp. 178–201.

56 O. T. J. Alpers, 'Looking forward: how will soldiers fare?' *Quick March* vol. 1, number 1 (25 April, 1918), p. 9.

57 Worthy, 'Communities,' p. 606.

58 *Evening Post* (Wellington), 26 April 1935, p. 13.

59 G. L. Kristianson, *The Politics of Patriotism: The Pressure Group Activities of the Returned Servicemen's League* (Canberra: Australian National University Press, 1966), pp. 1–25.

60 In 1930 the RSSILA forced the Labor government to rescind within a week of its issuance a Cabinet decision to give preference to trade unionists over returned soldiers in hiring for government-sponsored public works jobs. Alomes, *Modern Australia*, pp. 470–472.

61 Thomson, *Anzac Memories*, pp. 115–126.

62 *Argus* (Melbourne), 28 March 1930, p. 23.

63 See Fussell, *Great War*; Hynes, *War Imagined*.

64 Edmund Blunden, *Undertones of War* (London: Cobden-Sanderson, 1927), pp. v–vi.

65 Hynes, *War Imagined*, p. 424.

66 Gregory, *Silence*, pp. 118–119.

67 Robert Graves, *Good-bye to All That* (New York: Anchor Books, 1998 [Reprint]), p. 342.

68 See Hynes, *War Imagined*; Fussell, *Great War*.

69 Ford Madox Ford, *Parade's End* (New York: Alfred A. Knopf, 1928), pp. 306–307.

70 See Robert Wohl, *The Generation of 1914* (Cambridge, Mass.: Harvard University Press, 1979), p. 112.

71 Herbert Read, 'A Lost Generation,' *Nation and Athenaeum* (April 27, 1929), p. 116.

72 Charles Yale Harrison's *Generals Die in Bed* (1929) being the most notable one. *Iron in the Fire* (1934) by Edgar Morrow, and *Flesh in Armour* (1932) by Leonard Mann, both Australians, are others. Though not explicitly anti-war, one of the most literate and articulate war novels produced by any ex-soldier is *Frank Honywood, Private: A Personal Record of the 1914–1918 War* (1929), by Eric Partridge, a New Zealander who served in the AIF. As the historian Geoffrey Serle acknowledged in a forward to a 1987 re-issue of the book, Partridge's novel was almost entirely unnoticed in Australia or anywhere else when it was originally published.

73 H. R. Williams, *The Gallant Company: An Australian Soldier's Story of 1915–18* (Sydney: Angus & Robertson, Ltd., 1933), p. 127.

74 Ibid., pp. 273–274.

75 The December 1, 1932, issue of *Reveille*, the journal of the RSSILA reported that Maxwell's *Hell's Bells* was a bestseller [From a news-clipping contained in AWM 43, A580]. Similarly, a review of the Australian war author T. H. Prince's *Purple Patches* noted its popularity at three-penny libraries [AWM 43, A705].

76 Nathaniel A. Benson, *Saturday Night* 45(November 23, 1929) pp. 8–9.

77 *Courier* (Ballarat), 14 April 1933, p. 3.

78 Quoted in *Argus* (Melbourne), 28 March 1930, p. 23.

79 *Argus* (Melbourne), 10 May 1930, p. 23.

80 *Argus* (Melbourne), 29 May 1930, p. 30. War books were not the only works to fall vic-
    tim to the heavy hand of government censorship in Australia during these years. Aldous
    Huxley's *Brave New World* was banned in the Dominion, as were earlier classics such as
    Moll Flanders and the *Decameron*. The authoritarian narrow-mindedness of the govern-
    ment led to the formation in 1934 of the Book Censorship Abolition League, which
    later combined with other organizations to become the Australian Council of Civil Lib-
    erties. Crowley, *Australia*, p. 544.

81 Vance, *Death*, pp. 193–195.

82 Charles Yale Harrison, *Generals Die In Bed* (New York: William Morrow and Co., 1930),
    pp. 255–256.

83 Vance, *Death*, pp. 194–195.

84 Notice of the ban and the publisher's quote reproduced in *Argus* (Melbourne), 29 May
    1930, p. 11.

85 *Argus* (Melbourne), 19 February 1930, p. 12.

86 W. B. Milne, *Saturday Night* 44 (26 October 1929), p. 8.

87 *Morning Herald* (Sydney), 8 February 1930, p. 1.

88 Edgar Morrow, *Iron in the Fire* (Sydney: Angus and Robertson, 1934), Foreword.

89 Martin Caedel, 'The King and Country Debate, 1933: Student Politics, Pacifism and the
    Dictators,' *The Historical Journal* (Cambridge) 22 (June 1979), 2: 397–422.

90 See Gregory, *Silence*; King, *Memorials*.

91 P. M. Hamilton, *Our Australian Heritage: A Survey of Australian History in Note Form* (Mel-
    bourne: The Macmillan Company, 1931), p. 110.

92 O. E. Burton, *The Silent Division: New Zealanders at the Front, 1914–1919* (Sydney: Angus
    and Robertson, 1935), pp. 46–47.

93 Clutha Mackenzie, *The Tale of a Trooper* (London: John Lane the Bodley Head, 1938), p.
    87.

Bibliography

Primary sources

Archival records

Auckland War Memorial Museum (AWMM), MS 1497 (Anzac Diary of Percival Clennell Fenwick)

Australian War Memorial (AWM) 43, A580

AWM 43, A705

AWM 38 (C. E. W. Bean papers) 3 Donated Records List 6673.

AWM 93.

AWM 93, pt. 4

Canada, Parliament, *Parliamentary Debates* (Commons), vol. 127 (1917)

Commonwealth of Australia, *Parliamentary Debates* (Senate and House of Representatives) Vol. 111 (1925)

National Archives of Canada (NAC), RG 35/5, Vol. 1

NAC, RG 37, Vol. 366

NAC, RG 37, Vol. 352

NAC, RG 37, Vol. 302

Newspapers and other periodicals

Advocate (Australia)

Age (Melbourne)

Argus (Melbourne)

Australian Christian World (Sydney)

Australian Worker (Sydney)

Bathurst National Advocate (Bathurst, Australia)

Bulletin (Sydney)

Canadian Geographical Journal

Chronicle (Halifax)

Commonwealth Gazette (Australia)

Courier (Ballarat, Australia),

Courier (Brisbane)

Daily Express (London)

Daily News (St. John's, Newfoundland)

Daily Telegraph (Sydney)

Devoir (Montreal)
Direct Action (International)
Evening Telegram (St. John's)
Free Press (Manitoba)
Gazette (Montreal),
Globe (Toronto)
Herald (Sydney)
Labor Call (Melbourne)
Labor Call (Sydney)
Mercury (Hobart)
Morning Herald (Sydney)
Nation and Athenaeum (Great Britain)
Queen's Quarterly (Canada)
Saturday Night (Canada)
Times (London),
Vision (Australia)
West Australian Worker (Brisbane)
Workers' Weekly (Melbourne)

Books, articles and unpublished manuscripts

Adams, A. H., *Tussock Land: A Romance of New Zealand and the Commonwealth* (London: Fisher and Unwin, 1904)

Adams, Francis *The Australians: A Social Sketch* (London: T. Fisher Unwin, 1893)

Adcock A. St. John, *Australasia Triumphant* (London: Simpkin, Marshall, Hamilton, Kent and Co., 1916)

Anzac Memorial (Sydney: Returned Soldiers' Association of New South Wales, 1916)

Asquith, H. H. *Memories and Reflections* (Boston: Little, Brown and Co., 1928)

Bean, C. E. W. *Anzac to Amiens: A Shorter History of the Australian Fighting Services in the Great War* (Canberra: Australian War Memorial, 1952)

Bean, C. E. W. (ed.) *The Anzac Book* (London: Cassell and Co., 1916)

—— *The Official History of Australia in the War of 1914–1918 volumes I-VI* (Sydney, Angus and Robertson, 1929)

——, *Gallipoli Correspondent: The Frontline Diary of C. E. W. Bean* (Sydney: Allen and Unwin, 1983 [reprint])

—— *Letters from France* (Melbourne: Cassell and Company, 1917)

Bird, Will R. *Thirteen Years After* (Toronto: The Maclean Publishing Company, 1932)

Blunden, Edmund *Undertones of War* (London: Cobden-Sanderson, 1927)

Borden, Robert Laird *Memoirs*, vol. 2 (New York: The Macmillan Company, 1938)

Boulger, Demetrius C. *The Life of Gordon* (London: T. Fisher Unwin, 1897)

Bourassa, Henri *The Duty of Canada at the Present Hour* (Montreal: Le Devoir, 1914).

—— *Canadian Nationalism and the War* (Montreal: Le Devoir, 1916)

—— *Que Devons-Nous à L'Angleterre?* (Montreal: Le Devoir, 1915)

—— *The Duty of Canada at the Present Hour* (Montreal: Devoir, 1914)

—— *Win the War and Lose Canada* (Montreal: Le Devoir, 1917)

Brooke, Rupert *The Collected Poems of Rupert Brooke* (London: Sidgwick and Jackson, Ltd., 1924)

Burton, O. E. *The Silent Division: New Zealanders at the Front, 1914–1919* (Sydney: Angus and Robertson, 1935)

Buley, E. C. *Glorious Deeds of Australasians in the Great War* (London: Andrew Melrose, Ltd., 1916)

Canadian War Records Office, *With the First Canadian Contingent* (Toronto: Hodder and Stoughton, 1915)

———, *Canada in Khaki* (London: Canadian War Records Office, 1917)

Carlyle, Thomas *Past and Present* (New York: The Macmillan Company, 1927)

Cave-Browne, J., *The Punjab and Delhi in 1857* (London: William Blackwood and Sons, 1861)

Craig, Grace Morris *But This Is Our War* (Toronto: University of Toronto Press, 1981)

Croad, Nancy (ed.), *My Dear Home: The Letters of Three Knight Brothers Who Gave Their Lives During World War I* (Auckland: Nancy Croad, 1995)

Cutlack, F. M. *The Australians: Their Final Campaign, 1918* (London: Sampson Low, Marston & Co., Ltd., 1918)

DeBeck, A. M. 'How Canada Answered the Call,' *Canada in Khaki* (London: The Canadian War Records Office, 1916)

Digby, Kenelm, *The Broad Stone of Honour, or the true sense and practice of chivalry* (London: G. Quaritch, 1877)

Duguid, Colonel A. Fortescue *Official History of Canada in the Great War, 1914–1919* (Ottawa: J. O. Patenaude, 1938)

East, Ronald ed., *The Gallipoli Diary of Sergeant Lawrence of the Australian Engineers, 1st AIF, 1915* (Melbourne: Melbourne University Press, 1981)

Evans, W. Sanford *The Canadian Contingents and Canadian Imperialism* (London: T. Fisher Unwin, 1901)

Fitchett, W. H., *The Tale of the Great Mutiny* (London: John Murray, 1912)

Ford, Ford Madox *Parade's End* (New York: Alfred A. Knopf, 1928)

Fuller, J. F. C. *The Last of the Gentlemen's Wars* (London: Faber and Faber Ltd., 1937)

Gallishaw, John, 'Gallipoli: The Adventures of a Survivor,' *Century* , vol. 9, July 1916, 371–382

Gibbs, Philip *Realities of War* (London: W. Heinemann, 1920)

Gilliat,, Edward *Heroes of Modern India* (London: Seeley and Co., Ltd., 1910)

Graves, Robert *Good-bye to All That* (New York: Anchor Books, 1998 [Reprint])

Guide to the Australian War Memorial (Canberra: Australian War Memorial, 1941)

Gullet, Harry 'Australia', *United Empire: The Royal Colonial Institute Journal* (October 1914)

Haliburton, R. G. *The Men of the North and Their Place in History. A Lecture delivered before the Montreal Literary Club, March 31st, 1869* (Montreal: Montreal Gazette, 1869)

Hamilton, P. M., *Our Australian Heritage: A Survey of Australian History in Note Form* (Melbourne: The Macmillan Company, 1931)

Harrison, Charles Yale *Generals Die In Bed* (London: Douglas, 1929)

Hodson, W. S. R. *Twelve Years of a Soldier's Life in India* (Boston: Ticknor and Fields, 1860)

Hughes, Thomas, *Tom Brown's Schooldays* (London: Macmillan, 1857)

Hundevad, John *The Epic of Vimy* (Ottawa: The Legionary, 1936)

Huxley, Leonard (ed.), *Scott's Last Expedition: Being the Journals of Captain R. F. Scott* (Smith, Elder & Co., 1913)

Kaye, John William, *Lives of Indian Officers* (London: A. Strahan and Co., 1867)

Kaye, John William, *History of the Indian Mutiny* (London: W. H. Allen and Co., 1888)

Keynes, John Maynard *The Economic Consequences of the Peace* (New York: Harcourt, Brace and Howe, 1920)

Lawson, Henry *In the Days When the World Was Wide and Other Verses* (Sydney: Angus and Robertson, 1903)

Leacock, Stephen *Sunshine Sketches of a Little Town* (London: John Lane, 1912)

Lewis, Brian *Our War: Australia During World War I* (Melbourne: Melbourne University Press, 1980)

Lewis, Cecil, *Sagittarius Rising* (London: Giniger/Stackpole Books, 1936)

Livesay, J. F. B. *Canada's Hundred Days* (Toronto: Thomas Allen, 1919)

Logan, J. D., Donald G. French, *Highways of Canadian Literature* (Toronto: McClelland & Stewart, 1924)

Mackellar , Dorothea, *My Country: A Poem by Dorothea Mackellar with decorations and illustrations by J. J. Hilder* (Sydney: Greenhouse Publications, 1915)

Mackenzie, Clutha, *The Tale of a Trooper* (London: John Lane and the Bodley Head, 1938)

Mair, Charles *Canadian Poems* (Toronto: William Briggs, 1901)

Marquis, T. G. *Canada's Sons on Kopje and Veldt* (Toronto: The Canada's Sons Publishing Co., 1900)

Marshman John Clark, *Memoirs of Major-General Sir Henry Havelock* (London: Longmans, Green and Co., 1885)

Masterman, C. F. G. *England After the War* (New York: Harcourt, Brace and Co., 1923);

McCrae, John *In Flanders Fields, and Other Poems* (London: G. P. Putnam's Sons, 1919)

McKenzie, F. A. *Canada's Day of Glory* (Toronto: William Briggs, 1918)

Montague, C. E. *Disenchantment* (London: Chatto and Windus, 1922)

Morrow, Edgar, *Iron in the Fire* (Sydney: Angus and Robertson, 1934)

Newbolt, Henry *The Island Race* (London: E. Mathews, 1898)

Priestley, J. B. *Margin Released: A Writer's Reminiscences and Reflections* (New York: Harper and Row, 1962)

Repington, Charles, *The First World War* (London: Constable and Company, 1920).

Roy, Reginald H. ed. *The Journal of Private Fraser* (Victoria, B. C.: Sono Nis Press, 1985)

Sorley, Charles *The Collected Letters of Charles Hamilton Sorley* (London: Cecil Woolf, 1990)

Southey, Robert *Life of Nelson* (London: J. M. Dent & Sons, Ltd., 1813)

Stevenson, Lionel *Appraisals of Canadian Literature* (Toronto: The Macmillan Company, 1926)

Stewart, Col. H., *The New Zealand Division, 1916–1919: A Popular History Based on Official Records* (Auckland: Whitcombe and Tombs, 1921)

Treadwell, C. A. L., *Recollections of an Amateur Soldier* (New Plymouth, New Zealand: Thomas Avery and Sons, 1936)

Trotter, Lionel J. *The Bayard of India: A Life of General Sir James Outram* (London: William Blackwood and Sons, 1903

Waite, Fred, *The New Zealanders at Gallipoli* (Auckland: Whitcombe and Tombs, Ltd., 1921)

Wells, H. G., *Outline of History* (New York: The Macmillan Company, 1920)

Williams, E. P., *A New Zealander's Diary: Gallipoli and France, 1915–1917* (Christchurch: Cadsonbury Publications, 1998)

Williams, H. R. *The Gallant Company: An Australian Soldier's Story of 1915–18* (Sydney: Angus & Robertson, Ltd., 1933

Wright, David Mckee, *Station Ballads and Other Verses* (Dunedin: J. G. Sewell, 1897)

Secondary sources

Books, articles and unpublished manuscripts

Abrams, Ann Uhry, *The Valiant Hero: Benjamin West and Grand Style History Painting* (Washington, D.C.: The Smithsonian Institution Press, 1985)

Abrams, M. H., *The Norton Anthology of American Literature* (New York: W. W. Norton & Company, 1989)

Adams, Michael C. C., *The Great Adventure: Male Desire and the Coming of World War I* (Bloomington: Indiana University Press, 1990)

Adam-Smith, Patsy, *The Anzacs* (Melbourne: Thomas Nelson, 1978).

Alomes, Stephen *Australian Nationalism* (New South Wales: Angus and Robertson, 1991)

Anderson, Benedict, *Imagined Communities: Reflections on the Origins and Spread of Nationalism* (London: Verso, 1983)

Andrews, E. M. *The Anzac Illusion: Anglo-Australian Relations During World War I* (Cambridge: Cambridge University Press, 1993)

Armstrong, Elizabeth *The Crisis of Quebec* (McClelland and Stewart, Ltd., 1937)

Atkinson, Edward 'Colonel Doughty and the War Museum,' in *The Archivist* 16, (July–August, 1989)

Baker, Paul, *King and Country Call: New Zealanders, Conscription and the Great War* (Auckland: Auckland University Press, 1988)

Barrowman, Rachel, *A Popular Vision: The Arts and the Left in New Zealand, 1930–1950* (Wellington: Victoria University Press, 1991)

Barthorp, Michael, *Slogging Over Africa: The Boer Wars, 1815–1902* (London: Cassell, 2002)

Bateman, Philip *Generals of the Anglo-Boer War* (Cape Town: Purnell and Sons, 1977)

Beckett, J. V., *The Aristocracy in England, 1660–1914* (New York: Blackwell, 1986)

Belich, James, *Paradise Reforged: A History of New Zealanders from the 1880s to the Year 2000* (Honolulu: University of Hawaii Press, 2001)

Berger, Carl *The Sense of Power: Studies in the Ideas of Canadian Imperialism, 1867–1914* (Toronto: University of Toronto Press, 1970)

Bond, Brian (ed.), *Victorian Military Campaigns* (London: Hutchison, 1967)

Boyanoski, Christine, 'Selective Memory: The British Empire Exhibition and national histories of art,' Annie E. Coombs, (ed.), *Rethinking Settler Colonialism: History and Memory in Australia, Canada, Aotearoa New Zealand and South Africa* (Manchester: Manchester University Press, 2006)

Bracco, Rosa Maria *Merchants of Hope: British Middlebrow Writers and the First World War, 1919–1939* (Oxford: Berg Publishers, Ltd., 1993).

Brown, Robert Craig and Ramsay Cook, *Canada, 1896–1921* (Toronto: McClelland & Stewart Ltd., 1974)

Caedel, Martin, 'The King and Country Debate, 1933: Student Politics, Pacifism and the Dictators,' *The Historical Journal* (Cambridge) 22, (June 1979), 2:397–422.

Cannadine, David *The Decline and Fall of the British Aristocracy* (New Haven: Yale University Press, 1990)

——, (ed.), *Admiral Nelson: Context and Legacy* (New York: Palgrave Macmillan, 2005)

Caudill, Edward, *Darwinian Myths: The Legends and Misuses of a Theory* (Knoxville, University of Tennessee Press, 1997)

Cecil, Hugh *The Flower of Battle: British Fiction Writers of the First World War* (London: Secker & Warburg, 1995)

Chandos, John, *Boys Together: English Public Schools, 1800–1864* (London: Hutchison, 1994)

Chisolm, Alec H. *The Making of a Sentimental Bloke* (Melbourne: Georgian House, 1946)

Clark, Manning *A Short History of Australia* (Sydney: Tudor Distributors, 1963)

Coleman, Terry, *Nelson: The Man and the Legend* (London: Bloomsbury, 2001)

Colley, Linda *Britons: Forging the Nation, 1707–1837* (New Haven: Yale University Press, 1992)

Collier, Richard, *The Great Indian Mutiny* (New York: E. P. Dutton and Company, 1964)

Crook, Paul, *Darwinism, War and History* (Cambridge: Cambridge University Press, 1994)

Dawson, Graham and Bob West 'Our Finest Hour? The Popular Memory of World War II and the Struggle Over National Identity,' in Geoff Hurd, (ed.), *National Fictions: World War II in British Films and Television* (BFI Publishing, 1984)

Docking, Gil, *Two Hundred Years of New Zealand Painting* (Auckland: David Bateman, 1990)

Eddy, John and Deryck Schreuder, (eds.) *The Rise of Colonial Nationalism* (Sydney: Allen and Unwin, 1988)

Ely, Richard 'The First Anzac Day: Invented or Discovered?', *Journal of Australian Studies* 17, November 1985, pp. 41–58

Erickson, Edward J. *Ordered to Die: A History of the Ottoman Army in the First World War* (Westport, Conn.: Greenwood Press, 2001)

Fitzhardinge, L. F., *The Little Digger: William Morris Hughes, A Political Biography, vol. II* (Sydney: Angus and Robertson, 1979)

Freeman, Bill and Richard Nielson, *Far From Home: Canadians in the First World War* (Toronto: McGraw-Hill Ryerson, 1999).

Fussell, Paul, *The Great War and Modern Memory* (New York: Oxford University Press, 1975).

Gammage, Bill *The Broken Years: Australian Soldiers in the Great War* (Victoria, Australia: Penguin Books, 1975

Girouard, Mark, *The Return to Camelot: Chivalry and the English Gentleman* (New Haven: Yale University Press, 1981)

Gough, Paul 'Canada, Conflict and Commemoration: An Appraisal of the New Canadian War Memorial in Green Park, London and Reflection on the Official Patronage of Canadian War Art,' in *Canadian Military History* 5 (Spring 1996), 1: 29–30.

Granatstein, J. L. and J. M. Hitsman, *Broken Promises: A History of Conscription in Canada* (Toronto: Oxford University Press, 1977)

Green, H. M. *A History of Australian Literature, vol. II* (Sydney: Angus and Robertson, 1961)

Gregory, Adrian *The Silence of Memory: Armistice Day, 1919–1946* (Oxford: Berg Publishers, 1994).

Grey, Jeffrey *A Military History of Australia* (Cambridge: Cambridge University Press, 1990)

Griffith, Paddy *Battle Tactics of the Western Front: The British Army's Art of Attack, 1916–1918* (New Haven, Yale University Press, 1994)

——, (ed.), *British Fighting Methods in the Great War* (London: Frank Cass, 1996)

Gwyn, Sandra *Tapestry of War* (Toronto: Harper Collins, 1992)

Harris, Stephen J. *Canadian Brass: The Making of a Professional Army* (Toronto: University of Toronto Press, 1988)

Hibberd, Dominic *The First World War* (London: MacMillan Ltd., 1990)

Hibbert, Christopher, *The Great Mutiny* (New York: Viking Press, 1978)

Hickey, Michael *Gallipoli* (London: John Murray, 1995)

Higgonet, Margaret, et. al. (eds.) *Behind the Lines: Gender and the Two World Wars* (New Haven: Yale University Press, 1987)

Hobsbawm, Eric J., *The Age of Empire, 1875–1914* (New York: Pantheon Books, 1987)

Hobsbawm, Eric J. and Terence Ranger, eds, *The Invention of Tradition* (Cambridge: Cambridge University Press, 1983)

Hynes, Samuel, *A War Imagined* (New York: Collier Books, 1990)

Inglis, K. S. and Jock Phillips, 'War Memorials in Australia and New Zealand: A Comparative Survey' in J. Richard and P. Spearritt, (eds.) *Packaging the Past? Public Histories* (Melbourne: Melbourne University Press, 1991)

Inglis, K. S. 'The Anzac Tradition,' *Meanjin Quarterly* (March, 1965)

James, Robert Rhodes *Gallipoli* (London: Batsford, 1965)

Jauncey, L. C. *The Story of Conscription in Australia* (Melbourne: Macmillan, 1968)

Jones, Greta, *Social Darwinism and English Thought: The Interaction Between Biological and Social Theory* (Brighton, Sussex: Harvester Press, 1980)

Kilduff, Peter, *Richtofen: Beyond the Legend of the Red Baron* (New York: John Wiley and Sons, Inc., 1994)

King, Alex *Memorials of the Great War in Britain: The Symbolism and Politics of Remembrance* (Oxford: Berg, 1998)

King, Michael, *The Penguin History of New Zealand* (Auckland: Penguin Books, 2003)

Klinck, Carl F. *Literary History of Canada: Canadian Literature in English, vol. II* (Toronto: University of Toronto Press, 1965)

Kristianson, G. L. *The Politics of Patriotism: The Pressure Group Activities of the Returned Servicemen's League* (Canberra: Australian National University Press, 1966)

Lambert, Andrew, *Nelson: Britannia's God of War* (London: Faber and Faber, 2004)

Lavery, Brian, *Horatio Lord Nelson* (New York: New York University Press, 2003)

Laird, J. T. (ed.) *Other Banners: An Anthology of Australian Literature of the First World War* (Canberra: The Australian War Memorial, 1971)

Lee, John *A Soldier's Life: General Sir Ian Hamilton* (London: Macmillan, 2000)

Lloyd, David W. *Battlefield Tourism: Pilgrimage and the Commemoration of the Great War in Britain, Australia and Canada, 1919–1939* (Oxford: Berg, 1998).

Longworth, Philip, *The Unending Vigil: A History of the Commonwealth War Graves Commission* (London: Constable, 1967)

MacKenzie, John M. (ed.) *Popular Imperialism in the Military, 1850–1950* (Manchester: Manchester University Press, 1992)

Maclean, Chris and Jock Phillips, *The Sorrow and the Pride: New Zealand War Memorials* (Wellington: Historical Branch, Department of Internal Affairs, 1990)

Macnab, Roy, *The French Colonel: Villebois-Mareuil and the Boers, 1899–1900* (Cape Town: Oxford University Press, 1975)

Main, J. M. (ed.) *Conscription: The Australian Debate, 1901–1970* (Melbourne: Cassell Ltd., 1970)

Malthus, Cecil *Anzac: A Retrospect* (Christchurch: Whitcombe and Tombs, 1965)

Mangan, J. A. *Athleticism in the Victorian and Edwardian Public School* (Cambridge: Cambridge University Press, 1981)

Marshall, P. J. (ed.) *The Cambridge Illustrated History of the British Empire* (Cambridge: Cambridge University Press, 1996)

Martin, A. C., *The Concentration Camps: 1900–1902: Facts, Figures and Fables* (Cape Town: H. Timmins, 1957)

McCord, Norman *British History 1815–1906* (Oxford: Oxford University Press, 1991)

McKernan, Michael *Here is Their Spirit: A History of the Australian War Memorial, 1917–1990* (St. Lucia: University of Queensland Press, 1991)

McLaren, John *Australian Literature: An Historical Introduction* (Melbourne: Longman Cheshire, 1989)

McMinn, W. G. *Nationalism and Federalism in Australia* (Oxford: Oxford University Press, 1994)

McQueen, Humphrey 'Shoot the Bolshevik! Hang the Profiteer! Reconstructing Australian Capitalism, 1918–21' in E. L. Wheelwright and K. Buckley, (eds.), *Essays in the Political Economy of Australian Capitalism, vol. 2* (Sydney: Australian and New Zealand Book Company, 1978), pp. 185–206

Miller, Carman *Painting the Map Red: Canada and the South African War, 1899–1902* (Montreal and Kingston: McGill-Queen's University Press, 1993)

Miller, Geoffrey *Straits: British Policy Towards the Ottoman Empire and the Origins of the Dardanelles Campaign* (Hull: University of Hull Press, 1997

Moorehead, Alan *Gallipoli* (London: H. Hamilton, 1956)

Morgan, Kenneth O., (ed.) *The Oxford History of Britain* (Oxford: Oxford University Press, 1991)

Morton Desmond and Glenn Wright, *Winning the Second Battle: Canadian Veterans and the Return to Civilian Life, 1915–1930* (Toronto: University of Toronto Press, 1987)

Morton, Desmond and J. L. Granatstein, *Marching to Armageddon: Canadians and the Great War, 1914–1919* (Toronto: Lester & Orpen Dennys, 1989)

Morton, Desmond, *A Peculiar Kind of Politics: Canada's Overseas Ministry in the First World War* (Toronto: University of Toronto Press, 1982)

—— , 'From Subordinate to Ally: The Canadian Corps and National Autonomy,' *Revue Internationale d'histoire Militaire* 51 (1982)

—— , 'Junior but Sovereign Allies: The Transformation of the Canadian Expeditionary Force, 1914–1918,' *Journal of Imperial and Commonwealth History* 8 (1979)

Mosse, George *Fallen Soldiers: Reshaping the Memory of the World Wars* (New York: Oxford University Press, 1990)

Murrow, Casey, *Henri Bourassa and French-Canadian Nationalism* (Montreal: Harvest House, 1968)

Neillands, Robin *The Dervish Wars: Gordon and Kitchener in the Sudan* (London: John Murray, 1996)

Nicholson, G. W. L. *Canadian Expeditionary Force, 1914–1919* (Ottawa: R. Duhamel, 1962)

——— , *The Fighting Newfoundlander: A History of the Royal Newfoundland Regiment* (St. John's: Government of Newfoundland, 1964)

Nora, Pierre, *Realms of Memory: Rethinking the French Past* (New York: Columbia University Press, 1996)

Novick, Peter, *The Holocaust in American Life* (Boston: Houghton Mifflin, 1999)

Nutting, Anthony *Gordon of Khartoum: Martyr and Misfit* (New York: Clarkson N. Potter, 1966)

Onions, John *English Fiction and the Drama of the Great War, 1918–1939* (New York: St. Martin's Press, 1990)

Pakenham, Thomas, *The Boer War* (New York: Random House, 1979)

Pollock, John, *Gordon: The Man Behind the Legend* (London: Constable, 1993)

Pound, Reginald *Scott of the Antarctic* (New York: Coward-McCann, Inc., 1966)

Pugsley, Christopher, *The ANZAC Experience: New Zealand, Australia and Empire in the First World War* (Auckland: Reed Publishing Ltd., 2004)

Preston, Richard A., Alex Roland, Sydney F. Wise, *Men In Arms: A History of Warfare and its Interrelationship with Western Society* (Fort Worth: Holt, Rinehart and Winston, 1991)

Prior, Robin, Trevor Wilson, *Command on the Western Front: The Military Career of Sir Henry Rawlinson, 1914–1918* (Cambridge, Mass.: Blackwell, 1992)

Read, Daphne *The Great War and Canadian Society: An Oral History* (Toronto: New Hogtown Press, 1978)

Rickard, John *Australia: A Cultural History* (United Kingdom: Addison Wesley Longman, 1996)

Robson, L. L. *The First A.I.F.: A Study of its Recruitment, 1914–1918* (Melbourne: Melbourne University Press, 1982)

Ross, Jane *The Myth of the Digger: The Australian Soldier in Two World Wars* (Sydney: Hale & Iremonger, 1985).

Russell, Peter, (ed.) *Nationalism in Canada* (Toronto: McGraw-Hill, 1966)

Schreiber, Shane *Shock Army of the British Empire: The Canadian Corps in the Last 100 Days of the Great War* (London: Praeger, 1997).

Serle, Geoffrey *John Monash: A Biography* (Melbourne: Melbourne University Press, 1982)

Seymour, Alan and Richard Nile, (eds.), *Anzac: Meaning, Memory and Myth* (London: Sir Robert Menzies Centre for Australian Studies, 1991).

Sherman, Daniel, *The Construction of Memory in Interwar France* (Chicago: University of Chicago Press, 1999)

Sinclair, Keith, *A Destiny Apart: New Zealand's Search for National Identity* (Sydney: Allen and Unwin, 1986)

Skelton, O. D. *Life and Letters of Sir Wilfrid Laurier* (McClelland and Stewart, Ltd., 1965)

Souter, Gavin *Lion and Kangaroo: The Initiation of Australia, 1901–1919* (Sydney: Collins, 1976)

Spies, S. B., *Methods of Barbarism? Roberts and Kitchener and Civilians in the Boer Republics: January 1900-May 1902* (Cape Town: Hammer and Rousseau, 1977)

Stanley, George F. G. *Canada's Soldiers: A Military History of an Unmilitary People* (Toronto: The Macmillan Company, 1954)

Steel, Nigel and Peter Hart, *Defeat at Gallipoli* (London: Macmillan, 1994)

Stone, Lawrence and Jeanne C. Fawtier Stone, *An Open Elite? England 1540–1880* (Oxford: Oxford University Press, 1984)

Tanner, Thomas W. *Compulsory Citizen Soldiers* (New South Wales: Alternative Publishing Cooperative, Etd., 1980).

Thompson, John Herd and Allen Seager, *Canada, 1922–1939: Decades of Discord* (Toronto: McClelland and Stewart, 1985)

Thomson, Alistair, *Anzac Memories: Living with the Legend* (Oxford: Oxford University Press, 1994)

Thomson, Denise 'National Sorrow, National Pride: Commemoration of War in Canada, 1918–1945,' *Journal of Canadian Studies* 30:4 (March 1996), pp. 5–27.

Tippett, Maria *Art at the Service of War: Canada, Art, and the Great War* (Toronto: University of Toronto Press, 1984)

Tynerman, Christopher, *A History of Harrow School* (Oxford: Oxford University Press, 2000)

Vance, Jonathan E. 'The Great Response: Canada's Long Struggle to Honour the Dead of the Great War,' *The Beaver* (October-November, 1996)

—— *Death So Noble: Memory, Meaning and the First World War* (Vancouver: UBC Press, 1997).

Wallin, Jeffrey D. *By Ships Alone: Churchill and the Dardanelles* (Durham, N.C.: Carolina Academic Press, 1981)

Wannan, Bill, (ed.) *A Marcus Clarke Reader* (Melbourne: Landsdowne Press, 1963)

Ward, Russell *Australia* (Englewood Cliffs, New Jersey: Prentice Hall, 1965)

Watson, Janet S. K., *Fighting Different Wars: Experience, Memory and the First World War in Britain* (Cambridge: Cambridge University Press, 2004)

Wheelwright E. L. and K. Buckley, (eds.), *Essays in the Political Economy of Australian Capitalism, vol. 2* (Sydney: Australian and New Zealand Book Company, 1978)

Wiener, Martin J., *English Culture and the Decline of the Industrial Spirit* (Cambridge: Cambridge University Press, 1981)

Wilkinson, Rupert, *Gentlemanly Power: British Leadership and the Public School Tradition; A Comparative Study in the Making of Rulers* (London: Oxford University Press, 1964)

Winter, Denis *Death's Men* (London: Penguin Books, 1978)

—— *Haig's Command, A Reassessment* (London: Viking, 1991)

Winter, J. M., *The Great War and the British People* (Cambridge, Mass.: Harvard University Press, 1986)

Winter, Jay, *Sites of Memory, Sites of Mourning* (Cambridge: Cambridge University Press, 1995).

Wohl, Robert *The Generation of 1914* (Cambridge, Mass.: Harvard University Press, 1979)

Wood, Herbert Fairlie and John Swettenham, *Silent Witnesses* (Toronto: Canadian War Museum Historical Publications, 1974)

Worthy, Scott, 'Communities of Remembrance: Making Auckland's War Memorial Museum,' *Journal of Contemporary History* , 39/4 (2004)

Wright, Matthew, *Western Front: The New Zealand Division in the First World War, 1916–1918* (Auckland: Reed Publishing, 2005)

Index